# About This Book

### Why is this topic important?

The rapidly changing workplace continues to impact workplace learning and performance. This changing and evolving climate "raises the bar" for those who have responsibility for developing workers to contribute to the organization's success. Whether charged with the responsibility of training as part of their jobs or hired for full-time positions, people are often thrown into these positions to sink or swim with little or no formal instruction on how to train. Written primarily for the novice classroom-based trainer, this book provides a comprehensive, systematic approach to developing training skills and competencies.

### What can you achieve with this book?

This book offers a new trainer a simple game plan. The topic of "how to" train is covered from assessment to evaluation. At the same time, the "why" behind the "how" and "what" is included without getting bogged down in theory. It is designed to help the trainer "do it better and faster." Although best suited to the new trainer, this book is also a good reference for those with more experience. Experienced trainers will learn new tips and techniques to enhance their current skills and help them deliver on-target training that meets individual as well as organizational needs.

### How is this book organized?

The book's basic structure follows a commonly used approach to instructional design: analysis, design, development, delivery, and evaluation. In addition, the book includes chapters that address adult learning principles, learning styles, training styles, and insights into the complexity and diversity of today's training environment and audiences. Also included is a chapter on distance learning. Reflecting the changing role and function of training to performance consulting, there is a "bonus" chapter dealing with the business of consulting. This chapter addresses the consulting function from the perspective of both the internal and external consultant, including tips on managing the client-consultant relationship. This updated edition includes another "bonus" chapter that provides tips for training with limited resources.

# About Pfeiffer

Pfeiffer serves the professional development and hands-on resource needs of training and human resource practitioners and gives them products to do their jobs better. We deliver proven ideas and solutions from experts in HR development and HR management, and we offer effective and customizable tools to improve workplace performance. From novice to seasoned professional, Pfeiffer is the source you can trust to make yourself and your organization more successful.

**Essential Knowledge**  Pfeiffer produces insightful, practical, and comprehensive materials on topics that matter the most to training and HR professionals. Our Essential Knowledge resources translate the expertise of seasoned professionals into practical, how-to guidance on critical workplace issues and problems. These resources are supported by case studies, worksheets, and job aids and are frequently supplemented with CD-ROMs, websites, and other means of making the content easier to read, understand, and use.

**Essential Tools**  Pfeiffer's Essential Tools resources save time and expense by offering proven, ready-to-use materials—including exercises, activities, games, instruments, and assessments—for use during a training or team-learning event. These resources are frequently offered in looseleaf or CD-ROM format to facilitate copying and customization of the material.

Pfeiffer also recognizes the remarkable power of new technologies in expanding the reach and effectiveness of training. While e-hype has often created whizbang solutions in search of a problem, we are dedicated to bringing convenience and enhancements to proven training solutions. All our e-tools comply with rigorous functionality standards. The most appropriate technology wrapped around essential content yields the perfect solution for today's on-the-go trainers and human resource professionals.

www.pfeiffer.com

*Essential resources for training and HR professionals*

An Instructor's Guide is available at www.wiley.com/college/lawson.

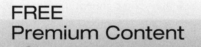

FREE
Premium Content

Pfeiffer®
An Imprint of
WILEY

This book includes premium content that can be
accessed from our Web site when you register at
**www.pfeiffer.com/go/karenlawson**
using the password *professional*.

**KAREN LAWSON**

# THE
# Trainer's
# HANDBOOK

## Updated Edition

Pfeiffer
A Wiley Imprint
www.pfeiffer.com

**Library of Congress Cataloging-in-Publication Data**

Lawson, Karen.
  The trainer's handbook / Karen Lawson.—[3rd] updated ed.
    p. cm.
  Includes bibliographical references and index.
  ISBN 978-0-470-40304-4 (pbk.)
  1. Employees—Training of—Handbooks, manuals, etc.
  2. Training—Handbooks, manuals, etc. I. Title.
  HF5549.5.T7L344 2009
  658.3'1243—dc22
                                        2008041495

Acquiring Editor: Matthew Davis                    Editor: Marcy Marsh
Director of Development: Kathleen Dolan Davies      Manufacturing Supervisor: Becky Morgan
Production Editor: Mary Garrett                     Editorial Assistant: Lindsay Morton
Printed in the United States of America
Printing  10  9  8  7  6  5  4  3  2  1

# Contents

# List of Tables, Exhibits, and Figures

# Contents of the Website

# Acknowledgments

I would like to thank the many people who have attended my training sessions throughout the years. In essence, they are the authors of this book. They have taught me what it means to be a training professional.

I am grateful to the many training professionals who have shared their tips and techniques from conference platforms and also one-on-one. Many of these colleagues have become my close friends. In particular, I thank Steve Sugar for his willingness to share ideas and materials. I also thank my dear friend, Harriet Rifkin, with whom I have shared the joy and pain of growing as a training professional, for her caring and sharing.

I particularly thank Dr. Mel Silberman for sharing his knowledge and experience. His influence has truly made a difference in my life.

Finally, to my husband, Bob Lawson, I can never adequately express how much I appreciate his love and support throughout the years. I thank him not only for his patience and understanding but for his belief in me even when I didn't believe in myself. He is my colleague and partner, my champion and much-needed critic, but most of all, he is my best friend.

# Introduction

The field of workplace learning is growing by leaps and bounds. Along with the growth of the industry comes the demand for trainers. For our purposes, "trainer" refers to anyone who is responsible for delivering classroom instruction. A trainer, therefore, might be an internal HRD professional employed by an organization and responsible for providing training to the organization's employees. A trainer can also be a subject-matter expert who has been enlisted as a full-time professional trainer. Another category of trainers includes those who deliver training on a part-time basis as part of their overall job responsibilities. The term also applies to the external practitioner who contracts with an organization to design and/or deliver training programs. Often the external trainer is a casualty of corporate downsizing or maybe someone who just wants a career change. In either case, this individual has turned to the training profession as a means of utilizing skills or expertise in a particular discipline or subject area.

Internal or external, full-time or part-time, the demand for trainers often exceeds the supply. To meet this need, organizations often turn to those in line positions as a talent pool for trainers. More and more, people are being asked to deliver training as part of their jobs. These "non-trainers" or subject-matter experts are expected to deliver training, not just present information. Unfortunately, these folks have received little or no formal instruction on how to train. They are thrown into the position to sink or swim. Left to their own devices, they find themselves training the way they were trained or taught. In many situations, that means a didactic approach in which the trainer stands in front of participants and dumps information on often-unhearing ears.

Although the approach just described never really worked as a sole method of training adult learners, it is even less effective today. Trainers are no longer viewed as merely disseminators of information. They are now expected to be facilitators, agents of learning, and performance consultants. These new roles require them to direct their efforts away from specific task-oriented instruction and to concentrate on helping people and organizations improve performance.

Trainers need to design, develop, and deliver training that encourages people at all levels of the organization to take responsibility for their own learning. The trainer becomes a catalyst, a resource person, and often a coach to help people through the discovery process.

The effective trainer will also have to understand business needs and identify how those needs are linked to learning and performance needs. Quite simply, the purpose of training is to help line managers solve business problems. Trainers must develop partnerships with those managers who are ultimately accountable for the success of training. Before this can happen, however, trainers must become proficient at the skills and competencies that define them as professionals. Every profession requires its practitioners to master a certain body of knowledge and a set of skills. The training profession should be no different.

To that end, this book, written primarily for the novice classroom-based trainer, presents a comprehensive, systematic approach to developing training skills and competencies. Those who are thrown into full-time, professional training positions with little or no formal training will be able to use this book to learn the fundamentals of training or supplement what they already know. They can be brought "up-to-speed" in a relatively short period of time. Although best suited to the new trainer, this book is a good reference for those with more experience. Experienced trainers will learn new tips and techniques to enhance their current skills and help them deliver on-target training that meets individual as well as organizational needs.

## How This Book Is Organized

The success of any training program or initiative depends on the use of a systematic approach to delivering effective instruction with high impact for both the participants and the organization. To that end, you, as the trainer, must understand various principles and concepts of learning and also follow a process that results in behavioral change. This process (reflected in the arrangement of this book) consists of five parts: *analysis, design, development, delivery,* and *evaluation.*

The analysis phase is covered in Chapters 1 through 4. In Chapter 1, you will learn how to conduct a needs analysis at both the organizational and individual levels. Chapter 2 addresses the principles of adult learning as well as learning styles. You will have an opportunity to learn about your own personal training style in Chapter 3. To round out the analysis phase, Chapter 4 provides additional insights and understanding of the complexity and diversity of today's training environment and audiences.

The second phase in the design process is addressed in the next two chapters. Chapter 5 explains how to write training objectives/learning outcomes, and Chapter 6 presents a step-by-step approach to developing a complete instructional plan.

After the program has been designed, the next step is to fully develop the program, selecting and creating activities and tools to create an exciting and effective learning experience. You will learn about specific active-training methods and techniques in Chapter 7.

The next step in the instructional process is delivery. Chapters 8 through 12 give creative tips and techniques for delivering a dynamic and professional training session. You will also learn how to deal with difficult people and situations. Chapter 10 specifically addresses distance learning delivery methods.

In Chapter 13 you will learn how to evaluate training and measure its effectiveness. You will learn how to go beyond the "smile sheet" at the end of a session and develop more tools and techniques to show the benefits of training to employees and the organization.

Chapter 14 is offered as a "bonus" for those who find themselves in either an internal or external consulting role. As a result of the movement or evolution of training to performance consulting, the training and development professional must learn to function as a true consultant. In this chapter, you will learn how to develop a client-consultant relationship that positions you as a valuable resource and business partner within the organization.

Finally, Chapter 15 offers strategies for training during tough economic times. You'll learn how to maximize your training dollars by adapting to change, using resources more efficiently, and becoming more business savvy.

By developing your skills in each of these areas, you will indeed become a master of your craft.

The book includes checklists, forms, and specific activities that you can use immediately in designing, developing, and delivering your own training programs. The book's website makes it easy to print the tables and exhibits included in this book. Not only will you find them useful as you develop your own programs, but you may also choose to use them in your own train-the-trainer programs.

# Chapter 1

# Assessing Needs

**LEARNING OUTCOMES**

In this chapter, you will learn

- To identify key steps in the needs-assessment process

- To select appropriate methods to gather data

- To develop questions for a variety of needs-assessment techniques

- To apply the needs-assessment process to a specific organization and situation

## Understanding the Needs-Assessment Process

Every year companies spend thousands and thousands of dollars in training programs that fail. Why? Because they fail to provide programs that meet the specific business needs of the organization and the specific professional development needs of the employee.

A needs assessment is the core of any training program. It gives you the basis for program development and establishes the criteria for measuring the success of the program after its completion.

## What Is a Needs Assessment?

Needs assessors are much like physicians, who ask a series of questions and order a battery of medical tests to uncover and treat the causes rather than the symptoms of an ailment. Needs assessment is the process of determining the cause, extent, and appropriate cure for organizational ills. The process addresses the organizational context and combines organizational analysis, data gathering, and interviewing techniques to identify and shrink the gap between desired and actual knowledge, skills, and performance. It is a careful study of the organizational context, the job itself, and the knowledge, skills, and abilities of the job incumbents.

Simply put, the process identifies the desired performance and the current performance. The difference or the gap between the actual and the desired level of performance becomes the training need and provides the basis for the training design. The correct problem identification (cause) is the key to developing and implementing appropriate corrective measures (proper cure).

## Why Conduct a Needs Assessment?

Before we address how to conduct a needs assessment, we need to take a look at the reasons for doing one. Overall, the purpose of a needs assessment is to prevent a quick-fix, bandage approach to business problems. Instead, a needs assessment, if you do it properly, will ensure that the solution(s) addresses the real issue(s) and effectively focuses the appropriate resources, time, and effort toward a targeted solution. The following are some valid reasons for conducting a needs assessment.

**To Determine Whether Training Is Needed.** Poor performance is not always a training issue. Often performance problems are the result of poor management practices, organizational barriers, or inadequate systems or equipment. A needs assessment, if conducted properly, will determine whether training is necessary and avoid the mistake of applying a training solution to a non-training problem. If it is determined that the problem does require training, the needs assessment will help you identify the performance issues that training should address.

**To Determine Causes of Poor Performance.** As noted above, poor performance can be the result of many other factors, including poor incentives, lack of internal motivation, the work environment, poor management, inadequate skills and knowledge, or the employees' lack of confidence. Sometimes, the cause may be poor management. Poor management practices might include poor hiring decisions, poor communication, unclear expectations, or inadequate coaching and feedback. For example, there is a saying that "ducks don't climb trees." Unfortunately, corporations are full of "ducks" in positions that require "cats," and no matter how hard they try, they will never succeed in their positions. In other words, if employees are put in positions for which they are unsuited, all the training in the world will not improve their performance. In other cases, managers fail their employees by not stating clearly their expectations or standards of performance.

Often employees do not know what is expected of them. They may have the knowledge, skills, and ability to do the job quite well but are not meeting the manager's expectations. If that is the case, then the training needs to be directed toward the manager rather than the manager's employees.

**To Determine Content and Scope of Training.** A needs assessment will help determine the type of training necessary to achieve results. Should it be workshop, self-study, or on-the-job? It will help you identify how long the training program should be and who the target audience is. It will also help you identify what should be included in the program and the degree of urgency.

**To Determine Desired Training Outcomes.** The needs assessment will help you determine what knowledge, skills, and attitudes need to be addressed during the training. It will also help distinguish "need to know" from "nice to know." By focusing on what the trainees actually need to know in order to do their jobs better, a program can be developed that will get results.

**To Provide Basis of Measurement.** A needs assessment provides a baseline against which to measure results or changes. It is simply a starting point.

**To Gain Management Support.** By involving line management and other key organizational players, you will find the support you need for the training program to succeed. Because they have had input, they will have a vested interest in the program. Management commitment comes if managers and supervisors see that you are developing training programs in direct response to their specific needs.

# Needs-Assessment Process

The needs-assessment process can be as detailed and involved as needed or desired. Many factors must be taken into consideration, including time, money, number of people involved, resources available, and so forth.

A full-blown needs assessment is both time-consuming and costly. Frankly, few organizations are willing to make that kind of investment. A typical alternative is to conduct an abbreviated form of needs assessment, using only two or three methods.

Table 1.1 offers a comparison between an in-depth and an abbreviated needs assessment.

## Whom to Assess

The people assessed depends on the goal and the required depth of the assessment. Consider the following categories of people and then decide which groups to target as data sources.

**Senior Management.**  To get a clear picture of the problem and its business impact, start with senior management. Ask more strategic questions that address the direction of the organization as well as anticipated industry changes. In other words, start

| Table 1.1. | In-Depth Versus Mini Needs Assessment | |
|---|---|---|
| | **In-Depth** | **Mini** |
| Type of Information | Quantitative | Qualitative |
| Methods | Multi-tiered approach<br>Surveys<br>Observation<br>Interviews<br>Focus groups<br>Document reviews | Interviews<br>Focus groups |
| Scope | Widespread organizational involvement<br>Broad-ranging objectives | Fewer people involved<br>Short-term focus |
| Length | Several months to a year | Few days to a week |
| Cost | Expensive | Inexpensive |
| Focus | Linked to defined outputs<br>Long-term | Immediate, quick results |
| Exposure/Visibility | High profile and risk | Lower risk |

with an organizational context. If you are an internal consultant, you should already have a good idea of the issues driving the need for training. If you are external, you will probably need to do some research first and then ask specific questions to gain better insight into the organizational issues that can be addressed through training.

Here are some questions that will help you gain a better understanding of the organization's business needs:

- "What is the vision of the organization?"
- "What is the mission of the organization?"
- "What are the primary goals and objectives, both short-term and long-term?"
- "What organization or industry issues are driving the need for training?"
- "What is your most critical concern right now?"

**Target Population.** It is also important to identify the target population, those who will receive the training. Often they are overlooked. They should be contacted to find out both their perceived and real training needs. If they are not consulted, it is unlikely they will have a sense of ownership or "buy-in," and they will most likely approach the training experience with resistance and resentment.

**Target Population's Managers.** Those who manage members of the target population are a critical source of data, since the purpose of the training is to help the line manager solve a business problem or meet a business need. These business needs may include improved productivity, decreased errors, fewer accidents, increased business, decreased turnover or absenteeism, or fewer customer complaints.

**Direct Reports.** When the target population consists of managers or supervisors, good sources of data are those who report to these people. Direct reports can often provide valuable insight into the skills that managers and supervisors need to improve.

**Co-Workers or Peers.** More and more organizations are using 360-degree feedback as part of their assessment process, providing employees with performance feedback from multiple sources. Talking with or surveying the target population's co-workers or peers, for example, can provide valuable insight into the skills necessary for a successful team environment. The more organizations that use cross-functional teams, the more critical the need becomes to involve other team members in the assessment process.

**Human Resource Personnel.** The human resources (HR) department is probably the best source of records and documents. They, of course, will have data on turnover, grievances, safety violations, and so forth, as well as performance appraisals and the like. The HR professionals can also provide interesting insight into the organization's culture.

**Vendors.** Vendors are a good source of qualitative data. They can share their perceptions of the organization or specific departments with which they interact, plus give some valuable insights into industry standards and practices.

**Customers (Internal and External).** Customer surveys provide quantitative data that can help pinpoint specific deficiencies, that is, gaps between desired and actual behavior. Survey data will provide information on the level of satisfaction relative to customer-service practices, the quality of the product or service, and delivery systems.

For example, an organization may survey external customers to determine customer satisfaction regarding a call center's activity, such as response time in answering the telephone, friendliness of the service representative, ability to solve the customer's problem, and turnaround time for a request. An internal customer satisfaction survey will include similar items but would be targeted to a specific department. The systems or information technology (IT) department, for example, may choose to send a survey to all the other internal departments it supports to identify how well IT is meeting the needs and expectations of its internal customers.

**Competitors.** Published competitor data such as sales results, market share, stock prices, and financial reports help to identify the organization's position in relation to its competitors and helps to pinpoint areas for improvement. Gather these data from an organization's annual report or from trade publications.

**Industry Experts or Observers.** Industry experts have their thumbs on the pulse of the business in which your organization is engaged. They identify trends and industry standards against which your organization can measure itself. Experts may be identified through trade publications, where they may have written about the industry or may have been cited by others as experts in the field. One can also learn about and from experts by attending their sessions at professional conferences and "surfing the Internet" for appropriate websites.

# How to Conduct a Needs Assessment

Exhibit 1.1 provides an overview of the needs-assessment process.

### Step One: Identify Problem or Need

A good place to start is to take a look at the organization's statements of vision, mission, values, and goals. Ask to look at the strategic plan. If these organizational data do not exist, suggest that these statements and documents be developed before addressing any training issues. Because the purpose of training is to help solve organizational problems, you must have a clear understanding of what the business problems are.

The first step is to identify the problem or need, stated in dollar terms, if possible. Find out what the problem is costing the organization in errors, turnover, lost business, or additional help. Remember that the *desired outcome minus the current outcome identifies the need.*

After the need has been determined, define the specific objective the training program should meet. The objective must state the desired performance or behavior and be measurable, observable, realistic, and "fixable." Working with line managers, determine what to measure and how to tie it to organizational goals. Outcomes relate to the specific need. For example, the goal or outcome of safety training is to reduce accidents by a particular percentage. Customer service training should result in fewer customer complaints.

While examining possible causes, it is important to ask, "Is the problem due to a lack of knowledge or skill or is it operational?" For example, improper telephone use may have been identified as the problem. Incoming calls are being disconnected when the person who answers the call tries to transfer his or her calls. At first glance, it might appear that the people handling inbound calls need telephone skills training. However, if the telephone system is not set up to handle multiple functions, then training will not solve the problem.

### Step Two: Determine Needs-Assessment Design

To determine the true causes, not just the symptoms, of the problem or need, employ several investigative tools and techniques, including interviews, surveys, questionnaires, observation, and document examination. Choose investigative or data-collection methods on the basis of their appropriateness to the problem. The

## EXHIBIT 1.1.   Needs Assessment Process

### Step One: Identify Problem or Need

- Determine organizational context
- Perform gap analysis
- Set objectives

### Step Two: Determine Needs Assessment Design

- Establish method-selection criteria
- Assess advantages and disadvantages of methods

### Step Three: Collect Data

- Conduct interviews
- Administer questionnaires
- Administer surveys
- Review documents
- Observe people at work

### Step Four: Analyze Data

- Conduct qualitative analysis
- Conduct quantitative analysis
- Determine solutions/recommendations

### Step Five: Provide Feedback

- Write report
- Make an oral presentation
- Determine next step

choice of methods will depend on various criteria such as time, cost, or available re-sources. These criteria, as well as the advantages and disadvantages of various data-collection methods will be explained later in Chapter 1.

## Step Three: Collect Data

Many methods are available for conducting a needs assessment.

### Data-Collection Methods and Tools

- Interviews
- Questionnaires
- Attitude surveys
- Observation
- Tests of proficiency
- Organizational statements and plans
- Turnover records
- Performance appraisals
- Procedures, handbooks, or audits
- Training evaluations
- Exit interviews
- Samples of work
- Job descriptions
- Complaints, error rates, and rejects
- Call reports, incident reports, and grievances
- Trade, government, and business publications

**Criteria for Selecting a Method.** From the rather extensive list of methods, select those most appropriate for the situation. Many factors will determine which methods to select. Look at the criteria in Exhibit 1.2, think about your own needs-assessment situation, and determine which criteria you believe should be taken into consideration.

| EXHIBIT 1.2.   Method Selection Criteria |
|---|

- Time
- Cost
- Number of people involved
- Workplace disruption
- Complexity
- Confidentiality
- Trust level
- Comfort level, knowledge, expertise of assessor
- Validity
- Reliability
- Adaptability
- Participant-friendly

*The Trainer's Handbook, Updated Ed.* Copyright © 2009 by Karen Lawson. Reproduced by permission of Pfeiffer, an imprint of John Wiley & Sons, Inc.

**Advantages and Disadvantages of Data-Collection Methods.** Data-collection methods fall roughly into six categories: open-ended questionnaires, closed-ended questionnaires, survey instruments, interviews, observation, and document examination.

To help determine which data-collection methods to use, it is a good idea to look at the advantages and disadvantages of each, as shown in Table 1.2. Weigh these considerations against your chosen criteria.

The most common approaches are covered in detail below.

**Interviews.** Whether for an in-depth or an abbreviated needs assessment, one-on-one and group interviews are valuable data sources. When developing interview questions, be sure to ask open-ended rather than closed-ended questions. Closed-ended questions can be answered with a simple "yes" or "no." For example, a question such as "Do you think there is a need for training?" elicits a one-word response. Probe further by asking an open-ended question. To get to the heart of the matter right away, ask a question that begins with "how" or "what" such as, "What would help you do your job better?" Try to avoid asking questions that begin with "why." First, people may not know why. Also, "why" questions tend to put people on the defensive.

| Table 1.2. | **Advantages and Disadvantages of Data-Collection Methods** | |
|---|---|---|
| | **Advantages** | **Disadvantages** |
| Open-Ended Questionnaires | Allow respondent to introduce new topics<br>Easy to develop<br>Inexpensive to administer | Communication is one-way<br>Respondents may not want to put comments in writing<br>Prone to ambiguity and opinions |
| Closed-Ended Questionnaires | Easier to answer<br>Inexpensive to administer<br>Feeling of anonymity and confidentiality ensured<br>Less time-consuming | Limited information<br>Require more skill and work to prepare<br>Items subject to misinterpretation<br>Difficult and time-consuming to construct |
| Instruments | Validated through research<br>Quickly and easily administered<br>Can be administered in groups<br>Scored quickly | Administration and coordination needed<br>Difficulty in choosing most appropriate<br>Difficult and time-consuming to construct<br>Need to research different types |
| Individual or Group Interviews | Can read nonverbal messages<br>Easier to talk<br>Build commitment for training<br>Clarifies expectations<br>Can introduce new topics<br>More detailed information | Time-consuming<br>Some people may feel threatened<br>Can be affected by interviewer bias<br>Difficult to organize and analyze data<br>People may be influenced by peers |
| Observation | Better understanding of variables<br>Provides real-life data and examples that can be used in course material<br>Real situations, highly relevant<br>Relatively low cost | Time-consuming<br>Requires some knowledge of the job<br>People may be anxious, nervous<br>Difficult to record data |
| Analysis of Existing Information | Factual, highly valid information<br>Easy access to many sources in one place<br>Inexpensive and not very time-consuming<br>Unobtrusive<br>Provides specific examples | May be outdated<br>May not cover all areas needed; too generic<br>Risks misinterpretation<br>May be biased |

**Sample Interview Questions.** Plan to take considerable time and care in writing questions. Not only should they be designed to elicit as much information as possible, but the questions must produce answers that will provide meaningful information. Although questions will vary according to the specific situation, some sample questions are included below that may help. After reading sample interview questions, make a list of questions you might ask. Be sure to identify your interviewees. Different sets of questions are required for the employees in the target audience and their managers.

### Questions for Target Audience

- "What is a typical day for you?"

- "With whom do you interact on a regular basis?"

- "What are the typical situations, customers, or projects that you deal with?"

- "What training have you received to prepare you for this position?"

- "What additional training do you think you need to help you do your job better?"

- "What are the most difficult aspects of your job?"

- "What do you like best about your job?"

- "How do you know you are doing a good job?"

- "What type of feedback do you receive about your job performance?"

- "How often do you receive feedback?"

### Questions for Managers of Target Audience

- "What would you like your employees to do differently?"

- "How would you describe the current level of performance in your department (or unit or team)?"

- "What are the important issues, problems, or changes your employees face at the present time?"

- "What skills, knowledge, or behaviors do you think your employees need to acquire or improve on in order to do their jobs better?"

- "What are the potential barriers that might get in the way of your training efforts?"

- "What methods do you use to measure employee performance?"

- "How often do you give feedback to your employees about their performance?"
- "What is the biggest challenge you face as a manager?"

As mentioned earlier, communication is critical throughout the process. Interviews must be carefully planned and executed. The following guidelines will help you to conduct interviews smoothly and efficiently.

- *Schedule in Advance.* Be respectful of people's time. Be sure to contact your interviewees well in advance of the interview and arrange meetings at their convenience. If they view an interview as an imposition and a disruption, they will probably not be as forthcoming or cooperative in responding to questions. It is also helpful to send the questions in advance so they can prepare or think about their answers. This preparation will enable the interview to move along more efficiently, and the interviewees' answers will be more meaningful.

- *Prepare an Agenda.* Good meeting management includes an agenda, prepared and sent out well in advance of the meeting. Needs-assessment interviews are no exception. Be sure to indicate the purpose and provide some direction or guidelines on how the interviewees can prepare for the interview. Of course, also include logistical information such as the date, location, and the time (both starting and ending).

- *Ensure Privacy.* This point should be a given; however, unless you take special care to arrange for a private meeting spot ahead of time, you might find yourself meeting in a less-than-ideal environment.

- *Eliminate Distractions and Interruptions.* Once again, planning is key. Take the necessary steps to ensure that you are not interrupted during the interview. In many cases, this means that you will need to communicate the importance of the interview session in advance and request that the interviewee do whatever it takes to maintain an interruption-free environment. If possible, try to conduct the interview away from the work site.

- *Clarify Purpose.* Begin the interview by clarifying the purpose of the meeting. Emphasize the importance of the needs assessment process and clearly explain the entire process and what you are going to do with the information. Give interviewees an opportunity to ask questions about the process before beginning the formal interview session.

- *Stress Confidentiality.* Assure all interviewees that their answers and remarks will be held in the strictest confidence. Be sure to explain how the information will be used. Focus groups, in particular, need to be reminded that, although the speaker's identity will be protected, what the person says will be recorded. It is critical that members of the focus group respect one another and not divulge any information shared within the group.

- *Use Good Communication Techniques.* To be an effective interviewer, hone your active listening skills, particularly your ability to clarify and confirm. Interviewees are prone to rambling and talking in generalities. Make sure that you understand clearly what the other person is saying. The following communication techniques will help you to gather the information you need:

  "Tell me more about. . . ."

  "Give me an example of. . . ."

  "Let me make sure I understand. What I heard was. . . ."

  "If I heard you correctly, you believe that. . . ."

  Whatever you do, don't say, "What you mean is. . ." or "What you're saying is. . . ." These statements imply that the speaker is not articulate enough to express himself or herself, and you have to help him or her out.

**Observation.** Observation involves a person who has received training in observation skills actually observing others on the job. Trained observers look for specific behaviors and are skilled in writing down their observations objectively in concrete behavioral terms. Observations are often used to validate information gathered by other methods such as interviews or questionnaires. Another observation technique makes use of an outside "shopper." Some organizations (banks, retail sales) hire outside professionals to conduct telephone or face-to-face shopping surveys. With this method, representatives from the consulting company go into a store or branch office and pretend to be customers. They note specific behaviors such as how they were greeted, friendliness, and knowledge level of the employees. They may look for evidence of cross-selling efforts or an offer of further assistance.

**Questionnaires/Survey Instruments.** An important consideration in using instruments is whether to develop them or purchase them. Questionnaires with open-ended questions are easy to construct, whereas questionnaires with closed-ended questions require more time and thought. Although published surveys can be costly, using them can not only save you time but will yield more accurate information because they have been tested for validity and reliability. Be aware, however, that published instruments may or may not be specific enough for a given situation. For both questionnaires and surveys, be sure to send a cover letter to participants explaining the purpose and what will be done with the results of the instrument. Make the instructions crystal clear.

## Step Four: Analyze Data

Data analysis can be simple or quite complex, depending on the methods chosen. For *qualitative* data, such as individual or group interviews, as well as open-ended questionnaires and observation, do a content analysis, sorting information into categories (for example, positive and negative reactions) and identifying common themes. The goal of the content analysis is to categorize and quantify the data as much as possible with minimal interpretation.

For *quantitative* data (survey instruments and close-ended questionnaires), do a statistical analysis. Keep it as simple as possible. Do not become engulfed in number-crunching activities. Look at the data in terms of mean (the average, calculated by adding all the values and dividing by the number in the group), mode (the number that occurs most frequently), and median (the middle number in a numerical listing).

If your research indicates that training is appropriate, specify the type of training called for. Should it be workshop training, on-the-job, self-study, computer-based, or what? Training must address the problem specifically, and the systems must be in place to support the training outcomes. For example, you may identify a customer-service training program as the solution to customer complaints and lost business. Participants in the training will learn how to handle customer complaints tactfully and respond to customer inquiries politely and efficiently. Yet the program will fail if slow delivery makes it hard for the customer to buy the product.

**Clarify and Define the Problem.** Although the problem may have been stated at the beginning of the needs assessment process by the key players in the organization, those are really *perceptions* of the problem. The data-collection process and subsequent analysis of that data will help to clarify and to define the *real* problem.

**NEEDS-ASSESSMENT EXAMPLE**

A client asked me to deliver a stress management program for a group of executive secretaries. In a discussion with my contact, the training director, I probed to uncover what events may have triggered the request. During a recent company-wide employee meeting, several secretaries were quite outspoken in expressing their dissatisfaction with the way they were being treated. As a result, senior management concluded that this group needed stress management. Although actual performance had not been affected, the morale and interpersonal relationships were deteriorating rapidly. I suggested that, before I developed a program specific to their situation, it would be a good idea to talk with a few members of the target audience. The training director agreed, and we arranged a focus group meeting with six of the secretaries. As I listened to the secretaries, it became increasingly clear that most of the stress the secretaries were experiencing stemmed from a single cause: the inability of the secretaries and managers to communicate effectively with one another. After listening to the secretaries' complaints and perceptions of the problem, I concluded that a stress management program was not the answer. In fact, it would be a waste of time and money. I suggested that we attack the cause of the problem, not its symptoms. I recommended that I design and deliver a program that would promote open, two-way communication between each secretary and her immediate supervisor by showing them how to improve their communication skills and to work more effectively as members of a boss/secretary team.

During the analysis phase, you will add to your perceptions of the problem through qualitative data such as interviews and focus groups. Verify your perceptions with survey results and other quantitative data. After categorizing the data, the next step is to identify priorities, always keeping in mind the business need. The prioritization process is extremely important since your needs assessment will probably result in a long list of training needs. Based on an analysis of the data, make your recommendations for specific training programs or interventions.

## Step Five: Provide Feedback

After the data have been collected and analyzed, identify the area(s) of need, design an action plan or strategies, and communicate your conclusions and recommendations to key personnel. This feedback should be delivered in both a written and an oral format. As you prepare to communicate your findings and recommendations, keep in mind that the goal is to get approval for your proposal. Plan a strategy for presenting the information in a positive light. Carefully think through what (and how much) to share, how to share, and with whom to share findings and recommendations.

**The Written Report.** The final report is a critical piece. It should be constructed in such a way that it presents the data in an easy-to-understand format along with conclusions and recommendations. The length of the final report, of course, depends on how extensive the assessment is. In any case, the written report should contain the following elements:

**Executive Overview.** Provide an overview of your proposal for executives, an abbreviated, concise representation of the larger document, limited to one page and distributed to the key decision makers.

**Description of the Process.** Provide appropriate background information, such as the problem statement or current situation and briefly describe the entire needs assessment process, including purpose, scope, methods used, and the people involved. Be sure to include your rationale, that is, your reason for conducting a needs assessment.

**Summary of Findings.** In this section, present your data clearly and concisely, highlighting patterns or significant results.

**Preliminary Conclusions.** Address the analysis of the data, focusing on key issues that have surfaced. It may be appropriate to show how the findings relate to or support your (or others') perceptions. Point out how the issues relate to the business need. Do not assume that readers will make the connection by themselves.

**Recommendations.** At this point, list your ideas and recommended solutions to the problem. When identifying training issues, be clear about what programs should be implemented, who should be involved, and how, when, and where the training will take place. Be careful not to lock yourself in by being too specific.

**Potential Barriers.** Solutions to problems are not without problems themselves. Take a proactive approach by addressing potential barriers up-front and suggesting ways to overcome them. Potential barriers can be almost anything, but the most common will probably be cost, time commitment, and the commitment of the target audience and/or their managers.

**Oral Presentation.** In addition to the written proposal, plan to present your information and recommendations to a selected audience. The oral presentation is an opportunity to hear reactions from the key players. Be prepared for questions and challenges. Anticipate what they may be and have responses and answers ready. Look at your presentation as a chance to sell your ideas. That means you will need to fine-tune your persuasion and influencing skills. Ask someone who is a skillful presenter and persuader to coach you before your presentation or, if you have the time and the opportunity, participate in a workshop on persuasive presentations.

**Selected Audience.** Your selected audience depends on a number of factors such as the corporate culture and internal politics. In general, include key decision makers and representative stakeholders such as members of the target audience, their managers, and anyone who may have a vested interest in the program's success. Also, the number of meetings and the levels involved in receiving the feedback should relate to the scope of the assessment. For example, if everyone in the organization completed an employee-opinion survey, then every employee should receive feedback. This is generally done in various group meetings, with the managers sharing the results of the survey along with the appropriate action plan.

**Length.** In many cases, you may have little control over the length of the presentation. Senior management will probably determine the time available based on their schedules, priorities, and other commitments. If they do not, then request an hour. That will give enough time to present your case and address any questions or concerns the executives might raise.

**Format/Approach.** The key here is to present findings in summary form. Use slides or transparencies of bulleted points and simple charts and graphs to illustrate and highlight important information.

# Developing an Action Plan

After presenting the information and making recommendations, solicit reactions and feedback from the key players. It is possible that they will immediately approve your proposal. More likely, however, you will be asked to make some modifications. In some cases, you may have to go back to the drawing board several times.

Once your proposal has been approved, map out a plan for the design, development, and delivery of the program(s). Include specific action items with a time line and appropriate task assignments.

The next step in the process of designing a program that meets the specific developmental needs of the participants and the business needs of the organization is to write learning outcomes or objectives, which are addressed in detail in Chapter 5. However, before you begin the design and development process, examine some critical elements that are often overlooked: how adults learn, the different learning styles of your participants, and your own training style. Finally, examine some of the diversity issues in today's workplace that will have an impact on how you design, develop, and deliver effective training programs. These important considerations will be addressed in Chapters 2, 3, and 4.

# Assessing Participants' Knowledge, Attitudes, Skills

So far, we have looked at the needs-assessment process that serves as the basis of training design, development, and evaluation. It may seem that after you receive the go-ahead to design and develop a program targeted to specific needs, the needs-assessment task is over. Not so! You also must assess the knowledge, attitudes, and skill level of the participants prior to each session. Different audiences may have different needs. For example, let's say the organization has decided to implement a management development program to include all levels of management from first-line supervisor to senior manager level. The needs of a first-line supervisor will be different from those of a mid-level manager, and certainly different from those of a senior manager. Therefore, participants at each level must be further assessed.

### Pre-Session Questionnaire

A short, simple, and straightforward questionnaire such as the one shown in Exhibit 1.3 can be an invaluable tool in fine-tuning your program.

The information you receive from such a questionnaire will help you in the following ways:

1. It can help to design the program at the appropriate level, not insulting participants' intelligence (and boring them to death) by dealing with content they already know. By the same token, you do not want to lose them by talking over their heads.

2. A questionnaire allows you to identify those participants who have greater familiarity with the training topic so you can draw on them as resources.

**EXHIBIT 1.3.   Confidential Pre-Session Questionnaire**

## Management Skills and Techniques: Part III

The purpose of this questionnaire is to provide the facilitator of this program with insights into your current skills in or knowledge about the subject of managing others. By knowing what new skills and knowledge you would like from the program, the facilitator will be better able to meet your needs.

Name: _____ Current Position: _____

Organization: _____ City, State: _____

Previous positions held:


Formal education beyond high school:


What management courses, workshops, or seminars have you attended?


Briefly describe the responsibilities of your current position:


How long have you managed or supervised others?


How many people do you directly supervise or manage?


What do you believe is the most difficult problem or challenge you face when managing people?


What one specific thing do you want to get out of this program?


What concerns do you have about participating in this learning experience?

---

Conversely, by identifying those with less familiarity with a topic, you will know who may need additional attention or encouragement.

3. The questionnaire will help to weed out those who do not belong in the session because they are under-qualified, over-qualified, or doing work for which the program is irrelevant. This is particularly important for voluntary, open-enrollment programs advertised to all employees in an organization. Unfortunately, no matter how well the course description identifies the target audience and learning outcomes, invariably those who do not read beyond the title will sign up for programs for which they are not suited. When that happens, take the person aside, explain that the session may not meet his or her expectations, and offer the person the option of leaving. Should the person choose to stay, you have at least been up-front about what the participant can and cannot expect.

4. The questionnaire can be used to gather information to use in creating real-life case studies, skill practices, and examples. The more relevant you can make your material, the more the participants will embrace the training. Of course, assure the participants that their contributions may be used but not identified.

5. The questionnaire can identify potential problems caused by negative attitudes so that you can take steps to overcome these barriers or pockets of resistance.

6. The questionnaire can create a positive learning environment even before the program starts. It can help participants be mentally prepared for the training. Also, your interest in finding out about them even before they come to your session will make them more receptive to you and what you have to offer.

## On-the-Spot Assessment

Regardless of how extensive your needs assessment is, it is also a good idea to conduct an informal, on-the-spot, individual needs assessment at the beginning of the first session. Start by asking the participants what they expect from the session. Their answers will give you an indication of whether or not your design is on target. This on-the-spot assessment will also provide an opportunity to clarify participants' expectations. Reinforce those expectations that are on target with the training design

## KEY POINTS

- A needs assessment serves as the basis for program development.

- A needs assessment identifies the gap between the actual and desired performance.

- A needs assessment provides criteria for measuring program success.

- Start with an organizational context, that is, the business impact of the training need.

- Use a variety of methods to assess training needs: surveys, interviews, observations, questionnaires, performance data, etc.

- Get input from various sources, including senior management, target population, target population's managers, direct reports, co-workers, customers, vendors, human resources professionals, competitors, and industry experts.

- Follow a prescribed five-step process to identify both the business needs of the organization and the developmental needs of the participants.

or make last-minute adjustments to the program, to make sure participants' needs are met. Sometimes, participants may have expectations that you cannot possibly meet in the session. Chapter 8 covers some specific interactive on-the-spot needs assessment activities.

Once you have completed the needs assessment and developed your action plan, the next step is to design the training program. Before doing so, however, you need to have a clear understanding of how adults learn so that you reflect adult-learning principles throughout your training program.

# Chapter 2

# Understanding Adult Learners

---

**LEARNING OUTCOMES**

In this chapter, you will learn

- To examine the basic principles of adult learning that all trainers should know before undertaking a training assignment

- To identify ways to overcome resistance to learning

---

## Andragogical Versus Pedagogical Model

People have been "brought up" on the pedagogical model of learning that has dominated education and training for centuries. Because that has been the standard, people use that approach when they are asked to teach or train others. In brief, the pedagogical model makes the following assumptions:

- The teacher is responsible for the learning process, including what and how learners learn. The learner's role is passive.

- Because the learner has little experience, the teacher is the expert, the guru, and it is his or her responsibility to impart his or her wealth of knowledge. This amounts to an "information dump" through traditional means such as lecture, textbooks, manuals, and videos in which other "experts" share their knowledge and experience.

- People are motivated to learn because they "have to" in order to pass a test, advance to the next level, or earn certification.

- Learning is information-centered. The teacher "covers" the material so that the learner can acquire the prescribed information in some type of logical order.

- Motivation to learn is largely external. Pressure from authority figures and fear of negative consequences drive the learner. The teacher, in essence, controls the learning through rewards and discipline.

## Understanding How and Why People Learn

Although adult education theorists differ on just how different adults are from children, most embrace the andragogical theory of adult learning. During the 1960s, European adult educators coined the term "andragogy" to provide a label for a growing body of knowledge and technology in regard to adult learning. The concept was introduced and advanced in the United States by Malcolm Knowles. The following assumptions underlie the andragogical model of learning, which Knowles now calls a model of human learning (Knowles, 1990):

### Assumption One

The first assumption involves a change in self-concept from total dependency to increasing *self-directedness.* The adult learner is self-directed. Adult learners want to take responsibility for their own lives, including the planning, implementing, and evaluating of their learning activities. This principle is often misinterpreted. Learner self-directedness does not mean the trainer abdicates responsibility for the plan or approach. From the beginning, the trainer establishes the training process as a collaborative effort. Throughout the process, the trainer and participant should be partners engaged in ongoing, two-way communication.

### Assumption Two

The second principle addresses the role of *experience,* a principle unique to the adult learner. According to Knowles, each of us brings to a learning situation a wealth of experiences that provide a base for new learning as well as a resource to share with others. These experiences may be good or bad, but they will impact the way in which an employee approaches a new learning experience. Because people base their learning on past experiences, the new information must be assimilated. The wise trainer will find out what the participants already know and will build on those experiences, rather than treating participants as though they know nothing and must be *taught* like small children.

## Assumption Three

The third assumption is that adults are ready to learn when they perceive a *need to know or do something* in order to perform more effectively in some aspect of their lives. The days of abstract theories and concepts are over for most adults. They want the learning experience to be practical and realistic, problem-centered rather than subject-centered. The effective trainer helps participants understand how learning a particular skill or task will help them be more successful, that is, how the employee can do the job quicker, easier, more efficiently.

## Assumption Four

Fourth, adults want immediate, *real-world applications.* They want the skills and knowledge to help them solve problems or complete tasks. People are motivated to learn when they see relevance to their real-life situations and are able to apply what they have learned as quickly as possible. Therefore, learning activities need to be clearly relevant to the immediate needs of the adult. To be effective, deliver just-in-time training and emphasize how the training is going to make participants' jobs easier.

## Assumption Five

Finally, adults are motivated to learn because of *internal factors* such as self-esteem, desire for recognition, natural curiosity, innate love of learning, better quality of life, greater self-confidence, or the opportunity to self-actualize.

## Principles of Adult Learning

As you begin to design and develop any training program for adults, keep in mind these additional principles regarding how adults learn:

- Adults must recognize the need to learn.
- Adults want to apply new learning back on the job.
- Adults need to integrate past experience with new material.

- Adults prefer the concrete to the abstract.

- Adults need a variety of training methods.

- Adults learn better in an informal, comfortable environment.

- Adults want to solve realistic problems.

- Adults prefer the hands-on method of learning.

# Learning Styles

Adults learn through a variety of ways. One person may learn better by listening; another may be visual or may prefer to read instructions. Someone else will need a demonstration.

Learning style refers to the way in which a learner approaches and responds to a learning experience. There are several learning style assessments available on the market including the following instruments, published in the Pfeiffer *Annuals*:

- Learning Style Inventory by Ronne Toker Jacobs and Barbara Schneider Fuhrmann (1984)

- The Learning Model Instrument by Kenneth L. Murrell (1987)

- The Dunn and Dunn Model of Learning Styles by Joanne Ingham and Rita Dunn (1993)

David Kolb's Learning Style Inventory (1991) is used widely as a basis for other models and instruments. These, among others, are all excellent tools to help you identify learning style. The self-assessment process heightens your awareness that different people learn in different ways and sensitizes people to the importance of designing training that addresses all learning styles.

## Determining Your Learning Style

To get a flavor for these style differences and to further your understanding of your preferred learning style, complete the learning style assessment in Exhibit 2.1, then score and study it.

**EXHIBIT 2.1. Learning Style Profile**

*Instructions:* For each of the numbered items below, rank alternatives A through D by assigning 4 to the phrase that is most like you, 3 to the one that next describes you, 2 to the next, and finally, 1 to the ending that is least descriptive of you.

1. When solving a problem, I prefer to. . .

    a. take a step-by-step approach

    b. take immediate action

    c. consider the impact on others

    d. make sure I have all the facts

2. As a learner, I prefer to. . .

    a. listen to a lecture

    b. work in small groups

    c. read articles and case studies

    d. participate in role plays

3. When the trainer asks a question to which I know the answer, I. . .

    a. let others answer first

    b. offer an immediate response

    c. consider whether my answer will be received favorably

    d. think carefully about my answer before responding

4. In a group discussion, I. . .

    a. encourage others to offer their opinions

    b. question others' opinions

    c. readily offer my opinion

    d. listen to others before offering my opinion

**EXHIBIT 2.1.  Learning Style Profile, Cont'd**

5.  I learn best from activities in which I. . .

   a.  can interact with others

   b.  remain uninvolved

   c.  take a leadership role

   d.  can take my time

6.  During a lecture, I listen for. . .

   a.  practical how-to's

   b.  logical points

   c.  the main idea

   d.  stories and anecdotes

7.  I am impressed by a trainer's. . .

   a.  knowledge and expertise

   b.  personality and style

   c.  use of methods and activities

   d.  organization and control

8.  I prefer information to be presented in the following way:

   a.  a model such as a flow chart

   b.  bullet points

   c.  detailed explanation

   d.  accompanied by examples

**EXHIBIT 2.1.  Learning Style Profile, Cont'd**

9.  I learn best when I. . .

   a.  see relationships among ideas, events, and situations

   b.  interact with others

   c.  receive practical tips

   c.  observe a demonstration or video

10.  Before attending a training program, I ask myself: "Will I. . .?"

   a.  get practical tips to help me in my job

   b.  receive lots of information

   c.  have to participate

   d.  learn something new

11.  After attending a training session, I. . .

   a.  tend to think about what I learned

   b.  am anxious to put my learning into action

   c.  reflect on the experience as a whole

   d.  tell others about my experience

12.  The training method I dislike the most is. . .

   a.  participating in small groups

   b.  listening to a lecture

   c.  reading and analyzing case studies

   d.  participating in role plays

| EXHIBIT 2.1.    Learning Style Profile, Cont'd |
|---|

## Scoring Sheet

*Instructions:* Record your responses on the appropriate spaces below, then total the columns. The higher the number, the more you prefer that particular style. Conversely, the lower the number, the less you prefer that style.

| Feeler | Observer | Thinker | Doer |
|---|---|---|---|
| 1c _____ | 1a _____ | 1d _____ | 1b _____ |
| 2b _____ | 2a _____ | 2c _____ | 2d _____ |
| 3c _____ | 3a _____ | 3d _____ | 3b _____ |
| 4a _____ | 4d _____ | 4b _____ | 4c _____ |
| 5a _____ | 5b _____ | 5d _____ | 5c _____ |
| 6d _____ | 6c _____ | 6b _____ | 6a _____ |
| 7b _____ | 7d _____ | 7a _____ | 7c _____ |
| 8d _____ | 8a _____ | 8c _____ | 8b _____ |
| 9b _____ | 9d _____ | 9a _____ | 9c _____ |
| 10d _____ | 10c _____ | 10b _____ | 10a _____ |
| 11d _____ | 11c _____ | 11a _____ | 11b _____ |
| 12c _____ | 12a _____ | 12d _____ | 12b _____ |
| Total _____ | Total _____ | Total _____ | Total _____ |

**EXHIBIT 2.1.    Learning Style Profile, Cont'd**

**Feelers.** Feelers are very people-oriented. They are expressive and focus on feelings and emotions. They enjoy affective learning and gravitate toward learning experiences that explore people's attitudes and emotions. Feelers thrive in an open, unstructured learning environment and appreciate the opportunity to work in groups and like activities in which they can share opinions and experiences.

**Observers.** Observers like to watch and listen. They tend to be reserved and quiet and will take their time before acting or participating in class. When they do decide to offer an opinion or answer a question, they are generally right on target. They enjoy learning experiences that allow them to consider various ideas and opinions, and they seem to thrive on learning through discovery.

**Thinkers.** Thinkers rely on logic and reason. They like the opportunity to share ideas and concepts. They prefer activities that require them to analyze and evaluate. They will question the rationale behind activities and will challenge statements that they perceive to be too general or without substance. The thinkers prefer to work independently and question the relevance of role plays and simulations.

**Doers.** Doers like to be actively involved in the learning process. They will take charge in group activities and tend to dominate discussions. They like opportunities to practice what they learned, and they are particularly interested in knowing how they are going to apply what they learn in the real world. They like information presented clearly and concisely and become impatient with drawn-out discussions.

Keep in mind that no one learning style is right or even better than another. The point is that each person learns differently. A variety of learning styles will be represented in any training session. To be effective, trainers must design their programs to accommodate style differences. Predictably, trainers use the styles they prefer. Although it is natural to use the style with which one is most comfortable, the most effective trainers will learn how to adapt their styles to meet the needs of all participants. You will have an opportunity to find out about your preferred training style in Chapter 3.

## Perceptual Modality

In addition to learning styles, an effective trainer must be able to understand the different perceptual modalities. According to M.B. James and M.W. Galbraith (1985), a learner may prefer one of the following six perceptual modalities, ways in which one takes in and processes information:

| | |
|---|---|
| Visual | Videos; slides; graphs; photos; demonstrations; methods and media that create opportunities for the participant to experience learning through the eyes |
| Print | Texts; paper-and-pencil exercises that enable the participant to absorb the written word |
| Aural | Lectures; audiotapes; methods that allow the participant to simply listen and take in information through the ears |
| Interactive | Group discussions; question-and-answer sessions; ways that give the participant an opportunity to talk and engage in an exchange of ideas, opinions, reactions with fellow participants |
| Tactile | Hands-on activities; model building methods that require the participant to handle objects or put things together |
| Kinesthetic | Role plays; physical games and activities that involve the use of psychomotor skills and movement from one place to another |

Research indicates that more adults are visual learners than any other perceptual style; however, a good training design incorporates all six modalities to ensure that all participants' needs are being addressed. Vary activities to create multi-sensory learning that will increase the likelihood of appealing to each participant's style.

This multi-sensory approach also helps each participant reinforce the knowledge or skills acquired through the preferred modality.

Learning should be presented in a way that complements each person's preferred modality. For example, let's look at a design for training several people in a group setting to use a personal computer. The trainer includes pictures of the computer screen, illustrating what the person should *see* when he or she strikes a particular key. The trainer also demonstrates how to perform certain functions on the computer *(visual)*. The training design includes print materials such as a manual and short application-oriented quizzes *(print)*. For review and reinforcement, the trainer prepares an audiotape *(aural)*. During daily instructional sessions, the trainer provides many opportunities for the trainee to answer as well as ask questions *(interactive)*. Of course, the design includes multiple opportunities for hands-on practice *(tactile)*. Finally, the trainer will create simulation activities in which the trainees will be asked to create "real-life" work-related documents such as spreadsheets, reports, graphs, etc. *(kinesthetic)*.

Another important consideration is that people generally learn by doing, not by being told how to do something. For example, a person learns more quickly how to reach a new location by driving the car rather than by observing as a passenger. So the more opportunities a person has to "try out" or apply the skills, the more likely he or she is to learn the skills.

Telling is not teaching or training. How many times have you said to yourself, "I've told him and told him how to do it, but he still gets it wrong"? Just because you tell someone how to do something doesn't mean he or she understands it or has developed the skill to do it.

Still other factors affect the speed at which people learn.

**Psychological.**  Some people prefer the "big picture," while others want a step-by-step process.

**Environmental.**  Sound, light, temperature, and seating can all impact learning. For example, sitting in a hard chair for several hours will put stress on the body, interfering with a person's ability to concentrate.

**Emotional.**  Participants' motivation for attending the session will influence the learning process. Those who attend because they want to are more likely to have a positive learning experience than those who are there because their supervisors required them to attend.

**Sociological.** People are by nature social beings. Although some people do learn better alone, studies show that most people learn better and experience greater satisfaction with the learning experience when they are in pairs or small groups.

**Physical.** People's physical condition, including hearing, sight, general health, and energy level, impact their ability to learn. Most people have less energy in the afternoon. Trainers should keep this in mind when designing and developing their programs.

**Intellectual and Experiential.** People in your sessions will vary greatly in educational background, life experiences, innate intelligence, and abilities. That is why it's important to find out as much as possible about your participants before they attend training sessions.

**Age.** One of the frequent issues that comes up in train-the-trainer and coaching courses relates to the impact of age on the learning process. Managers, supervisors, and trainers often say that older workers are slower and more difficult to train.

To set the record straight, researchers are somewhat divided on the issue of age and one's ability to learn, depending on one's interpretation of learning. In general, research on adult learning shows that adults continue to learn throughout the years; however, they may take longer to learn new things (Sterns & Doverspike, 1988). Although younger folks seem to be more efficient when it comes to memorizing information, older people are better able to evaluate and apply information. Research findings show that change in adulthood is a procession of critical periods during the fifty plus years following childhood and youth. These periods consist of marked changes and experiences during which some of the most meaningful learning may occur.

Adults have a potential for continuing learning and inquiry that conventional wisdom has sometimes failed to recognize. Researchers, however, do recognize that physical changes play a part in the learning process. As we age, we may experience some hearing loss, lower energy levels, and slower reaction time. These factors should be taken into consideration; however, they should not be regarded as proof that older people are slower or have greater difficulty learning. By observing adult-learning principles as well as basic concepts of individual differences and accommodating them accordingly, a trainer can effectively train any adult.

## Cognitive Overload

Our minds are like sponges as we soak up knowledge and information. When sponges are saturated, any additional water will run right through. Just as the sponge is overloaded, a learner can experience cognitive overload of his or her working memory. This working memory—the center of conscious thinking—has an estimated limited capacity of seven "chunks" or pieces of information. The limits on our working memory depend on the knowledge we have stored in long-term memory. A person who is quite comfortable with and knowledgeable about a subject can easily overwhelm those who are less familiar with the information. The challenge to the trainer is to present information in such a way that the participants do not experience overload.

## Preventing Cognitive Overload

To prevent cognitive overload, use the following strategies when designing, developing, and delivering your training:

- *Minimize the use of lecture.* Boil down information into key learning points, checklists, charts, graphs, or other visuals.

- *Have the participants do most of the work.* When the participants do the work, they transfer new information into long-term memory, much like storing data in a computer. The working memory is now free to absorb the next chunk of information.

- *Create chunks of content or information, and distribute or communicate it incrementally.* Use a variety of activities to communicate the material.

- *Design workbooks and other participant materials that present information in an easy-to-follow and easy-to-understand format.*

- *Create job aids for use during and after the training.*

# Application of Learning Principles

These concepts have certain implications for the trainer. The traditional or pedagogical orientation is concerned with content. Trainers are concerned with "covering" material in the most efficient way possible. In contrast, the andragogical orientation focuses on process, being attentive to the factors that either promote or inhibit learning.

Based on what you know about the adult learner and how learning takes place, take those principles and concepts and translate them into practical applications in your training programs. Consider the following points as you create a learning experience for your participants:

- Create a comfortable, non-threatening learning climate in which people are treated as responsible adults.

- Involve participants in planning their training through interviews, advisory committees, and other up-front activities.

- Allow participants to engage in self-diagnosis by using questionnaires and assessment instruments both before and during sessions.

- Give participants an opportunity to set their own objectives by soliciting their input through pre-session questionnaires and assessment activities at the beginning of sessions.

- Give them an opportunity to evaluate their own learning through a variety of activities throughout the training program.

- Help them understand the "big picture" by pointing out how the particular training program relates to the business objectives and/or problems.

- Make the learning relevant to them, that is, show how it will help them, by using "real-world" examples and activities that connect with their frames of reference.

- Use their experience by asking them to share examples from their own situations.

- Actively involve the participants in the learning process by using learner-centered activities and structured experiences and by providing them with many opportunities to master the content.

The more you understand about how and why adults learn, the better equipped you will be to design training programs that meet participants' needs and obtain the results you want.

---

### KEY POINTS

- Training adults is different from teaching children.

- Adults need to be involved in planning, implementing, and evaluating their learning.

- Adults base their learning on past experiences.

- Adults expect training to be directly relevant to them and want real-world application.

- Adults learn in various ways.

---

Before you begin to develop your training program, you also need to have a clear understanding of how your own style and approach to training may impact the participants' learning experience.

# Chapter 3

# Training Styles

**LEARNING OUTCOMES**

In this chapter, you will learn

- To identify your own training-style preference

- To identify ways to increase your style flexibility

- To distinguish between learner-centered and information-centered training

- To define your own role in the success of the training experience

## Trainer Characteristics and Competencies

Recall your *best* and *worst* learning experiences from any time in your life (elementary school, high school, college, organizations, work). For each experience, briefly describe the highlights and list what factors made that experience good or bad.

Description of Good Experience:

Factors That Made It Good:

Description of Bad Experience:

Factors That Made It Bad:

Think about your feelings and reactions to both the good and bad experiences. How effective was the learning experience? To what degree did the training or learning experience contribute to your success?

During discussions of these questions in train-the-trainer programs, participants are quick to respond that the single most important factor in the success or failure of the learning experience was the instructor. People often share that the positive experiences had a positive impact on their success in life and how the negative experiences created major obstacles to further education and training. In some cases, the negative experience prevented them from seeking or taking advantage of opportunities that could have led to career advancement.

## Are You Trainer Material?

Being good at your job does not guarantee that you will be good at training someone else how to do it. To be effective, trainers must perfect their competencies in the following areas:

- First and foremost, training professionals must have a business orientation. They must concern themselves with improving performance and focus on business outcomes.

- Training professionals must also be able to recognize and admit when training is not the appropriate solution for a problem.

- To succeed in a diverse environment, trainers must fine-tune their interpersonal skills and be able to adapt to a variety of people, cultures, and situations.

- Those responsible for training others in a workshop setting must develop and master training skills. True professionals spend their entire lives honing their craft and perfecting their skills, learning new skills, and they keep up-to-date on the latest trends, concepts, and application to the field.

Over the years, educational research has identified personal and professional characteristics or attributes that are associated with successful teachers. These same attributes can be ascribed to trainers as well. Review the checklist in Exhibit 3.1 to identify those characteristics you bring to your role as a trainer. Place a check mark next to those that describe you.

# Training Style

Even if you have never done any formal training or teaching, you have already developed a training style, a combination of training philosophies, methods, and behaviors, as the result of the experiences you have had as a learner and as an

## EXHIBIT 3.1. Characteristics of Effective Trainers

| | |
|---|---|
| _____ Knowledge of subject | _____ Articulate |
| _____ Genuine | _____ Empathetic; understanding |
| _____ Well-organized | _____ Sense of humor |
| _____ Goal-oriented | _____ Uses a variety of methods |
| _____ Strong presence; poise | _____ Warm; approachable |
| _____ Professional appearance | _____ Tactful |
| _____ Ability to relate content to participants' situations | _____ Good voice quality |
| | _____ Enthusiastic |
| _____ Good listener | _____ Positive self-concept |
| _____ Patient | _____ Honest and open |
| _____ Flexible; spontaneous | _____ Participant-centered |
| _____ Positive attitude | _____ Respectful of participants |
| _____ Credible | _____ Emotional stability |
| _____ Ability to relate to others at all levels | _____ Diagnostician |
| | _____ Objective |
| _____ Coach and counselor | |

*The Trainer's Handbook, Updated Ed.* Copyright © 2009 by Karen Lawson. Reproduced by permission of Pfeiffer, an imprint of John Wiley & Sons, Inc.

unofficial trainer. The way in which you give directions to others (co-workers, friends, family members), present information, or explain how to do something reflects a preferred training style.

## Style Flexibility

Just as you have a preferred style of learning, you have a preferred approach to presenting content and relating to participants. Although you may have a strong preference for one style over another, you can and should learn to use the entire range of styles to connect with participants and facilitate the learning process.

Much like management or leadership styles, inherent in training styles is the need to balance continually concern for task or content with concern for people. This is further complicated by the fact that different training styles impact different types of learners in different ways.

## Identifying Your Training Style

To heighten your awareness of your own style preferences, complete the assessment instrument in Exhibit 3.2, using your most recent training assignment as a frame of reference. You are evaluating yourself as "the trainer" and thus ranking statements in terms of how you think you behave. To gain a more accurate and complete picture of your training style, ask others to evaluate you by completing the assessment, and then compare results.

# Increasing Effectiveness

As mentioned in the description of styles in the interpretation section of the Instructional Styles Diagnosis Inventory, the "coach" is probably the most appropriate style for a true training situation. This style and its underlying philosophy are reflected throughout this book. The coaching style supports and reinforces the cooperative learning approach to training adults.

Keep in mind, however, that the coaching style is not going to be appropriate for every learner. The challenge is to increase style flexibility and learn to assess what style or approach is the most appropriate with a particular situation, group, or individual learner. Flexibility is the key to success, that is, changing and adapting throughout the training program as you are faced with new challenges from the participants. Trainers have trouble when they either cannot or will not adapt to the styles and needs of the participants.

**EXHIBIT 3.2.   Instructional Styles Diagnosis Inventory**

*Instructions:* Think of your most recent learning experience with the trainer who is being evaluated. Each of the twenty items that follows contains four statements about what instructors can do or ways in which they can act.

Rank each set of statements to reflect the degree to which each statement in the set describes the trainer's instructional style. Assign a ranking of four (4) to the statement most characteristic or descriptive of the trainer; assign a three (3) to the next most descriptive statement; a two (2) to the next most descriptive statement; and a one (1) to the statement that is least descriptive of the trainer. Record your response for each statement in the blank next to it.

For some items, you may think that all statements are very descriptive or that none fit very well. To give the most accurate feedback, force yourself to rank the statements as best you can.

## "When Instructing Adults, This Person Would Be Most Likely to . . ."

1. ____ a. Allow extended practice or discussion in areas of particular interest to learners.

   ____ b. Judge trainer's effectiveness by how well the prepared materials are covered.

   ____ c. Sit down with learners while instructing them.

   ____ d. Set trainer up as a role model and encourage learners to emulate trainer.

2. ____ a. End a training session by summarizing the key subject matter and recommending that learners find ways to apply it on the job.

   ____ b. Arrange the room so as to provide for better discipline and control.

   ____ c. Use specific course objectives to inform learners as to what they should expect to be able to do.

   ____ d. Focus learners' attention more on themselves and their own performance than on trainer.

| EXHIBIT 3.2. | Instructional Styles Diagnosis Inventory, Cont'd. |
|---|---|

3. \_\_\_\_ a. Gain supervisors' involvement by providing ideas on how to support learners' attempts to apply new skills.

     \_\_\_\_ b. Let the group "handle" difficult learners or privately explore reasons for problems.

     \_\_\_\_ c. Evaluate learners by giving examinations to test their retention of presented materials.

     \_\_\_\_ d. Carefully lead and control any group discussions.

4. \_\_\_\_ a. Put his or her primary focus on giving a technically polished presentation.

     \_\_\_\_ b. Avoid reducing impact by not disclosing any course materials prior to the program.

     \_\_\_\_ c. Show willingness to learn from learners by admitting errors or lack of knowledge when appropriate.

     \_\_\_\_ d. Collect background information and adjust the level of content material for each particular group.

5. \_\_\_\_ a. Involve learners in activities designed to stimulate critical or reflective thought.

     \_\_\_\_ b. Communicate positive expectations to slower learners through feedback and encouragement, in order to help them improve.

     \_\_\_\_ c. Motivate learners with enthusiastic talks, humorous stories, and entertaining or inspirational videos.

     \_\_\_\_ d. Maintain punctuality of published program schedules.

6. \_\_\_\_ a. Make occasional use of media tools to support other primary learning activities.

     \_\_\_\_ b. Present materials in the most logical order.

     \_\_\_\_ c. Allow learners to influence or prioritize course content and objectives.

     \_\_\_\_ d. Ensure that learners perform and apply newly learned skills as instructed.

**EXHIBIT 3.2.   Instructional Styles Diagnosis Inventory, Cont'd.**

7. \_\_\_\_ a. Thoroughly cover all subject-matter areas in the scheduled time allotted.

\_\_\_\_ b. Change course materials or training methods based on feedback about performance changes after training.

\_\_\_\_ c. Maintain a consistent pace of presentation throughout the program.

\_\_\_\_ d. Express concern for and interest in individual learners and their problems.

8. \_\_\_\_ a. Judge trainer's effectiveness based on learners' "liking" of trainer.

\_\_\_\_ b. Allow learners to make mistakes and learn from session experiences.

\_\_\_\_ c. Expose learners to traditionally accepted subject matter and correct procedures.

\_\_\_\_ d. Ask learners questions designed to guide them to self-discovery of key points.

9. \_\_\_\_ a. Frequently assess learners' body language and emotional states and adjust activities or schedule appropriately.

\_\_\_\_ b. Explore content-related controversial issues as potential learning experiences.

\_\_\_\_ c. Plan and structure course materials in considerable detail.

\_\_\_\_ d. Begin program by informing learners of trainer's experience or qualifications and trainer's goals for the program.

10. \_\_\_\_ a. Cite a bibliography of resources concerning materials discussed for further learner self-development.

\_\_\_\_ b. Use position as instructor to quickly resolve "difficult learner" problems (e.g., monopolizers, side conversations, sharpshooters, etc.).

\_\_\_\_ c. Encourage casual or comfortable dress to increase the informality of the learning environment.

\_\_\_\_ d. Avoid potentially time-wasting tangents by dealing with learners' questions quickly and moving on.

**EXHIBIT 3.2.    Instructional Styles Diagnosis Inventory, Cont'd.**

11. ____ a. Direct learners' attention primarily to trainer and to what is being said or demonstrated.

____ b. Frequently redirect learners' questions to other learners to be answered.

____ c. Send out self-study "prework" materials to spark learner interest and formation of course expectations.

____ d. Consistently cover the same material with each group.

12. ____ a. Arrange the room so as to promote group activities and discussions.

____ b. Always stand in front of the class while instructing.

____ c. Send learners' bosses an overview of course subject matter.

____ d. Judge trainer's effectiveness based on how proficient learners are in performing new skills or applying new concepts on the job.

13. ____ a. Project a professional image by maintaining a separation between trainer and learners.

____ b. Help learners motivate themselves by developing new skills through involvement and participation.

____ c. Closely direct learners' activities.

____ d. Allow learners to analyze materials and draw their own conclusions.

14. ____ a. End a training session by helping learners create action plans to apply course content to real-world problems.

____ b. Criticize slow learners to help them improve.

____ c. Avoid controversy as a potential distraction or turnoff.

____ d. Coach learners as they practice new skills.

**EXHIBIT 3.2.   Instructional Styles Diagnosis Inventory, Cont'd.**

15. _____ a. Encourage detailed note taking by learners.

_____ b. Encourage learners to challenge outdated course materials or concepts of questionable value on the job.

_____ c. Sequence activities so as to stimulate and hold learner interest.

_____ d. Use media (video, slides, overheads, etc.) extensively to increase the professionalism of the presentation.

16. _____ a. Use an introductory overview to inform learners of the subject matter to be covered.

_____ b. Judge trainer's effectiveness based on learners' increase in confidence and self-esteem.

_____ c. Maintain a formal dress code to establish a more serious atmosphere.

_____ d. Encourage creativity in the performance and application of course concepts.

17. _____ a. Change course materials or training methods based on update of expertise in the subject matter.

_____ b. Begin a program by having learners introduce themselves to one another and communicate to trainer what their expectations are.

_____ c. Adjust time schedules during the program in response to learners' interests and concerns.

_____ d. Enhance credibility with learners by answering all questions quickly and accurately.

18. _____ a. Avoid potentially embarrassing questions and protect material by keeping content resources confidential.

_____ b. Highlight key points in detail, speaking from carefully prepared notes.

_____ c. Vary pace of the program to adjust to natural daily highs and lows in learners' energy levels.

_____ d. Evaluate learners based on their abilities to perform specific objectives.

| **EXHIBIT 3.2.** | **Instructional Styles Diagnosis Inventory, Cont'd.** |
|---|---|

19. ____ a. Defend trainer's expertise and credibility when challenged by a learner on a content issue.

____ b. Emphasize establishing open, two-way communication.

____ c. Leave the structure of the program loose to respond to the specific needs of the group.

____ d. Aim the level of sophistication of course material at the "average" learner.

20. ____ a. Listen attentively and observe group discussion of content issues or problem applications.

____ b. Ensure that learners reach the right conclusions and accept the key points or concepts presented.

____ c. Explore reasons that learners ask questions, to bring out individual concerns and hidden agendas.

____ d. Project confidence and assurance by using effective gestures, posture, and vocal dynamics while instructing.

**EXHIBIT 3.2.    Instructional Styles Diagnosis Inventory, Cont'd.**

# INSTRUCTIONAL STYLES DIAGNOSIS INVENTORY SCORING SHEET
(To be completed by trainer)

***Step 1.*** *Instructions:* Transfer the rankings from the ISDI to the Scoring Chart below. Note that the letter items in each set are **not** in alphabetical order.

**Scoring Chart**

|     | A | B | C | D |
|-----|---|---|---|---|
| 1   | d | a | c | b |
| 2   | b | c | d | a |
| 3   | d | a | b | c |
| 4   | a | d | c | b |
| 5   | c | a | b | d |
| 6   | b | c | a | d |
| 7   | c | b | d | a |
| 8   | a | b | d | c |
| 9   | d | b | a | c |
| 10  | b | a | c | d |
| 11  | a | c | b | d |
| 12  | b | d | a | c |
| 13  | a | d | b | c |
| 14  | b | a | d | c |
| 15  | d | b | c | a |
| 16  | c | d | b | a |
| 17  | d | c | b | a |
| 18  | b | d | c | a |
| 19  | a | c | b | d |
| 20  | d | c | a | b |
| Total | ____ | ____ | ____ | ____ |

***Step 2.*** Determine the sum of the rankings in each column and record them at the bottom of that column.

***Step 3.*** Subtract the lower of the Column A or C totals from the higher.

*The Trainer's Handbook, Updated Ed.* Copyright © 2009 by Karen Lawson. Reproduced by permission of Pfeiffer, an imprint of John Wiley & Sons, Inc.

## EXHIBIT 3.2.   Instructional Styles Diagnosis Inventory, Cont'd.

*Step 4.* Subtract the lower of the Column B and D totals from the higher.

*Step 5.* Plot the result from Step 3 on the vertical scale of the graph that follows. If the "A" total is higher, plot the result below the midpoint "O." If the "C" total is higher, plot the result above this point.

*Step 6.* Plot the result from Step 4 on the horizontal scale. If the "B" total is higher, plot the result to the right of the midpoint "O." If the "D" total is higher, plot the result to the left of this point.

*Step 7.* Extend lines from the plotted points on each scale to the point where the two lines intersect.

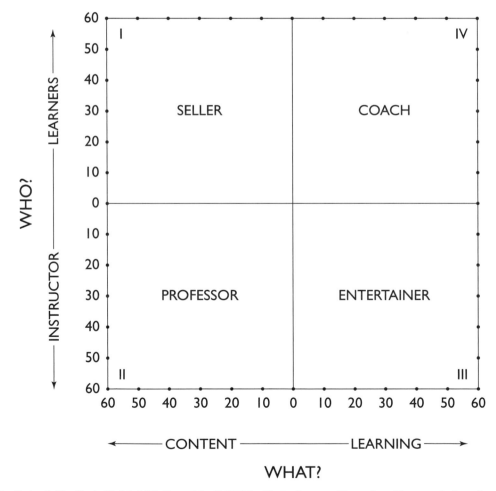

*The Trainer's Handbook, Updated Ed.* Copyright © 2009 by Karen Lawson. Reproduced by permission of Pfeiffer, an imprint of John Wiley & Sons, Inc.

**EXHIBIT 3.2.** Instructional Styles Diagnosis Inventory, Cont'd.

# INSTRUCTIONAL STYLES DIAGNOSIS INVENTORY INTERPRETATION SHEET

(For the trainer)

## Components of Instructional Styles

The styles that trainers use in developing and presenting learning experiences are based on their personal beliefs about what the purposes of instruction are and how they can best contribute to achieving those purposes.

The ISDI attempts to determine training style as the interactive product of two dimensions: *what* the trainer's attention is focused on and *who* is the focus of attention while the trainer is instructing. Each dimension is a function of two sets of concerns.

The *what* dimension (the horizontal scale) represents the tradeoff between:

1. Concern for content quality and thoroughness of presentation coverage (represented by the Column D total); and

2. Concern for the actual learning that takes place with learners who are working with the content (represented by the Column B total).

The *who* dimension (the vertical scale) represents the tradeoff between:

1. Concern for the trainer and how polished, impressive, or entertaining his or her delivery is (represented by the Column A total); and

2. Concern for the learners and how effectively or positively they are receiving, practicing, considering, discussing, or applying new skills (represented by the Column C total).

No model of this type is perfect. For instance, you may be able to think of trainers who are able to balance a high concern for content with a high concern for the learning that the content produces. However, for most instructors, it is realistic to expect that balancing the two involves influencing one at the expense of the other. The same may be said for the who dimension.

## Interpreting Your Scores

The point on the graph at which the scores of these two dimensions intersect represents your overall training style.

| EXHIBIT 3.2.  Instructional Styles Diagnosis Inventory, Cont'd. |
|---|

To interpret your results, you must consider three things:

1. The comparative strengths of the four individual column totals,

2. The position of each of the two dimension scores, and

3. The direction and distance from the center of the point where the two dimension scores intersect.

For instance, were the four column totals high and low or were they close to one another? This indicates whether you tend to balance each aspect of training style equally or whether some aspects differ greatly to you in degree of importance. This directly effects the position of the dimension scores, which is the next consideration. If a dimension score is far toward one extreme or the other, this indicates a higher degree of tradeoff between the two sets of concerns involved. Dimension scores more near the middle represent a balanced degree of tradeoff, regardless of individual emphasis.

The intersection of the two dimension scores represents your overall training style, the product of your attempt to achieve balance among concerns for content, learning, delivery, and reception. The further this point is from the center of the graph, the more extreme your training style tends to be. The closer to the center this point is, the more "balanced" it tends to be.

## Descriptions of Styles

Following are short descriptions of the types of behaviors, attitudes, tendencies, and preferences that characterize each of the four styles.

 ### I. "The Seller"

A person who has the "seller" instructional style is primarily concerned with the content and how positively it is received and understood. Learning is the participant's responsibility, and it may or may not happen as a result. Because getting the message across and creating a good attitude toward it are the primary goals, "seller" instructors tend to focus their attention on the learners and the learners' receptivity to the message.

**EXHIBIT 3.2.   Instructional Styles Diagnosis Inventory, Cont'd.**

They build a receptive atmosphere by creating a comfortable learning environment, encouraging learners, answering questions, varying the pace of the program, and so on. They tend to use lectures or prepared media presentation methods, interspersed with discussion to hold interest and attention. Note taking is encouraged to aid retention of material.

Homework, prework, and course-summary materials are used extensively to communicate or reinforce the content. Pass/fail or nongraded examinations are preferred to assess retention without turning the learners off.

The "seller" style is common in public schools and is probably more appropriate for building general educational backgrounds than for developing specific skills. It may also be appropriate for situations in which the selling of a technique, concept, or product is more important than the learners' becoming proficient in it. It is not as appropriate when learners are expected to perform better or differently as a result of the training.

## II. "The Professor"

Instructors who have a high concern for both content and delivery probably see themselves primarily as presenters. The "professor" types tend to be highly concerned about such things as their image, their technique and smoothness of speaking, and creating a proper impression. They prefer to have the spotlight on themselves, because this focuses the learners' attention on them. The atmosphere in their sessions tends to be formal, and the separation between the presenter and the audience is emphasized.

"Professor" types are, at the same time, concerned with the adequacy of what they are presenting. Their presentations are usually well-researched, often impressively footnoted and referenced, planned and organized in detail, and well-rehearsed. Time is important because it reflects on their images as presenters (i.e., punctuality is impressive) and on their ability to cover all important content.

Their preferred teaching method is to lecture, as this allows them to focus attention on themselves, to control time, and to cover the content they believe is important. There is a tendency to overuse or inappropriately use media such as video, slides, or overheads because of their perceived ability to impress, entertain, and present large amounts of information in short time spans.

**EXHIBIT 3.2.   Instructional Styles Diagnosis Inventory, Cont'd.**

Typical situations where the "professor" style would be appropriate are making a speech, delivering an after-dinner talk, communicating a report, and presenting or selling ideas to decision makers. This style usually is not as effective where actual skill development or behavioral change is expected from the learners. It may be appropriate for attitude change purposes; however, change produced by this method typically is short-lived unless constantly reinforced.

## III. "The Entertainer"

Instructors who use the "entertainer" style focus on the results of training but also feel that people will learn best from instructors they like, respect, or admire. They have many of the same personal-image concerns as "professors." They are very concerned with their credibility and whether the learners have confidence in their expertise.

"Entertainers" are concerned about involvement in the learning process, but more with their own than with the learners'. Thus, methods such as watching a role model (the instructor) demonstrate proper technique are preferred over self-discovery or group learning activities. When more participatory methods are used, these instructors tend to exercise close control and make themselves an integral part of the learning process.

Because these instructors generally believe that learners need to be "inspired" if they are going to perform differently, sessions often are designed to be highly motivational or entertaining. This can be effective but has the potential limitation of making what is learned instructor-dependent. When this occurs, learners can suffer drops in motivation when attempting to apply new skills on the job because the dynamic instructor is not there.

The fact that they are personally influencing learners is often more important to these instructors than the specific change that takes place or the input that causes it. Thus, specific content is not an important issue.

This style probably is most appropriate for personal growth seminars, sales meetings, and programs that are meant to "recharge learners' batteries."

In its worst case, the "entertainer" style could be likened to a medicine-show huckster who dazzles you and takes your money before you have a chance to judge the value of his product.

**EXHIBIT 3.2.    Instructional Styles Diagnosis Inventory, Cont'd.**

## IV. "The Coach"

Instructors who are oriented both to learning and to the learners tend to have the spotlight reversed so that the learners' attention is focused on themselves most of the time. These trainers see their role more as facilitators of learning experiences than as presenters of information. They see value in course content only insofar as it enables learners to perform in new ways.

The focus of most coaching activities is on skill development, confidence building, and application, rather than on retention of information. Learners are evaluated, but mostly through observation of performance or behavioral change rather than through written tests. Grades usually are ignored, because most instruction is aimed at upgrading everyone's skills to a minimum or improved level rather than on determining who is most proficient.

There is less concern for polished delivery because "coach" instructors spend much less time "delivering." Also, because of the informal atmosphere created, there is less pressure on the instructor to perform, motivate, or entertain. Use of a high ratio of self-discovery and group-learning activities allows the learners to motivate and entertain themselves. The responsibility to perform is, in effect, shifted from the instructor to them.

Separation between the instructor and the learners is de-emphasized. The prevailing philosophy typically is that the best instructor is the one who sets high expectations, guides and coaches the learners, and then gets out of the way so they can perform.

The instructor has a message, but the message is determined more by specific learner needs and less by what the instructor thinks might be good for the learners. Rather than forcing learners to understand and accept new ideas, "coaches" use questions, discussions, self-study, group work, and other involving techniques to lead learners to conclusions, but they allow the learners to make the commitments on their own.

The "coach" style tends to be most effective in bona fide training situations where skill building and behavioral change are the primary concerns. Potential problems with this style are tendencies to ignore time constraints, skip over important content issues, lose control of the class, turn off learners who are used to more traditional instructional styles, or be overly influenced by learners' perceptions of their own needs.

| EXHIBIT 3.2. | Instructional Styles Diagnosis Inventory, Cont'd. |
|---|---|

## A Quick Reference Sheet

The following figure provides an overview of the instructional styles measured by the Instructional Styles Diagnosis Inventory.

### ISDI QUICK REFERENCE GUIDE

| SELLER | COACH |
|---|---|
| Sellers are: Task-oriented | Coaches are: Learner-oriented |
| They see themselves as: Taskmasters/persuaders | They see themselves as: Facilitators/guides |
| Sellers' main concern is: Product/content | Coaches' main concern is: Results/performance |
| They strive to be: Driving, aggressive, enthusiastic, convincing | They strive to be: Driving, accepting, empathic, supportive |
| Programs are structured to be: Informal but inflexible | Programs are structured to be: Informal and flexible |
| Leading to sessions that are: Informative, productive, efficient, complete, persuasive | Leading to sessions that are: Involving, encouraging, constructive, developmental |
| Learners are evaluated by: Objective testing | Learners are evaluated by: Comparing behaviors or performance objectives |
| **PROFESSOR** | **ENTERTAINER** |
| Professors are: Instructor-oriented | Entertainers are: Relations-oriented |
| They see themselves as: Presenters/experts | They see themselves as: Role models/stars |
| Sellers' main concern is: Process/delivery | Entertainers' main concern is: Reactions/feelings |
| They strive to be: Impressive, polished, professional, aloof | They strive to be: Dynamic, animated, charismatic, outgoing, inspirational |
| Programs are structured to be: Formal and inflexible | Programs are structured to be: Formal but flexible |
| Leading to sessions that are: Scheduled, controlled, organized, disciplined | Leading to sessions that are: Motivated, lively, fun, entertaining |
| Learners are evaluated by: Subjective testing and instructor judgement | Learners are evaluated by: Assessment of their feelings and opinions |

WHO? — LEARNERS / INSTRUCTOR

WHAT? — CONTENT / LEARNING

*The Trainer's Handbook, Updated Ed.* Copyright © 2009 by Karen Lawson. Reproduced by permission of Pfeiffer, an imprint of John Wiley & Sons, Inc.

**EXHIBIT 3.2.   Instructional Styles Diagnosis Inventory, Cont'd.**

## Sources of Answers

Obviously, the preceding descriptions are those of the more extreme examples in each quadrant. The closer the intersection of the two scales to the center of the graph, the closer one would tend to be to a more "middle of the road" style with aspects of all four dimensions.

If you think that some respondents ranked you as more to the "ideal" than the "real," it would probably be worth your time to go back and rank the items yourself, being brutally honest, to get a more balanced picture of yourself.

The following shows the location of the polar statements for each item measured by the ISDI.

WHAT

Content ◄─────────────► Learning

### Application of Skills

L  16.  d.   Encourage creativity in the performance and application of course concepts.

C   6.  d.   Ensure that learners perform and apply newly learned skills as instructed.

### Punctuality of Scheduling

L  17.  c.   Adjust time schedules during the program in response to learners' interests and concerns.

C   5.  d.   Maintain punctuality of published program schedules.

### Currency and Applicability of Materials

L  15.  b.   Encourage learners to challenge outdated course materials or concepts of questionable value on the job.

C   8.  c.   Expose learners to traditionally accepted subject matter and correct procedures.

**EXHIBIT 3.2.   Instructional Styles Diagnosis Inventory, Cont'd.**

### Degree of Program Structure

L  19.  c.  Leave the structure of the program loose to respond to the specific needs of the group.

C  9.  c.  Plan and structure course materials in considerable detail.

### Evaluation of Learners

L  18.  d.  Evaluate learners based on their abilities to perform objectives.

C  3.  c.  Evaluate learners by giving examinations to test their retention of presented materials.

### Direction of Activities

L  8.  b.  Allow learners to make mistakes and also learn from session experiences.

C  13.  c.  Closely direct learners' activities.

### Handling of Controversy

L  9.  b.  Explore content-related controversial issues as potential learning experiences.

C  14.  c.  Avoid controversy as a potential distraction or turnoff.

### Role of the Learner

L  5.  a.  Involve learners in activities designed to stimulate critical or reflective thought.

C  15.  a.  Encourage detailed note taking by learners.

### Updating Methods or Materials

L  7.  b.  Change course materials or training methods based on feedback about learners' performance changes after training.

C  17.  a.  Change course materials or training methods based on update of expertise in the subject matter.

**EXHIBIT 3.2.  Instructional Styles Diagnosis Inventory, Cont'd.**

### Probing Individual Concerns

L  20.  c.  Explore reasons that learners ask questions, to bring out individual concerns and hidden agendas.

C  10.  d.  Avoid potential time-wasting tangents by dealing with learners' questions quickly and moving on.

### Determining Level of Material

L  4.  d.  Collect background information and adjust the level of content material for each particular group.

C  19.  d.  Aim the level of sophistication of course material at the "average" learner.

### Sharing Resources

L  10.  a.  Cite a bibliography of resources concerning materials discussed for further learner self-development.

C  18.  a.  Avoid potentially embarrassing questions and protect material by keeping content resources confidential.

### Controlling Learner Expectations

L  11.  c.  Send out self-study "prework" materials to spark learner interest and formation of course expectations.

C  4.  b.  Avoid reducing impact by not disclosing any course materials prior to the program.

### Flexibility of Course Content

L  1.  a.  Allow extended practice or discussion in areas of particular interest to learners.

C  7.  a.  Thoroughly cover all subject-matter areas in the time allotted.

## EXHIBIT 3.2.   Instructional Styles Diagnosis Inventory, Cont'd.

### Instructor Evaluation

L  12.  d.  Judge trainer's effectiveness based on how proficient learners are in performing new skills or applying new concepts on the job.

C   1.  b.  Judge trainer's effectiveness by how well the prepared materials are covered.

### Gaining Learner Commitment

L  13.  d.  Allow learners to analyze the materials and draw their own conclusions.

C  20.  b.  Ensure that learners reach the right conclusions and accept the key points or concepts presented.

### Maintenance of Learned Behavior

L  14.  a.  End a training session by helping learners create action plans to apply course content to real-world problems.

C   2.  a.  End a training session by summarizing key subject matter and recommending that learners find ways to apply it on the job.

### Communicating Course Intent

L   2.  c.  Use specific course objectives to inform learners as to what they should expect to be able to do.

C  16.  a.  Use an introductory overview to inform learners of the subject matter to be covered.

### Involving Learners' Bosses

L   3.  a.  Gain supervisors' involvement by providing ideas on how to support learners' attempts to apply new skills.

C  12.  c.  Send learners' bosses an overview of course subject matter.

**EXHIBIT 3.2.    Instructional Styles Diagnosis Inventory, Cont'd.**

### Responding to Learners' Needs

L   6.   c.   Allow learners to influence or prioritize course content and objectives.

C  11.   d.   Consistently cover the same material with each group.

WHO

DELIVERY ⟵⟶ RECEPTION

### Communication of Expectations

I   9.   d.   Begin program by informing learners of trainer's experience or qualifications and trainer's goals for the program.

S  17.   b.   Begin a program by having learners introduce themselves to one another and communicate to trainer what their expectations are.

### Dress/Atmosphere

I  16.   c.   Maintain a formal dress code to establish a more serious atmosphere for the learning environment.

S  10.   c.   Encourage casual or comfortable dress to increase the informality of the learning environment.

### Motivation of Learners

I   5.   c.   Motivate learners with enthusiastic talks, humorous stories, and entertaining or inspirational videos.

S  13.   b.   Help learners motivate themselves by developing new skills through involvement and participation.

### Improving Learner Performance

I  14.   b.   Criticize slow learners to help them improve.

S   5.   b.   Communicate positive expectations to slower learners through feedback and encouragement, in order to help them improve.

**EXHIBIT 3.2.    Instructional Styles Diagnosis Inventory, Cont'd.**

### Establishing Program Pace

I    7.    c.    Maintain a consistent pace of presentation throughout the entire program.

S   18.    c.    Vary pace of the program to adjust to natural daily highs and lows in learners' energy levels.

### Building Communication Patterns

I    4.    a.    Put primary focus on giving a technically polished presentation.

S   19.    b.    Emphasize establishing open, two-way communication.

### Use of Media

I   15.    d.    Use media (video, slides, overheads, etc.) extensively to increase the professionalism of the presentation.

S    6.    a.    Make occasional use of media tools to support other primary learning activities.

### Method of Presentation

I   18.    b.    Highlight key points, in detail, speaking from carefully prepared notes.

S    8.    d.    Ask learners questions designed to guide them to self-discovery of key points.

### Building Instructor Credibility

I   19.    a.    Defend trainer's expertise and credibility when challenged by a learner on a content issue.

S    4.    c.    Show willingness to learn from learners by admitting errors or lack of knowledge when appropriate.

### Guiding Learner Performance

I    1.    d.    Set trainer up as a role model and encourage learners to emulate trainer.

S   14.    d.    Coach learners as they practice new skills.

**EXHIBIT 3.2.    Instructional Styles Diagnosis Inventory, Cont'd.**

### Sequencing Activities

I   6.   b.   Present materials in the most logical order.

S  15.   c.   Sequence activities so as to stimulate and hold learner interest.

### Positioning the Instructor

I  12.   b.   Always stand in front of the class while instructing.

S   1.   c.   Sit down with learners while instructing them.

### Evaluating Instructor Effectiveness

I   8.   a.   Judge trainer's effectiveness based on learners' "liking" of trainer.

S  16.   b.   Judge trainer's effectiveness based on learners' increase in confidence and self-esteem.

### Use of Body Language

I  20.   d.   Project confidence and assurance by using effective gestures, posture, and vocal dynamics while instructing.

S   9.   a.   Frequently assess learners' body language and emotional states and adjust activities or schedule appropriately.

### Arranging the Room

I   2.   b.   Arrange the room so as to provide for better discipline and control.

S  12.   a.   Arrange the room so as to promote group activities and group discussions.

### Focusing Learners' Attention

I  11.   a.   Direct learners' attention primarily to trainer and to what is being said or demonstrated.

S   2.   d.   Focus learners' attention more on themselves and their own performance than on trainer.

**EXHIBIT 3.2.    Instructional Styles Diagnosis Inventory, Cont'd.**

### Personal Concern for Learners

I   13.   a.   Project a professional image by maintaining a separation between trainer and learners.

S   7.   d.   Express concern for and interest in individual learners and their problems.

### Controlling Activities

I   3.   d.   Carefully lead and control any group discussions.

S   20.   a.   Listen attentively and observe group discussion of content issues or problem applications.

### Maintaining Discipline

I   10.   b.   Use position as instructor to quickly resolve "difficult learner" problems (e.g., monopolizers, side conversations, sharpshooters, etc.).

S   3.   b.   Let the group "handle" difficult learners or privately explore reasons for problems.

### Handling Learners' Questions

I   17.   d.   Enhance credibility with learners by answering all questions quickly and accurately.

S   11.   b.   Frequently redirect learners' questions to other learners to be answered.

*Source:* Greg Cripple. *The 1996 Annual: Volume 1, Training.* San Francisco: Pfeiffer, 1996.

# Learner-Centered Versus Information-Centered

To better understand the difference between learner-centered and information-centered learning, study Table 3.1.

Notice that, with learner-centered training, the primary focus is on what the learner or participant is able to take away from the learning experience. The learner is actively involved in the process and, therefore, is much more likely to retain the information and be able to apply it on the job.

**Table 3.1. Learner-Centered Versus Information-Centered Training**

| | Learner-Centered | Information-Centered |
| --- | --- | --- |
| Stated Objective | To improve performance of participants | To cover the material; present content |
| Underlying Objectives | Meet participants' need to know and do | To establish trainer as expert |
| Role of Trainer | Facilitator; coach | Imparter of information; lecturer |
| Methods | Trainer asks questions; does no more than 50 percent of the talking | Trainer lectures, explains, demonstrates; does most of the talking while participants listen and watch |
| Participant's Role | Active participant in learning process; learns by doing | Passive learner; absorbs information |
| How Feedback Is Obtained | Opportunities to apply skills through role plays, case studies, simulations, and other structured experiences | Asking participants whether they have any questions; asking participants questions about what trainer has said |
| Purpose of Feedback | To see whether participants can apply what they learned; to see whether they need more practice or remedial instruction | To see whether participants understand the information; to test their retention |

## Advantages and Disadvantages

Both learner-centered training and information-centered training have advantages and disadvantages, as seen in Table 3.2. Although research supports learner-centered instruction over information-centered, the reality of life is that sometimes "the powers that be" apply pressure on trainers to put massive numbers of people through so-called "training" in a short period of time. Although we know this "cattle car" approach to training is not effective, it is often difficult to convince others. Regardless of whether you are an internal or an external practitioner, if your client—that is, the decision maker—insists on what amounts to the simple dissemination of information, you may want to suggest an alternative approach. Alternatives may include sending required reading material to employees, creating an audiotape or videotape of a presentation, or even communicating via the organization's intranet system. Be sure to stress that these other approaches should not be mistaken for training. They are one-way communication methods designed to present information.

## Recognizing Learner-Centered Behavior

To test your understanding of learner-centered versus information-centered behavior, complete the activity in Exhibit 3.3. You could also use this checklist as a reminder of what you need to do to become more learner-centered in your training sessions. Answers are provided in Appendix A.

# Key Elements of a Trainer's Style

As you work through this text, you will be challenged to examine and perhaps even modify your own beliefs and practices. Should you decide to make some changes in your current thinking or behaviors, realize that change is not easy. In fact, it can be downright painful. When it seems that changing the way you train (or had planned to train) is just too much work, ask yourself the following questions: "Am I as effective a trainer as I would like to be?" and "Am I obtaining the results I want?" If the answer to either of these questions is "no," then be open to

| Table 3.2. | Advantages and Disadvantages | |
|---|---|---|
| | **Learner-Centered** | **Information-Centered** |
| Advantages | Two-way communication<br>Participants directly involved in learning; opportunities to apply learning<br>Participants receive immediate feedback through application opportunities<br>Greater satisfaction with learning experience<br>Increased understanding and retention<br>Addresses different learning styles | Efficient in that more information presented in short period of time<br>Effective in presenting "nice to know" rather than "need to know" information<br>Cost-effective in that one trainer can present to many people at once |
| Disadvantages | Takes longer because participants have opportunities to practice<br>Less content covered in a given time period<br>Can be expensive because of smaller class size | One-way communication<br>Participants have no opportunity to apply learning during the training session and receive feedback<br>Participants' questions often are not addressed<br>Information overload often results in poor retention<br>Less satisfaction with learning experience<br>Limited effectiveness in appealing to differences in learning styles |

**EXHIBIT 3.3.    Learner-Centered or Information-Centered Behavior**

*Instructions:* For each of the following items, indicate whether it is descriptive of learner-centered (LC) or information-centered (IC) behavior.

1. _____ The job of an trainer should be to present the material in a clear, logical, well-organized manner.

2. _____ At the beginning of a training session, the trainer clearly identifies the session or course objectives.

3. _____ The trainer encourages participants to ask questions when they need clarification.

4. _____ Visual aids are used minimally.

5. _____ The trainer uses tests to find out how well the participants retained the material.

6. _____ The trainer begins a session by reviewing ground rules dealing with breaks.

7. _____ The most important factor to consider when evaluating packaged training programs is the amount of content.

8. _____ The best trainer is one who involves the participants.

9. _____ The room is arranged classroom style with participants seated in rows, all facing the trainer.

10. _____ Good trainers are experts in their subject matter.

11. _____ Experience and knowledge of subject are more important than the ability to involve the participants in the learning experience.

12. _____ The trainer asks participants what they want to know and learn.

13. _____ The trainer builds in many opportunities to try out new skills and ideas.

14. _____ The trainer establishes himself or herself as the expert or authority on the subject.

15. _____ The trainer's role is to facilitate the learning process.

16. _____ The trainer frequently puts participants into small groups to discuss questions or solve problems.

17. _____ The trainer chooses a variety of learning methods or approaches.

18. _____ The primary role of the participant is to receive information from the trainer or subject-matter expert.

learning and trying out new ways of structuring and conducting your training sessions.

Use the following list of behaviors as a reminder for creating participant-centered training:

- Organize the program and behave in such a way that participants feel they have "ownership" of the program.

- Create many opportunities for participants to discover things for themselves.

- Establish both participant and trainer expectations at the very beginning of the program.

- Create a supportive learning environment in which people feel free to take risks, to ask questions, and to try out new ideas and ways of doing things.

- Be sensitive to the communication process, including your own body language as well as that of your participants.

- Maintain a high energy level throughout the session. It becomes contagious.

- Accept ideas you may not agree with, and accept the fact that some people will not agree with you.

- Show respect to all participants, no matter how difficult they may be.

- Don't be afraid to admit what you don't know; be willing to find out the information and pass it on to the participants later.

- Use positive reinforcement throughout the session.

- Look at every training experience as an opportunity to learn from your participants.

- Make the learning experience enjoyable.

- Seek feedback from the group about your own behavior so you can further grow and develop as a trainer.

You will learn specific strategies throughout the book that reflect participant-centered trainer behavior and will help you create a powerful learning experience for all.

**KEY POINTS**

- The trainer determines the success or failure of a training program.

- Effective trainers are those who learn how to flex their style according to the needs of the participants.

- Effective training is learner-centered rather than information-centered.

Now that you have gained some important insight into the way in which you approach the training experience, it is important to understand the complexities of today's learning environment and the challenges of training an increasingly diverse workplace population.

# Chapter 4

# Understanding Today's Learner

**LEARNING OUTCOMES**

In this chapter, you will learn

- To identify the diversity issues that impact the design, development, and delivery of training

- To use tools and techniques to create a risk-free and bias-free learning environment

## The Changing Training Environment

Organizational training and workplace learning have changed dramatically in the last two decades and will continue to change in order to meet the needs and demands of the workplace. A more diverse workforce has not only changed the way companies do business but also the way they train their workers. In addition to different learning styles, differences such as age, gender, race, ethnicity, lifestyles, religion, language, disabilities, and literacy impact how trainers design, develop, and deliver training. The challenge of meeting the individual needs of participants often seems overwhelming. Armed with an understanding of today's learners and equipped with a toolkit of tips, techniques, and tools, you as a change agent and influencer of behavior will be able to create an environment that both respects and celebrates differences.

# Self-Awareness

To be effective in meeting the needs of a diverse audience, first examine your own attitudes, beliefs, and behaviors toward those who are different from you. Your own unintentional biases and inadvertent insensitivity may undermine your attempts to create an environment that values the individual and promotes learning. To increase your self-awareness of the ways in which your behavior and beliefs are transferred to the session, complete the Diversity-Awareness Inventory in Exhibit 4.1.

| **EXHIBIT 4.1.    Diversity-Awareness Inventory** |
|---|

*Instructions:* This inventory is designed to increase your awareness of the ways in which you judge, stereotype, and sometimes discriminate. Please respond to each of the following questions by placing a check mark in the appropriate column.

| Do I... | no | yes | sometimes |
|---|---|---|---|
| 1. Recognize that I have prejudices and biases? | ____ | ____ | ____ |
| 2. Make efforts to get to know people from cultures and races other than my own? | ____ | ____ | ____ |
| 3. Accept that other people may not share my values, views, or lifestyle? | ____ | ____ | ____ |
| 4. Try to learn about other cultures by reading and asking questions? | ____ | ____ | ____ |
| 5. Try not to judge others by my behavior or standards? | ____ | ____ | ____ |
| 6. Help people from other cultures learn about mine? | ____ | ____ | ____ |
| 7. Respect other cultures' traditions and practices? | ____ | ____ | ____ |
| 8. Make certain that I include examples, case studies, and other types of activities that reflect the diversity in my classroom? | ____ | ____ | ____ |
| 9. Create a classroom environment in which all students feel free to express and be themselves? | ____ | ____ | ____ |
| 10. Make a special effort to become familiar with the verbal and nonverbal communications of other cultures? | ____ | ____ | ____ |

There is, of course, no score for this assessment. Its purpose is to help you identify areas in which you might need to acquire information or make a concerted effort to modify your behavior.

# Diversity Issues

The most important thing to remember is that you are training individuals who just happen to be in a group setting. Before you deal with specific design and delivery considerations, let's look at some specific diversity issues.

Although many diversity categories may be represented in a training session, let's focus on those that have the greatest impact on the session climate.

## Age Differences

The so-called "generation gap" seems to be widening more and more throughout the world, particularly in corporate America. At one end of the workplace continuum are the young professionals in their early twenties; at the other end are the older employees, for whom the idea of an early, comfortable retirement is no longer viable. The result is a much greater age span in the workplace than ever before.

## Meeting the Training Needs of Older Participants

As noted in Chapter 2, the ability to learn does not diminish with age. There are those, however, who believe that anyone over forty cannot learn new skills. Forty, the somewhat arbitrary number that separates "younger" workers from "older" workers, seems to stem from the Age Discrimination in Employment Act of 1967, designed to protect workers over forty from unfair employment policies and practices. Trainers make statements such as, "Older workers don't catch on as quickly" or "Older people can't adapt to change." These beliefs are bound to be reflected in the trainer's behavior toward older participants. According to Harvey Sterns, director of the Institute for Lifespan Development and Gerontology (Sterns & Doverspike, 1988), many people over forty may indeed take longer to learn new skills, primarily because they have to first unlearn the way they are currently doing things. Younger employees who have grown up with computers and video games will, of course, find it easier to learn new computer systems and software programs than will their older colleagues who learned to use typewriters and carbon paper.

One of the biggest barriers to older workers learning new skills is their lack of confidence or fear of failure, created, in part, by society's myths and stereotypes about aging. So the trainer's first challenge is to build older participants' confidence by encouraging them. Hands-on learning is even more critical for those over forty, as well as using materials and methods that are directly job-focused and relevant to the participants' work situations. Because older adults experience a decline in vision or hearing, the trainer must pay attention to the room arrangement, lighting, and the use of larger print on visual aids and even in participant workbooks.

Those forty and older are interested in receiving training that is relevant, immediately applicable, and in an easy-to-absorb format. Participants over forty are in a hurry to learn. They realize that they must keep up and, in some cases, catch up in order to survive in today's fast-paced, high-pressured, and rapidly changing work environment.

## Connecting with Younger Participants

Younger workers, the so-called "Generation X" born during the years 1965 to 1978, present a different challenge. Many erroneous assumptions are made about them as well. Trainers as well as managers may think that these younger workers have a short attention span, are disrespectful, apathetic, lazy, and think they know it all. The truth is that they are enthusiastic, confident, and achievement-oriented. They can process large amounts of data at a time; however, they want information presented to them in abbreviated forms such as sound bites and checklists. These characteristics create different challenges as well as opportunities for trainers.

During the training event, these participants need many opportunities to apply their knowledge and solve problems through group discussion, simulations, case studies, and so forth. They like to be challenged but also to receive immediate and meaningful feedback. They are bored easily and, therefore, programs must be designed that offer a variety of learning experiences. The entertainment factor cannot be overlooked. Remember: This is the MTV generation. They expect high-quality materials, including participant workbooks, videos, and other visual aids. They also expect more technology-based learning opportunities and experiences.

Because they like to challenge as well as be challenged, they will question and demand proof of what is being said. They will not accept your word at face value just because you are the trainer. Be prepared with facts and figures to support your statements and explain why they are learning a particular skill or piece of information, focusing particularly on outcomes and results. They do not like to be told what to do, so provide opportunities for them to discover things on their own through structured experiences and self-assessment instruments.

## SAMPLE ATTITUDES OF YOUNGER WORKERS

I conducted a problem-solving and decision-making session for new associates in a Wall Street investment firm. These recent college graduates were the "cream of the crop"—intelligent, well-educated, energetic, enthusiastic, and clearly "fast-trackers." They came to the session with the confidence and bravado that are typical of the uninitiated. They expressed early on that they thought this session was a waste of time because they knew how to make decisions and solve problems. Rather than argue with them, I put them into small groups and gave them a rather complicated business simulation in which they had to analyze six problem situations and come up with solutions. They were given fifteen minutes to solve each problem and then were given the recommended solution so they could score their teams before moving on to the next situation.

Without exception, all five groups quickly arrived at the solution to the first problem and waited impatiently for the correct answer. Much to their surprise, they all got it wrong. Thinking this was just a fluke, they quickly solved the next problem and were wrong on that one, too. Getting the message that this was not as easy and simplistic as they first thought, they began to buckle down and took the time to look beneath the surface and beyond the obvious. When they finished the last four problems, they were not only exhausted but humbled because they realized and readily admitted that they had not known as much about solving problems as they thought they did.

An even younger group of workers entering the workplace learning environment is referred to as "Gen Yers," "Nexters," or "Echo Boomers" (born after 1978). Even more than their slightly older counterparts, "Gen Yers" need technology and multimedia. They want information presented in sound bites, and they expect rewards such as prizes for their participation. More than any other group, the "Gen Yers" crave interaction of any and all sorts. They also have a greater need to be entertained and to have fun. According to Susan El-Shamy, author of *How to Deliver Training for the New and Emerging Generation* (El-Shamy, 2004), to meet the needs of this younger audience, trainers need to increase the speed and interaction of the training, make the training more relevant to the learners, give learners more options and choices, use more technology, and make learning fun.

Because many grew up as latch-key kids, today's younger participants have learned to be self-reliant and independent problem solvers. To function in the current work environment, they need to be involved in learning experiences that will help them develop the interpersonal and team skills they lack.

It is even more critical that these younger employees participate in planning the training program and that self-study and projects outside the structured class environment be included.

Today's audiences, regardless of age, are conditioned by television, and consequently, they expect to take frequent "commercial breaks" of sorts. The training design must reflect the participants' need to stand up and move around or at least experience a change in venue or delivery methods. To better understand how to meet the training needs of participants in all age groups, refer to Table 4.1, Generational Differences.

## Gender Differences

Gender issues continue to exist in corporations and find their way into the corporate training. As a role model, you must demonstrate appropriate behavior at all times. Make sure task assignments are evenly distributed to both genders, preventing participants from falling into traditional roles such as a woman recording and a man leading the discussion. The trainer must also avoid sexist remarks or using examples and activities that appeal more to one gender.

Help bridge the gender gap by providing opportunities to heighten awareness of the different perspectives each gender brings to the same situation. Promote this exchange of perspectives through small-group activities, making sure all groups include both men and women. During general discussions, solicit ideas and reactions from both men and women.

## Cultural Differences

Today's corporate training room is a patchwork quilt of many cultures that can enrich the learning experience. Learn how to draw on the experience and background of these participants to add value to training, regardless of the topic. You have a responsibility to understand and meet the learning needs of those whose experiences and frames of reference may be quite different from yours. Create opportunities for participants from different backgrounds to learn about each other by working together in structured experiences.

## Accommodating Cultural Differences

Cultural differences include ethnicity, race, gender, age, and chosen affiliations. When planning your training session, be sure to keep the following issues in mind.

**Table 4.1. Generational Differences**

| Preferences | Veterans (Also Called Mature) 1922–1945 | Baby Boomers 1946–1964 | Gen Xers 1965–1978 | Gen Yers 1979–1984 |
|---|---|---|---|---|
| Learning Environment | Traditional classroom; risk-free; orderly | Interactive; non-authoritarian; interaction; teamwork; networking opportunities | Self-directed learning; two-to-four-hour segments; honest feedback; fun; personal; fast-paced | Teamwork with technology; cooperative learning |
| Type of Trainer/ Facilitator | Traditional; shows respect for their experience | Views participants as equals; shares personal examples | Gets right into material; gives solid examples and real-life cases; demonstrates their expertise | Authority figure who provides structure |
| Motivation for Learning | Tied to good of the organization | Will help them be stars at work | Adds to their marketability | Learn skills and information that makes work less stressful; increases their marketability; helps them deal with difficult people |
| Preferred Activities | Straightforward presentation | Interactive; hate role plays; want skill-building activities | Simulations; role play; learn by doing; discovery method | Entertaining; creative; incorporate games, music, art |
| Training Materials | Well-organized; summaries; *Reader's Digest* format | Readily accessible information (like Internet); *USA Today* format | Few words; chunks of information; lots of visual stimulation such as headlines, subheads, quotes, graphics, lists; *Fast Company* format | Lively and varied; graphics; include reprints of articles and job aids |

Adapted from "Generation on Gaps in the Classroom" by Ron Zemke, Claire Raines, and Bob Filipczak. *Training,* November 1999. *The Trainer's Handbook. Updated Ed.* Copyright © 2009 by Karen Lawson. Reproduced by permission of Pfeiffer, an imprint of John Wiley & Sons, Inc.

On the WEB

**Materials.** When selecting both methods and materials, you must make sure you choose videos, case studies, and other activities that are inclusive and reflect your diverse audience. Eliminate gender-specific language such as chairman, mailman, fireman, or salesman. Instead, use chairperson, postal carrier, firefighter, or salesperson. Role plays and case studies should reflect various cultures in the choices of names and situations. If you are writing your own, be careful not to create profiles or situations that illustrate and thus perpetuate stereotypes. For example, in a role play or case study illustrating an interaction between a manager and an employee, make sure that the manager is not always identified as a white male and the employee as a female or a minority person.

For case studies, select names that clearly reflect the diversity in your organization such as Kwan Lee, Jose, Rosa, Tamera, Antonio, Amalia. For role-play assignments, use gender-neutral names like Robin, Pat, Chris, or Kim, or indicate that the role can be either gender by expressing both: Robert or Roberta, Sam or Samantha, Michael or Michele.

If you buy a packaged program or use published materials authored by someone else, make sure they meet these same criteria or alter them as needed. Use similar care in choosing videos that reflect diversity. The same holds true for graphics you might add to your participant workbooks or those included in materials purchased from a training vendor.

**Trainer Behavior.** Think about the different ways in which people from various cultures communicate both verbally and nonverbally, so that you can prevent communication miscues. For example, you may interpret head nodding to mean that the participant is agreeing with what you are saying. In some cultures, however, nodding one's head is only an indication that the person is listening and is also encouraging the speaker to continue. In U.S. culture, people often make negative judgments about those who do not engage in direct eye contact. Once again, other cultures view direct eye contact as challenging or disrespectful. It is important that you not misinterpret a participant's behavior that may be culturally based.

Learning about your participants also includes learning how to pronounce their names and addressing them correctly during the session.

### SAMPLE OF IMPORTANCE OF USING NAMES

I learned the importance of using people's names the hard way in a session on influencing skills for a group of new associates in a bank. The members of the group were in their early twenties with an equal distribution of women and men. The group, however, was quite diverse in terms of cultural backgrounds with a mix of those from North America, Asia, the Middle East, and the Indian subcontinent. One young man from Afghanistan was particularly interesting and very participative. He spoke with me at length at breaks and at lunch, and seemed to have developed rapport with me. I was, therefore, quite surprised when I read in his session evaluation that he was offended because I had not made any attempt during the day to say his name. He was not the only person I did not address specifically by name. In his culture, however, addressing a person by name is very important, and I had demonstrated disrespect by not doing so.

To avoid similar incidents, make an effort to learn about those from other cultures by talking with them and asking them questions about their customs. Ask them the correct pronunciation of their names and then practice saying their names. Read articles and books about intercultural communication so that you are somewhat familiar with the cultures that are most frequently represented in your training sessions.

**Activities.** Keep in mind that in many cultures, the approach to learning is very traditional. The trainer is regarded as an authority figure. Participants are expected to assume a passive role, with the trainer delivering content in a very structured and rigid manner. As a result, some people may be uncomfortable with the participative and interactive approach to learning. These participants may need a little more nudging and encouragement to help increase their comfort level with the learning process. Cooperative-learning techniques such as asking them to discuss a question or problem in pairs or small groups are effective ways of involving those who are not accustomed to interactive learning.

## Participants with Disabilities

Today's training audiences represent a variety of special needs and considerations. Some participants may have one or more disabilities. As with other differences, be sensitive to their situation, accommodate their special needs, but at the same time, be sensitive to their need to be treated just like everyone else.

**Accommodating Disabilities.** It is incumbent on you to learn how to adapt your training methods and materials to accommodate the needs of participants with physical, mental, and even medical impairments. Find out in advance about those who may have special needs and accommodate those needs in the initial design.

For example, if a hearing-impaired person will be attending the session, find out whether an interpreter will be accompanying the individual or, if not, to what degree the participant can read lips. If lip reading is required, make sure the participant is positioned in such a way that he or she is able to see your face. You, of course, must make sure that you turn toward that individual when speaking. When other participants respond to a question or make a comment, remind them to do the same, if possible.

Be sensitive to those who may have learning disabilities, literacy problems, or for whom English is a second language. Choose or create materials written at an appropriate reading level. This is where a pre-session questionnaire or other needs-assessment methods can be quite helpful. Know as much as you can about the individuals who will be attending your session! Do not make assumptions about people just because they hold particular jobs or are at certain levels within the organization.

## EXAMPLES OF ACCOMMODATING DISABILITIES

I was asked to conduct a multi-session business-writing program for bank managers and assistant managers. About halfway through the program, just at the time when assignments became more complex, one of the participants (a branch manager) came to me after a session and explained that she was having a very difficult time writing the assigned letters and memos. She had dyslexia, and not only did no one in the bank know about her learning disability, but she did not want them to know. I worked with her one-on-one either before or after each session.

In another situation, I was conducting a four-session supervisory-training program for twelve first-line supervisors in a manufacturing environment. At the first session, eleven of the twelve came to the training session. The next evening, the man who had missed the first class called me at home. He apologized for missing class, and he wanted to explain why. He said that he had heard from the others that the session was really good and he wanted to come but was afraid to because he would have to read "stuff" and discuss it. He then explained that he was concerned because he could not read, and he didn't want the others to know. I assured him that I would make sure he would be able to participate and that his colleagues would never know. To accommodate his special need, I either read or paraphrased the assignment before they broke into small groups.

**Activities.** It is also a good idea to provide written materials and to write instructions for activities and exercises on a flip chart or transparency. Be sure to think through the logistics of activities, keeping in mind participants with special needs. Be aware that you cannot anticipate everything. No matter how well you plan, sometimes you will be caught off guard.

### EXAMPLE OF FLEXIBILITY

I had been contracted by the Pennsylvania Industries for the Blind and Handicapped to present a customer-service program to their employees who staffed the photo license centers throughout Pennsylvania. Many of the participants had some visual impairment, and several were in wheelchairs.

Because I used many small-group activities throughout the day, requiring people to change groups, I arranged the room so that those in wheelchairs would be able to move about the room as easily as possible. I also accommodated the needs of those who were visually impaired by reading materials as appropriate. Despite all my planning and preparation, there was still a surprise. At one of the sessions, one of the participants was deaf and her interpreter did not show up. Although the participant was able to read lips, I had to make a last-minute adjustment in an activity that was designed to illustrate poor listening skills.

**Adapting Materials.** Many special needs are obvious, but there are many others that are difficult to detect unless someone brings them to our attention. One good technique to move people quickly into small groups is called a "grouping card," which will be explained in more detail in Chapter 12. Each person receives a card that includes a colored dot. To form a specific small-group arrangement, ask participants to group themselves according to the color of their dots. This works well until you have someone who is color blind. An alternative is to use various shapes and symbols instead.

As a trainer, you have a responsibility to create a learning environment in which all participants feel free to express and be themselves. Begin to create this environment when you design a program, taking into consideration all types of differences, including learning style differences. Not only respect the individual differences of those in your sessions, but make sure you incorporate into your program design a variety of methods and materials that will accommodate those differences.

---

## KEY POINTS

- Diversity issues impact the design, development, and delivery of training.

- The trainer is responsible for creating a risk-free and bias-free learning environment.

- An effective trainer is one who is aware of and sensitive to diversity issues.

- Both methods and materials must reflect your diverse audiences.

- The trainer's own behavior can have a profound impact on participants' reactions.

---

Armed with knowledge of adult learning principles, learning styles, and diversity issues, as well as an understanding of yourself as a trainer, your next step is to develop specific objectives, that is, learning outcomes for your training program.

# Chapter 5

# Writing Instructional Objectives

**LEARNING OUTCOMES**

In this chapter, you will learn

- To determine the desired performance-based outcomes based on the needs analysis
- To write properly constructed learning objectives
- To use outcomes or objectives as the basis for program design and development

## What Are Learning Objectives?

After the needs assessment has been completed and the data gathered, analyzed, and reported to the appropriate people, the next step is to design the training program. The first step in the design process is to write learning objectives.

Learning objectives or outcomes state what the learner will be able to do at the end of the training program or at the end of a phase of training. They describe the planned outcome of the training rather than the training process—results rather than procedure.

## Why Set Objectives?

Objectives serve as a type of contract. If participants know the program or session objectives from the beginning, they will know what they are expected to learn. Objectives give participants a sense of direction. They know what to expect from you and what you expect from them.

Objectives serve as the basis for the design and development of the program, that is, the instructional plan. They help the trainer focus clearly on the desired outcomes and determine what the participants need to know and do in order to meet those objectives. The concept of designing a training program is analogous to planning a trip: the objectives are the destination and the instructional plan is the itinerary. First decide where you want to go (objectives) and then decide how you are going to get there—how long the trip will take and what means of transportation you will use (methods and materials).

Objectives should be written from the participant's point of view, not the trainer's. The emphasis should not be on what you want to cover but on what you want the participant to value, understand, or do with the subject, information, or skills after the training program is over.

Objectives are used to measure success. Because they describe what the participant will be able to do at the end of the training, the objectives automatically become the standard against which success is measured.

Finally, objectives are a sales tool. Develop the program objectives based on the needs assessment you conducted earlier. Then use these objectives to tell the participants' managers exactly what your training will do for their employees. These managers will have a much better understanding of what the training will and will not do.

## Types of Objectives

Objectives fall into three categories of development: attitude (affective), skill (behavioral), and knowledge (cognitive).

**Attitude Development—Feel.** Objectives that address attitude development deal with attitudes, values, or feelings. These objectives are appropriate when you want to change people's attitudes or increase their awareness of or sensitivity to certain issues or ideas.

**Skill Development—Do.** Objectives for skill development deal with behavior. These are much easier to identify and to determine whether they have been met. They focus on a person being able to perform a task or procedure.

**Knowledge Development—Think.** Knowledge-development objectives have to do with content or cognitive learning. They relate to the ability to demonstrate acquired knowledge, to comprehend information, and to analyze concepts.

## Essential Characteristics of Objectives

For objectives to be useful, they must meet certain criteria. They must be

- *Objective and measurable.* Objectives should describe exactly what the participants will be able to do at the end of the training session, that is, specify the kind of behavior (if possible) that will be accepted as evidence that the participants have achieved the objective.
- *Results-oriented, clearly worded, and specific.*
- *Focus only on important aspects of the job.*
- *Measurable with both qualitative and quantitative criteria.*
- *Action-oriented statements.* They must outline specific activities and how performance will be measured.
- *Written in terms of performance.* The trainer can then select the most appropriate methods and activities.
- *Specific about what the participants will be able to do.* They must be specific about results, rather than describing the trainer or the experience of the session.
- *Descriptive of the participants' behavior or performance.* Objectives should not describe what participants must know or understand, but what participants must do to demonstrate their understanding, knowledge, or skill.
- *Descriptive of desired competence at the end of the training.*
- *Specific about the conditions under which the participants will be performing.*
- *Indicate the minimum level of performance acceptable.*

## Components of an Objective

Writing objectives is not an easy task. The first challenge is to think of objectives from the participants' viewpoints, and the second challenge is to write them as performance outcomes. The easiest way to write an objective is to start by examining its three components: *performance, condition,* and *criteria.*

**Performance.** Ideally, the objective should describe behavior that can be observed, that is, what the participants will be able to do as a result of the training. This is not always possible, particularly when dealing with attitude or affective objectives.

When the objective is not observable, specify the consequences of the learned behavior that can be accepted as evidence of achievement. For example, for a diversity training program, an objective might be that the participants will "explore their feelings about workplace diversity issues."

The objective must use specific action verbs that are not subject to various interpretations. Words such as *understand, know,* and *learn,* for example, are not acceptable. You cannot observe those behaviors. Table 5.1 offers a few action verbs for each of the desired learning outcomes.

| Table 5.1.   Reference Chart for Objectives | | |
|---|---|---|
| **Learning Type** | **Related Action Verbs** | |
| Attitude Development | adjust | decide |
| | analyze | evaluate |
| | assess | pick |
| | choose | select |
| | criticize | |
| Skill Development | assemble | prepare |
| | compute | process |
| | construct | prove |
| | copy | record |
| | count | repair |
| | demonstrate | solve |
| | design | speak |
| | develop | transcribe |
| | draw | type |
| | measure | write |
| | operate | |
| Knowledge Development | cite | identify |
| | compare | list |
| | contrast | name |
| | define | quote |
| | describe | recite |
| | detect | recognize |
| | differentiate | relate |
| | distinguish | repeat |
| | enumerate | reproduce |
| | explain | |

For example, a performance component for a sales training objective might be that the participants will be able to "suggest other bank services to the customer."

**Condition.** The objective explains the circumstances under which the participant will be performing the activity. It also describes the equipment, supplies, and job aids that may or may not be used on the job. Furthermore, the objective describes the work setting and any information used to direct the action. For example, a statement such as "Using open-ended questions to identify customer needs, the participant will. . ." identifies the materials the participant will use to help him or her perform an action.

**Criteria.** Finally, the objective specifies the level or degree of proficiency that is necessary to perform the task or job successfully. It indicates the quality of the performance required to achieve objectives. Thus, information in the criteria is used to evaluate performance. The objective may involve speed, accuracy with a margin of error, maximum of mistakes permitted, productivity level, or degree of excellence. Keep in mind that not all standards can be quantified. Following the sales example, the criteria might be to identify how many or which services the participant would tell the customer about. Putting it all together, the objective reads: "Using open-ended questions to identify the customer's needs (*condition*), the participant will suggest (*performance*) at least two additional products or services to every customer (*criterion*)."

In many cases, the trainer will need to rely on input from subject-matter experts and/or supervisors to establish the criteria, especially if the objective relates to specific tasks that can be measured. This standard of performance is usually determined by the line manager and thus directly links the training to real-world projects and job expectations.

To gain a better understanding of the format and components of an objective, take a look at the following examples:

- "Using brochures and desk-top charts (condition), customer-service representatives will answer (performance) all customer questions about standard products and services (criteria)."

- "Employees will answer the telephone (performance) within three rings (criterion) using the standard identification message and greeting (condition)."

- "Following prescribed bank procedures (condition), employees will balance the teller windows (performance) each day within twenty minutes (criterion)."

- "Using PowerPoint® software (condition), employees will create (performance) a thirty-minute presentation that includes animation and sound (criteria)."

- "Managers will write (performance) a two-page, error-free request proposal (criteria) following the proposal format introduced in the business writing workshop (condition)."

# Writing Learning Objectives

To help you gain a better understanding of how to write learning objectives, complete the activity in Exhibit 5.1. Suggested solutions are provided in Appendix A.

## Using an Objective Worksheet

To better understand and master the objective-writing process, take a look at the Sample Objective Worksheet in Exhibit 5.2, which identifies the component parts of a well-written objective.

On the left are the components of a well-written objective along with a brief explanation of what information is included in each component. To the right of each component is an example of the specific piece(s) of information that would satisfy that component. In this example, the subject is "leadership characteristics." The objective (taken from the previous activity) "Know the characteristics of a leader" is not specific enough. In fact, this objective does not even come close to meeting the criteria listed earlier.

In this particular example, the trainer will be giving the participants "results from several recent studies" (condition). Having given that information, the trainer then expects the participants to be able to "identify" (behavior) "six characteristics of effective leaders in a team environment" (criteria). As you can see, the worksheet can help you identify the components more easily. You can then put those components together to create a useful and meaningful learning objective: "Using the results of several recent studies on leadership, participants will identify the six characteristics of effective leaders in a team environment."

## Writing Your Own Objectives

Choose a particular topic from your own situation and write three learning objectives that include all three components. Use the Objective Worksheet in Exhibit 5.3.

## EXHIBIT 5.1.  Editing Learning Objectives

*Instructions:* Examine each of the following objectives from a leadership program and decide whether it is a well-stated learning objective. If not, change it so that it is acceptable, noting what component needs to be added.

- Develop an understanding of the leader's role.

- Know the difference between authority of rank and authority of respect.

- Understand the theories of motivation.

- Know the characteristics of a leader.

- Know the role of the manager in a team environment.

- Appreciate the advantages and disadvantages involved in group decision making.

- Identify ways to motivate employees.

**EXHIBIT 5.2.   Sample Objectives Worksheet**

Subject: Leadership Characteristics

*Instructions:* In the box to the right of each component, write the specific piece(s) of information that satisfy that component.

| | |
|---|---|
| **Condition**<br>• What participant will be given<br>• Tools, supplies, equipment<br>• Use of notes, simulated situation | **Results from several recent studies** |
| **Behavior/Action**<br>• What participant will be doing<br>• Emphasis on verb<br>• What can be observed | **Identify** |
| **Criteria**<br>• What standards apply<br>• Time limits<br>• Degree of accuracy<br>• Level of performance | **Six characteristics of effective leadership in a team environment** |

| **EXHIBIT 5.3.   Objectives Worksheet** |
|---|

Subject:

*Instructions:* In the box to the right of each component, write the specific pieces(s) of information that satisfy that component.

| | |
|---|---|
| **Condition**<br>• What participant will be given<br>• Tools, supplies, equipment<br>• Use of notes, simulated situation | |
| **Behavior/Action**<br>• What participant will be doing<br>• Emphasis on verb<br>• What can be observed | |
| **Criteria**<br>• What standards apply<br>• Time limits<br>• Degree of accuracy<br>• Level of performance | |

## KEY POINTS

- Learning objectives serve as the starting point and basis for program design and development.

- Objectives are outcome-based, written from the participants' point of view.

- Objectives fall into three categories: attitude, skill, and knowledge.

- An objective should describe behavior that can be observed.

- An objective may also explain the circumstances under which the participant will be performing the activity.

- An objective specifies the level of proficiency required to perform the task or job.

At first, the practice of writing objectives may seem difficult, tedious, and time-consuming. With practice, though, it will become easy. After you have determined your learning outcomes and written objectives, you are ready to design your training program.

# Chapter 6

# Writing an Instructional Plan

---

**LEARNING OUTCOMES**

In this chapter you will learn

- To develop a clear and complete design matrix

- To write an instructional plan

- To select appropriate methods of instruction

- To determine how to sequence content and activities

- To develop and select appropriate participant and trainer materials

---

## Design Philosophy

The training approach described in this book can be summarized in one word: *active*. The underlying philosophy, as described in Chapter 2, is that adult participants are actively involved throughout the training session. The design and development strategies, therefore, reflect an active, experiential approach to training, allowing participants to discover ideas, principles, and concepts through a series of well-planned and well-executed structured experiences. Because the adult, in particular, learns by doing, not by being told, the design and development process includes very few didactic elements.

## Time Needed to Develop a Training Program

The most frequently asked question in train-the-trainer sessions is "How long does it take to design and develop a training program?" The answer: "It depends." As frustrating as that might be to those who want and need to know how much time they must devote to this effort, there are just too many variables to give an accurate answer. A "rule of thumb" is ten to twenty hours of development for every hour of delivery.

However, this figure can change dramatically. In the September 1996 issue of *Training & Development,* published by the American Society for Training and Development, author Karen White tells the reader that a good estimate is "forty to one hundred hours of development for each hour of an instructor-led course." The May 1997 issue of *Training* magazine cites a study by the U.S. Office of Personnel Management, which offers the following estimates for development hours per classroom hour for an instructor-led course (Zemke & Armstrong, 1997):

| | |
|---|---|
| Formal technical course | 5 to 15 hours |
| Self-contained, ready for handoff to other instructors | 50 to 100 hours |
| Conventional management development | 20 to 30 hours |

As you can see, all estimates have a wide range. Contributing variables include the designer's skill and experience, the complexity of the content, and whether one develops activities or uses those already developed. Will you use an "off-the-shelf" case study, or will you write your own? Do you have the skills to write a case study? If you choose to use one already written, will you use it as written, or will you modify it for a specific situation? Also, can you readily find an appropriate case study, or will you have to spend time looking through various resources to find one that serves your purposes? These are all critical decisions that involve varying amounts of time required to produce the training session.

The reality of life is that others will often dictate how much time is available to develop the training program. Because situations change so rapidly and unexpectedly, you may not have the luxury of developing a training program the way you would like. For a new product launch, for example, your client or decision maker may require you to put together a training session, sometimes literally overnight.

Also, like it or not, your client may also dictate how long the session can be. Based on your needs assessment and your training experience, you may know that a customer-service training program should be at least two days. This would give you enough time to present the content and give participants many opportunities to assimilate the information through experiential activities and to fine-tune their skills through a variety of skill-building activities. More often than not, however, you will be told that the training must be limited to one day. This is where it is extremely important for you to identify your objectives quite clearly. Be realistic about what you can and cannot accomplish within the prescribed time frame.

The time constraints will also impact your choice of methods. For example, if you had to deliver a time-management program in three hours, it is highly unlikely you would be able to use a structured experience that takes an hour and a half.

## Cost Considerations

Cost is another factor in the design and development of a training session. For a customer-service program, you may want to demonstrate the proper way of handling an irate customer. In your research, you might have come across a video that would be perfect. However, limited budget might preclude you from using it. Videos are expensive to buy or even to rent. Unless you can demonstrate that buying the video will be cost-effective because you will be using it numerous times, you may find yourself searching for another means of communicating your message. (Cost issues are discussed further in Chapter 7.) All is not lost, though. A less costly alternative is to write a scripted role play demonstrating the correct approach to handling an irate customer. During the training session, you can ask for two volunteers to read the role play, and then you can lead a discussion, just as you would following the video. The downside is that it takes time to write the script, and it probably will be considerably shorter than the video.

## Major Components of Design

Designing a training program is much like planning a trip. In both cases, you must ask yourself the following questions:

|  | **Trip** | **Training Session** |
|---|---|---|
| *WHO* | Who is going? | Who should participate? |
| *WHEN* | When are we going? | When will I conduct the training? |
| *WHERE* | Where are we going? | Where am I taking the participants (in terms of outcomes)? |
| *WHY* | Why have we chosen this destination | Why am I conducting this training? |
| *WHAT* | What do we want to see and do? | What do I want the participants to know or be able to do? |
| *HOW* | How will we get there? | How will I communicate the information or develop the participants' skills? |

An instructional plan identifies what you are going to accomplish (*learning outcomes for the participants*), what will be said or presented (*content*), and how content will be communicated (*methods and media*). The purpose of the initial design document is to organize one's thoughts and sequence the material and activities to create the optimum learning experience and meet learning outcomes.

After determining the objectives and before writing a detailed instructional plan, it is helpful to first design or lay out the course using a design matrix. This is truly the planning phase of the development process.

## Creating a Design Matrix

A design matrix (Exhibit 6.1) is used to visualize the course or session. It enables you to take a broad view of what you want to accomplish and how to meet the learning outcomes. The design matrix provides a framework or skeleton for the course. You will then "put the meat on the bones" as you make decisions about methods and materials and prepare your instructional plan. The design matrix consists simply of four parts: duration, content or learning points, methods or activities, and materials or aids.

**EXHIBIT 6.1.  Design Matrix**

| Duration | Content/Learning Points | Methods/Activity | Materials/Aids |
|---|---|---|---|
| | | | |
| | | | |
| | | | |
| | | | |
| | | | |
| | | | |
| | | | |
| | | | |
| | | | |
| | | | |
| | | | |
| | | | |
| | | | |
| | | | |
| | | | |
| | | | |

The design matrix is a rough sketch of the training session. Use it to identify and sequence content subtopics; estimate the amount of time devoted to each subtopic; consider the methods to communicate the content; and identify potential training materials and aids.

## Determining Content

Content flows naturally from the learning outcomes or objectives. The important point to remember when developing or determining content is that you want to focus on what the participants "need to know" versus what's "nice to know." This is particularly important when there are time constraints.

Many trainers new to the profession with little or no experience in designing a training program often ask: "Where do I start?"

## Research the Topic

Unless you are a subject-matter expert, start by researching the topic. Search the Internet, read books and articles to gather facts and other important information, and, whenever possible, work with subject-matter experts, especially for job-specific content. Approach the research process in much the same way you collected information for a research paper in school. In this case, however, be careful to collect information that is vital to the program, always keeping in mind your learning objectives and the "need-to-know" concept. In other words, don't go overboard collecting information. Read and distill the material. Make sure you cite sources of specific data and give credit for proprietary models. Include a full reference for every source cited, including the author's or editor's initials and last name, the title of the book (and article, if applicable), the city of publication, the name of the publisher, and the year of publication. Concentrate on recent sources—ones that have been published within the last three to five years.

## Mind Mapping

Often trainers have no idea where to start in terms of what specific subtopics they should include. One way to begin thinking about your content is by using a variation of brainstorming called mind mapping. Start by putting the title of your program in the center of a piece of paper. Draw a circle around it to give it focus. Then just start generating ideas related to your topic and writing them down (anywhere on the paper). When the ideas have stopped flowing, begin combining ideas into natural groupings, which become subtopics. Determine which are "need to know" and which are "nice to know." Decide whether to include or eliminate the "nice to know" topics based on time parameters. After determining the subtopics, the next step is to sequence them.

## Sequencing

After you have determined the major content and learning points for the training, determine the order in which you will present the content. This is the time to organize. Several ways can be used, depending on the type of training and what you are trying to accomplish. Although there are no hard-and-fast rules for sequencing, the following guidelines may help you as you make decisions about the order of content and activities.

- Start with easy activities and move to more complex.
- Use less risky activities before those that some participants might find threatening.
- Vary your activities and methods in terms of length and format.
- Present easy concepts first.

## Sequencing Example

As a result of a mind mapping process, let's assume that the following subtopics will be used for a one-day customer-service training session:

- Irate customers
- Internal service
- Telephone skills
- Communication problems
- Professional image
- Definition of customer service
- Personal action plans

Think about the logical arrangement of the topics and, based on knowledge of the subject, you might arrange the topics in the following order:

1. Definition of customer service
2. Professional image
3. Telephone skills

4. Communication problems

5. Irate customers

6. Internal service

7. Personal action plans

## Sequencing Activity

Assume that you are going to develop a time-management program, and you have identified the following subtopics. Determine the order in which you are going to address each one by numbering them from 1 to 7.

_____ Personal action plans

_____ Tips and techniques for managing time

_____ Assessing how you spend time

_____ Barriers to good time management

_____ Dealing with interruptions

_____ Overcoming procrastination

_____ Determining priorities

## Approaches to Organizing Training

Present the information in a way that will maximize the learning. You want the participants to retain the knowledge (*cognitive*), develop the skills (*behavioral*), or heighten their awareness (*affective*), and at the same time enjoy the learning experience.

Many of your designs will be variations of the behavior-modeling approach introduced in the 1970s by James Robinson and William Byham (Pescuric & Byham, 1996): content, positive role modeling, skill practice, feedback, and application on the job. There are, however, other ways to organize your session, depending on your intent. The following are other approaches to consider:

**Sequential.**  Sequential designs present a step-by-step process leading to a conclusion. For example, in a sales-training seminar, the content might be presented in this order: (1) establishing rapport, (2) identifying customer needs, (3) matching product benefits to needs, (4) overcoming objections, and (5) closing the sale. With this approach, the subtopics follow the pattern of the process that serves as the training focus.

**Job Order.** This approach teaches tasks as they occur on the job. For example, a bank teller-training program might present subtopics for opening procedures in the following order: (1) getting cash drawer from vault, (2) verifying cash, (3) ordering cash, (4) logging on the computer, and (5) preparing settlement sheet.

**Priority.** Skill or knowledge essential to the completion of a task is taught first as a prerequisite to the training that will follow. Returning to the teller-training example, trainees would need to have knowledge about how to log on to the computer before learning how to complete other transactions.

**Topical.** This approach addresses job knowledge in terms of topics rather than sequence of activity. Sales representatives, for example, would have to learn about the products before they could sell them; however, they would not have to learn about those products in any particular order.

# Purpose of an Instructional Plan

The instructional plan is a detailed guide to delivering a training program. It serves a number of purposes:

- It forces you to organize material or content and present it in a logical manner.

- It identifies what materials are needed, learning points, and how content will be communicated.

- It helps you stay on track, make the points you want to make, and avoid spending too much time on a particular topic.

- In the long run, it saves time. After it is created, file it away until the next time you have to present this particular subject. Rather than "reinvent the wheel," review the plan, assemble the necessary materials, and go.

The ability to create a detailed instructional plan will also help you in your own career development. First, it gives you credibility, enhancing your image as a trainer. Second, once you have designed and developed a complete program, you will find it easier to create subsequent programs.

# Components of an Instructional Plan

An instructional plan consists of two parts: (1) the program overview and (2) the instructional guide.

## Program Overview

The program overview details the components of the course or training session. It consists of the following:

1. *Title.* The title should be brief but descriptive.

2. *Course Description.* Identify the overall goal of the course, along with a brief description of the content.

3. *Learning Outcomes.* List exactly what the participants should be able to do as a result of this program.

4. *Length.* Give the length of the course in terms of the number of sessions, number of hours in each session, frequency, time of day and/or day of week, if appropriate.

5. *Format/Methodology.* Describe the approach and methodology you will use, such as case studies, role plays, experiential learning activities, discussion, and so forth.

6. *Audience.* Identify who should attend (in terms of levels, job titles, or job duties) as well as group size.

7. *Participant Preparation.* If applicable, identify any pretraining assignments such as reading, completing assessment instruments, or meeting prerequisites.

8. *Instructional Materials and Aids*

   • Document list: handouts, transparencies, textbooks, instruments, etc., along with the source.

   • Equipment list: computer, LCD projector, flip charts, chalkboards, overhead projector, video equipment, whiteboards, and markers.

   • Media list: video titles (include name of producer and length of video), audiotapes, or software.

9. *Reference List.* Identify sources used in putting the program together such as books and articles. This is particularly helpful if someone else delivering the program wants further information.

10. *Facility Checkoff List.* Reminders or "To Do's" such as table setup, water pitchers and glasses, refreshments, markers for flip chart and transparencies, pointers, extension cords, and participant materials (folders, paper, pencils, name tents).

Exhibit 6.2 is an example of Part I of an instructional plan for a customer service training program.

## Instructional Guide

Part II is the real meat of the plan. It consists of the following four parts: time frames, content outline, training aids and materials, and trainer notes. Let's take a look at each of these in detail.

**Time Frames.** Identify how much time each major content section takes. Indicate a time frame for each by listing the number of minutes required (for example, 15 minutes) or express time as a digital clock (0:15).

**Content Outline.** This section outlines in detail the ideas, principles, concepts, or skills the participants are to learn. There are many possible formats; however, an outline is best as it helps you see relationships as well as the sequence of topics and subtopics. Although you do not have to worry about adhering religiously to the rules of outlining, it is important to observe some basic rules or guidelines:

- Main points and subpoints follow the order of general to specific.
- Subdivisions or subpoints must flow logically from the each main point.
- Use the standard system of numerals, letters, and indentations as follows:

I. Roman Numerals

  A. Capital Letters

    1. Arabic Numerals

      a. Small Letters

        (1) Arabic numerals in parentheses

          (a) Small letter in parentheses

- If you have the heading "I", you must have "II." By the same token, if you have an "A", you must have a "B", and so forth. There cannot be just one point under a heading.

**EXHIBIT 6.2.   Instructional Plan, Part I**

1. *Title:* Ensuring Quality Service and Customer Satisfaction.

2. *Course Description:* To provide participants with the tools and techniques to help them enhance and fine-tune their telephone customer-service skills as well as build and improve the performance of their individual work teams.

3. *Learning Outcomes:* Participants will learn how to. . .

   • Create a positive initial contact

   • Ensure effective two-way communication with each customer

   • Solve customer problems effectively and efficiently

   • Handle customer complaints and difficult situations confidently and professionally

   • Develop a personal strategy for satisfying customer needs and building good will

   • Use customer-service skills in their interactions with internal customers

   • Develop a customer-focused mindset

   • Build a quality service team

4. *Length:* The standard program is designed as two full-day sessions. This is subject, however, to modification based on client requirements.

5. *Format/Methodology:* The workshop format will use interactive and experiential activities, including customized role plays, case studies, group discussions, assessment instruments, and lecturettes. The exercises and activities are designed to ensure both individual and group participation.

6. *Audience:* For all employees in a primary customer-contact position; maximum twenty participants

7. *Participant Preparation:* Pre-session questionnaires and interviews: A questionnaire will be designed by the trainer and sent to each participant prior to program implementation. The purpose of this survey is to identify participants' perceptions of customer service and identify areas in which they would like skill development. The data collected from this will be used to develop customized role plays, case studies, and activities.

**EXHIBIT 6.2.   Instructional Plan, Part I, Cont'd.**

8. *Instructional Materials and Aids*

   a. Document List

   - Participant workbooks containing reference materials and learning exercises

   - Custom-designed role plays and case studies based on participant input

   - Various individual assessment surveys and inventories

   - Simulations

   - Skill practice using individual audio feedback and trainer critique

   b. Equipment List

   - Flip chart

   - Overhead projector

   - VCR and monitor

   c. Media List: *Passion for Customers*, CRM Films, Running Time: 25 minutes

9. *Reference List*

   - Davidow, William H., and Bro Uttal. *Total Customer Service: The Ultimate Weapon.* New York: Harper & Row, 1989.

   - Lele, Milind M., with Jagdish N. Sheth. *The Customer Is Key.* New York: John Wiley & Sons, 1987.

   - Sanders, Betsy. *Fabled Service: Ordinary Acts, Extraordinary Outcomes.* San Francisco: Pfeiffer, 1995.

10. *Facility Checkoff List:*

    - Tables

    - Facilitator: Water and glass, extension cord, course materials, markers for flip chart and for overhead transparencies

    - Participants (four tables of five seats): Water and glasses, tent cards, folders, and pens

    - Break Table: Coffee, tea, soft drinks, Danish

**Training Aids and Materials.** Training aids and materials include assessment instruments, videos, transparencies, slides, computer-generated visual aids, audiotapes, games, and evaluation tools. Include brief notations to cue you when to use a slide, an overhead projector, video, handout. To make it easy for you (or someone else) to see at a glance what to do, you might use abbreviations or icons. The following are some ways to indicate your training aid without writing it out.

| Training Aid | Abbreviation | Icon |
|---|---|---|
| Slide | SL | |
| Transparency | TR | |
| Workbook | WB | |
| Flip Chart | FC | |
| Handout | HO | |
| Video | V | |

**Trainer's Notes.** In essence, your trainer's notes are your "stage directions" and methods. They tell you how you will communicate the content. They might include specific questions to ask the group or instructions for activities. Here are some possible "stage directions" you might choose to use:

| | |
|---|---|
| Distribute. . . | Write. . . |
| Conduct role play | Show video |
| Demonstrate. . . | Ask. . . |
| Discuss. . . | Instruct participants to. . . |
| Break into subgroups | Explain. . . |

# Instructional Methods

Instructional methods are the various means by which content or material is communicated. They include the use of assessment instruments; activities such as role plays, case studies, and simulations; and a host of cooperative-learning or active-training techniques (which are explored in detail in Chapter 7). Some of the issues to consider when using some of the standard experiential methods are discussed below.

When selecting training methods, remember that there is no one best method; however, do try to use a combination of strategies. In selecting your methods of delivering instruction, consider the following:

- Subject matter

- Group's knowledge of the subject

- Training objectives

- Available time

- Group size

- Kind of participation desired

- Equipment available

- Type of room

- Cost

- Comfort zone of the trainer

- Comfort zone of the participants

- Participants' learning styles and perceptual modalities (see Chapter 2)

Table 6.1 lists the advantages and disadvantages of the various instructional methods. Study it to help determine which methods you want to use.

When deciding which methods to use, determine your purpose. Refer to Table 6.2 as another guide for when to use any particular method to communicate your content.

**Table 6.1. Instructional Methods**

| Method | Advantages | Disadvantages |
|---|---|---|
| Role Playing: Acting out real-life situations in a protected, low-risk environment | Develops skills<br>Opportunity for participants to practice what they learn<br>Participants gain insight into their own behavior | Some participants are resistant<br>Contrived situations<br>Requires considerable planning |
| Games: An activity governed by rules entailing a competitive situation | Promotes active learning<br>Provides immediate feedback<br>Boosts interest<br>Stimulates excitement<br>Increases learning<br>Improves retention | Time-consuming<br>May lead to loss of facilitator control; sometimes difficult to monitor<br>Some degree of risk |
| Simulations: Activity designed to reflect reality | Promotes high level of motivation and participation<br>Provides immediate feedback<br>Approximates real-world environment | Can be costly<br>Time-consuming<br>Requires significant planning and excellent facilitation skills<br>May require more than one facilitator |
| Observation: Watching others without directly participating; give constructive feedback | Generates interest and enthusiasm<br>Is less threatening than other methods<br>Promotes sharing of ideas and observations | Focus could easily shift from learning factor to entertainment factor<br>Demonstrators may not do adequate job<br>Requires skilled facilitator |

*The Trainer's Handbook, Updated Ed.* Copyright © 2009 by Karen Lawson. Reproduced by permission of Pfeiffer, an imprint of John Wiley & Sons, Inc.

**Table 6.1. Instructional Methods, Cont'd.**

| Method | Advantages | Disadvantages |
|---|---|---|
| Instruments: Paper-and-pencil device used to gather information | Personalized; helps to achieve participant buy-in and commitment<br><br>Helps focus on most appropriate material<br><br>Helps clarify theory, concepts, terminology | Some participants might be fearful<br><br>Participants might argue with data<br><br>Time-consuming<br><br>Requires skilled facilitator<br><br>Participants may feel stereotyped or "pigeonholed" |
| Mental Imagery: Visualize situations; mentally rehearse putting skills into action | Everyone can participate<br><br>Stimulates thinking, imagination | Some participants may be uncomfortable or impatient<br><br>No way to monitor participation |
| Writing Tasks: Worksheets in conjunction with materials; list and evaluate information | Everyone can participate<br><br>Particularly effective for shy participant | Individual task; little or no interaction<br><br>Time-consuming<br><br>Some people have aversion to writing |
| Lecturette: Short, structured, one-way communication from trainer to participants | Trainer controls what material is covered<br><br>Saves time | Participant in passive mode<br><br>May be boring to participants<br><br>One-way communication |

*The Trainer's Handbook, Updated Ed.* Copyright © 2009 by Karen Lawson. Reproduced by permission of Pfeiffer, an imprint of John Wiley & Sons, Inc.

**Table 6.1. Instructional Methods, Cont'd.**

| Method | Advantages | Disadvantages |
|---|---|---|
| Small Group Discussion: Small groups formed from larger group; composed of five to seven individuals; assigned to discuss a certain topic within certain time limit | Increases participation<br><br>Creates risk-free environment<br><br>Stimulates thinking<br><br>Draws on knowledge and experience of all group members<br><br>Helps participants to assess their understanding of material | One participant might dominate<br><br>No guarantee that all will participate; some may choose to remain in passive role<br><br>Easy for group to get "off track"<br><br>Time-consuming |
| Case Study: Written description of a problem or situation trainees might be faced with on the job; working in small groups, trainees read and discuss the case to determine the pertinent facts, identify problem, suggest alternative solutions, and agree on a final solution | Allows participants to discover learning points by themselves<br><br>Participants apply new knowledge to specific situations<br><br>Stimulates discussion and participation<br><br>Participants receive immediate feedback | Contrived situation<br><br>No opportunity to solve real problem<br><br>Can cause frustration because there is no one "right" answer<br><br>Time-consuming |
| Task Exercise or Activity: Participants are divided into small groups of five to seven and work on a specific task or activity; often present results to the total group | Stimulates thinking<br><br>Promotes group interaction | Time-consuming<br><br>Difficult to keep groups on track |

*The Trainer's Handbook, Updated Ed.* Copyright © 2009 by Karen Lawson. Reproduced by permission of Pfeiffer, an imprint of John Wiley & Sons, Inc.

On the WEB

**Table 6.2. Instructional Methods and When to Use Them**

| Method | Purpose | When to Use |
|---|---|---|
| Role Playing | Help participants practice skills used in interactions | To practice newly acquired skill<br>To experience what a particular situation feels like<br>To provide feedback to participants about their behavior |
| Games | Provides non-threatening way to present or review course material | To help grasp total program content<br>To present dry material in an interesting way<br>To add a competitive element to the session |
| Simulations | Re-creates a process, event, or set of circumstances, usually complex, so that participants can experience and manipulate the situation without risk and then analyze what happened | To integrate and apply a complex set of skills<br>To elicit participants' natural tendencies and provide feedback on those tendencies<br>To provide a realistic, job-related experience |
| Observation | Certain participants act out or demonstrate behaviors, tasks, or situations while others observe and give feedback | To show group how to perform procedure or apply a skill or behavior<br>To increase participants' observation, critiquing, and feedback skills<br>To demonstrate behavior modeling |
| Instruments | Provide feedback; self-assessment | To identify areas for improvement<br>To establish a baseline for future growth |
| Mental Imagery | Helps participants increase understanding, gain insight | To address affective learning<br>To stimulate thinking, imagination<br>To replace role playing |
| Writing Tasks | Helps participants reflect on their understanding of concepts, information, ideas | To provide for individual input |

*The Trainer's Handbook, Updated Ed.* Copyright © 2009 by Karen Lawson. Reproduced by permission of Pfeiffer, an imprint of John Wiley & Sons, Inc.

**Table 6.2. Instructional Methods and When to Use Them, Cont'd.**

| Method | Purpose | When to Use |
|---|---|---|
| Lecturette | Conveys information when interaction or discussion is not desired or is not possible | To convey information quickly within short time period<br>To communicate same information to large numbers of people<br>To provide basic information to a group that is not knowledgeable |
| Small-Group Discussions | Offers opportunity for participants to express opinions, share ideas, solve problems, interact with others | To generate ideas<br>To find out what participants think about a particular subject<br>To increase level of participation<br>To encourage group interaction and build group cohesiveness |
| Case Study | Allows participants to discover certain learning points themselves | To apply new knowledge to a specific situation<br>To practice problem-solving skills |
| Task Exercise or Activity | Allows participants to work with the content in small groups | To test participants' understanding of concept or process<br>To promote group collaboration<br>To increase participants' confidence in their ability to apply learning on the job |

*The Trainer's Handbook, Updated Ed.* Copyright © 2009 by Karen Lawson. Reproduced by permission of Pfeiffer, an imprint of John Wiley & Sons, Inc.

Always keep your objectives and desired outcomes in mind as you design a training session. Table 6.3 will help you match the methods to the desired outcomes.

| Table 6.3. Matching Methods to Desired Outcomes | |
|---|---|
| **Desired Outcome** | **Suggested Training Method** |
| Knowledge | Textbook |
| | Lecture |
| | Small-group discussion |
| | Games |
| | Computer-assisted instruction |
| | Videotape |
| Attitudes/Values | Guided discussion |
| | Small-group discussion |
| | Role play |
| | Dramatization |
| | Business games |
| | Case study |
| | Videotape |
| | Simulation |
| | Debate |
| Understanding | Guided discussion |
| | Small-group discussion |
| | Role play |
| | Business games |
| | Videotape |
| | Computer-assisted instruction |
| | Case studies |
| | Demonstration/Dramatization |
| Skill Development | On-the-job performance |
| | Role play |
| | Business games |
| | Skill practice |
| | Simulation |
| | In-basket activity |

# Developing Materials

Writing training materials is a time-consuming process. Not only do you have to create the participant materials, but you also have to create materials for yourself—or for another trainer, if applicable. Always keep your purpose in mind. Don't get carried away by including everything you know about a particular subject. It is also a good idea to have someone who is unfamiliar with the topic take a look at the materials to determine whether they are understandable and user-friendly.

## Participant Materials

When creating participant materials, remember what you know about adult learners. First and foremost, keep in mind that you are dealing with a sophisticated audience with high expectations of the trainer, the course content, the methods used, and the materials they receive. The materials should be high quality, easy to read, and visually appealing. Also provide ample space on handouts and workbooks for participants to take notes. Workbook materials should be presented in "chunks" so that the participants can quickly and easily digest the information. To make participant materials even more useful and meaningful, include specific work-related examples. Create memory aids (called mnemonic devices) such as rhymes, acronyms, or pegging (associating words with images) to help people remember lists or important points. Create models or flow charts to present processes and procedures. Use the checklist (Exhibit 6.3) to ensure that your materials are easy to understand and use.

**EXHIBIT 6.3.   Checklist for a Quality Participant Workbook**

_____ Headings and subheadings

_____ Bullets

_____ Boxes

_____ Short paragraphs

_____ Wide margins

_____ Graphics/illustrations; cartoons

_____ Space for note-taking

_____ Exercises

_____ Checklists

_____ Conversational tone

Participant materials also include other ancillary pieces and job aids that help reinforce the learning. These takeaway pieces may include checklists, pocket-size reminder cards that list key points, or computer screen savers.

## Trainer Materials

Trainer materials include the detailed instructional plan; master copies of the slides or transparencies and participant materials; background reading; and copies of the leader's guides for videos, games, and other activities. In some cases, you may want to include an actual "script" that would tell the person who delivers the training exactly what to say. This may be necessary if someone other than the designer/developer is going to conduct the training session. My personal philosophy and approach is that you prescribe what the trainer is to address or cover, but the actual wording is left to the trainer.

The amount of detail in the trainer's guide depends on several factors:

- Who is going to use it
- The experience level of the trainer(s)
- The budget
- Amount of detail required by the key decision maker

Regardless of how elaborate the finished product needs to be, it should contain these basic components:

- Table of contents
- Introductory material providing background information
- Presentation guide that includes facilitation tips
- Instructional plan
- Master copies of handouts, participant workbook, transparencies
- List of materials
- Resources

## KEY POINTS

- You should determine "need-to-know" versus "nice-to-know" before designing the program.

- The design of an instructional plan should reflect an active, experiential approach to training.

- An instructional plan begins with a design matrix that includes learning outcomes, a brief content outline, methods, materials, and timeframes.

- An instructional guide includes a detailed content outline and trainer's notes in addition to specifics on how to deliver the training and facilitate activities.

- Participant materials should be high-quality and user-friendly.

Before you complete the instructional plan, study and select from the many active training methods presented in Chapter 7 to help you create a training program that achieves the results you want.

# Chapter 7

## Selecting, Designing, and Developing Active-Training Methods

**LEARNING OUTCOMES**

In this chapter, you will learn

- To use active-training methods to increase retention, build understanding, and improve skills

- To involve all participants in the learning process

- To adapt active-training methods to any course content

## The Case for Active Training

Based on what we know about adult learning, learning styles, and the characteristics of today's learner (as presented in Chapters 2 through 4), active training is the most effective means of delivering training. Research shows that people understand concepts better and retain information longer when they are actively involved in the learning process

Active-training expert Mel Silberman, author of several books on active-training techniques, defines active training as *the process of getting the participants to do the work.* To illustrate the active training philosophy and its powerful impact, Silberman has developed the "Active Training Credo" based on an old Chinese proverb (Silberman, 2006).

> **The Active Training Credo**
>
> What I hear, I *forget.*
>
> What I hear and see, I *remember* a little.
>
> What I hear, see, and ask questions about or discuss with someone else, I begin to *understand.*
>
> What I hear, see, discuss, and do, allows me to *acquire* knowledge and skill.
>
> What I teach to another, I *master.*

This chapter deals with developing and selecting specific activities and materials. The chapter provides an in-depth look at the methods introduced in Chapter 6, tells where to locate materials and activities, gives some examples of active training designs, and finally provides some guidelines for selecting and using active-training techniques in the overall design. Chapter 8 describes how to use these techniques.

We know from experience and through research that active training works. The active-training approach, however, requires the trainer to think through the design thoroughly. The trainer must spend time visualizing how the activity will play out, deal with logistics, anticipate participants' reactions, and identify potential problems. Active training is based on a well-researched, proven approach to learning called cooperative learning.

# Cooperative Learning

Cooperative learning is the "instructional use of small groups so that students work together to maximize their own and each others' learning" (Johnson, Johnson, & Smith, 1991). This approach to learning is based on two assumptions: (1) learning by nature is an active endeavor and (2) different people learn in different ways.

Cooperative learning is not simply putting people in pairs or groups and asking them to work on an assignment. The approach must be carefully planned and orchestrated by a skilled facilitator who composes and arranges learning experiences. Participants work in concert, encouraging and facilitating one another's efforts to achieve, complete tasks, and reach the group's goals. For this to happen, the trainer must function as an observer, advisor, coach, and consultant throughout the cooperative learning activity.

## Benefits of Cooperative Learning

The beauty of cooperative learning is that it can be used in any setting and adapted for content and individual differences. Because it focuses on individual differences, cooperative learning addresses the concerns voiced by women and culturally diverse participants, echoing the changes we are experiencing in society and the workplace. As more culturally diverse individuals enter the workforce, managers and trainers are being challenged to re-examine old assumptions and look for new approaches to developing their employees.

Cooperative learning also addresses the real-world issues of interdependence, conflict, and change. Group learning serves as an introduction to project teams and self-directed work groups found in many businesses. Organizations have found that work teams must be trained to function effectively as units.

## Research Data

Research on cooperative learning began in the late 1800s. Since then, more than 575 experimental and one hundred correlational studies have been conducted comparing the relative effects of competitive, cooperative, and individual efforts on instructional outcomes. Studies show that cooperative learning produces higher achievement, more positive relationships among participants, and healthier psychological adjustment than do individual experiences (Johnson, Johnson, & Smith, 1991). Involving participants in the learning process results in more higher-level reasoning, more frequent generation of new ideas and solutions, and greater transfer of what is learned from one situation to another. Furthermore, cooperative learning results in greater productivity.

# Creating an Active-Learning Environment

For an active learning environment, the instructional design should maximize the effectiveness of instruction for both the learner and the trainer.

## Physical Setting

A safe, positive environment is critical to a successful learning experience. The creation of such an environment begins with the physical setting. By using music, posters, and props, the trainer creates a mood and sets the tone for the learning experience. Beginning the session with an icebreaker, opener, or other active-learning technique will help learners focus on the course content and involve them immediately (Silberman, 2006). Other techniques such as showing a film clip or displaying a photo, artifact, or cartoon and asking participants to comment is an excellent way to build interest and prepare the participants for the learning that follows.

An integral part of the physical environment is the actual seating arrangement, which we will discuss in detail in Chapter 8. Because room size and configuration are often less than ideal, it is important to determine the type of interaction desired, then arrange the seating to achieve the desired results. For example, research conducted by the 3M Company with the Wharton School of Business found that the U-shape configuration is very effective in promoting group interaction with a minimum of trainer control (Meyers & Jones, 1993).

Another way in which trainers can create a positive learning environment is to find out what participants think and feel about the subject well in advance so that this information can be used to design active-learning activities that take into account individual differences and levels of experience. This can be accomplished through pre-session surveys and phone calls to participants. On-the-spot assessment through opening activities can also help the trainer learn about participants' knowledge, attitudes, and experience (Silberman, 2006).

## Strategies and Techniques

Based on learning, teaching, and motivation theories as well as research findings primarily at the pre-college level, the following strategies and techniques appear to characterize the successful implementation of cooperative learning in an adult training environment.

**Structure and Organization.** As noted above, cooperative learning is characterized by structured learning groups. The trainer places participants in specific groups and gives specific assignments with clear instructions and time limits. These assignments may include group tasks as well as individual roles such as recorder, timekeeper, or spokesperson. Cognizant of the different ways in which individuals perceive and process information, the trainer should first form the groups to avoid confusion and then give instructions in both oral and written form by displaying them on a flip chart, a transparency, or a handout.

**Moderate Level of Content.** Because cooperative-learning programs focus more on process than on content, trainers should be guided in their design by determining "need to know" rather than what would be "nice to know." Content is no longer limited to facts, dates, formulas, definitions, and so on. It has been redefined to include skills and understanding, thus ensuring a balance among the cognitive, affective, and behavioral domains of learning (Meyers & Jones, 1993). By clearly defining what participants will know and be able to do by the end of the sessions, trainers clarify content and select appropriate learning strategies. It is imperative that these expectations be communicated clearly to the participants at the beginning of the session—and preferably before. One strategy for communicating expected outcomes is to send a memo to the participants welcoming them to the session and briefly outlining learner-centered course objectives and content as well as instructions for any pre-work.

**High Level of Participation.** As mentioned earlier, the trainer's role is that of a facilitator whose primary function is to manage the learning process. Participants are actively engaged in activities from the start, continually involved in doing, discussing, and reflecting.

**Interdependence.** One of the primary purposes of cooperative learning is to create interdependence among group members. In order to facilitate that outcome, the trainer requires all group members to master the content of the assignment. This might be accomplished by a jigsaw design (discussed later in this chapter) in which the learning activity is structured in such a way that each group member is responsible for learning a specific piece of the content and then teaching it to the rest of the participants.

**Minimal Lecture.** Although there is a place for lecture as a training method, it should be used in small doses of ten to fifteen minutes. Based on research conducted during the 1960s, lengthy, uninterrupted periods of leader-centered discourse result in confusion, boredom, and low retention (Johnson, Johnson, & Smith, 1991). Lectures, however, need not relegate learners to a passive role. Participants can be involved through various interactive techniques that promote both understanding and retention (Silberman, 2006). These techniques are addressed later in this chapter.

**Use of Small Groups.** "Small groups" may consist of pairs, trios, or groups of five to seven. Small groups are very effective. Not only do they incorporate all the elements of active learning, but they help participants to develop interpersonal skills and provide those who might be reticent to participate a risk-free environment in which they can express opinions or ask questions. This helps participants gain confidence and develop the self-direction central to the adult learner.

**Peer Teaching.** We know from our study of adult-learning theory that adults bring a wealth of experience and expertise to the learning environment. Encouraging them to draw on and share their experiences with others in the group can be rewarding for both the trainer and participants.

**Variety of Methods.** By using a variety of methods including role plays, case studies, simulations, games, and other experiential activities, participants are actively engaged in the learning process.

**Iterative Process.** Throughout the session, the trainer uses activities that build on and overlap concepts and skills learned earlier. In this manner, learning is reinforced and participants have more opportunities to digest and integrate what they learn.

**Real-World Application.** Through many of the methods described above, participants are able to use real-life situations when learning new concepts and skills. Sometimes the trainer solicits examples of hypothetical or real problems for the participants to use throughout the session. In addition, before the session ends, the trainer gives participants the opportunity to develop individual action plans, identifying how they are going to apply what they have learned in the real world.

# Designing Active-Training Activities

After you have decided the content and have some idea of the methods and materials you want to use, the next step is to come up with specific activities or structured experiences and specific training aids.

The term "design" was used in Chapter 6 to describe the process of planning or laying out the training session or program. "Design" is also used in conjunction with the methods and materials chosen. Each technique or activity must be carefully thought out prior to actually developing the activity.

## Design Principles

As you begin to develop your activities and materials, keep in mind the following three principles:

- One design can accomplish two things at once. For example, an icebreaker can build group cohesiveness and assess group needs.

- The same design can often be used for different purposes.

- Published designs can often be modified to suit your own needs.

Think about your training design as an accordion. Accordion designs are activities that can be stretched, compressed, or eliminated, depending on the time available and the experience of the participants.

Before moving on to specifics, let's address a critical issue in course development: the decision whether to use materials and activities already developed or to create your own.

Many trainers, particularly those new to the field and often those faced with time and cost constraints, choose to use "off-the-shelf" training materials that they integrate into their own designs. In this chapter, you will learn how to select or develop individual activities, exercises, assessment instruments, and so forth.

Most trainers use a combination of developing their own, buying, customizing, and tailoring. For example, using published assessment instruments helps to maintain the integrity and professionalism of the program, providing a high degree of validity and reliability. Also, purchasing simulations is wise because of their complexity and their proven success. In general, customizing or tailoring published role plays and case studies to clients' specific situations is easier and less time-consuming than writing your own.

## Factors to Consider

Before jumping headlong into investigating resources for activities and materials or developing your own, consider several key factors that will influence your decision.

**Time.** Course or program development takes time—a lot of time. Coming up with your own activities, exercises, assessment instruments, role plays, case studies, and so forth can take hours, days, or even weeks. Many people are surprised to discover, however, that the process of locating the most appropriate activity or even a video for a given situation is also extremely time-consuming.

**Cost.** Cost plays an important role also. If you develop your own materials, take into consideration your salary per hour as well as the salaries of any support personnel involved. Even if you select published material, factor in the cost of your research time and remember that there are costs associated with purchasing or licensing that you will incur each time you deliver the program.

**Quality.** The quality of the materials and activities is also important. Quality can relate to the actual appearance of the materials, the credibility of the content, or the level of detail provided.

**Suitability.** Your biggest concern should be the appropriateness of the material for your purposes. Take into consideration the audience, the topic, and your objective. Does each proposed activity or material do what you want it to do?

**Your Experience and Expertise.** Also evaluate your own skills and abilities. If you want to develop your own role play or case study, for example, consider your level of creativity as well as your writing ability.

To help you decide whether to create, buy, or adapt materials, refer to Appendix C: Criteria for Selecting Packaged Programs.

# Common Methods and Materials

Even if you develop many of your own active-training activities, you will still need to use other sources for methods and materials such as videos and assessment instruments. In some situations you must lecture. All of these tried-and-true instructional methods, even lecture, can be redesigned to involve the participants more actively, which is discussed further in this chapter.

## Videos

New or inexperienced trainers will often develop training programs designed around videos. Videos can be very helpful in communicating a message. They appeal to visual learners and also to those who are part of the MTV generation. A video is often quite effective as a method of demonstrating skills or presenting concepts. Selecting the right video is also time-consuming, and then, of course, videos are costly to buy or even rent.

Ignoring the cost issue, though, let's look at what is involved in selecting the right video for the right situation.

### Do's and Don'ts

- Keep in mind that the purpose of a video is to complement, enhance, or reinforce your message. A video is not meant to stand alone.

- Quality is very important. Today's media-sophisticated audiences have high expectations. Make sure the video you choose is not "dated" or "hokey." Participants expect a professional production.

- A training video should reflect the diversity of today's business world. The characters should not be stereotypes; they should represent a variety of races, nationalities, and ages and have gender balance.

- Be sure the video meets your needs and satisfies your objectives. In their catalogues, video producers always provide brief descriptions as well as the objectives of the videos.

### Benefits

- Videos offer models of positive behavior, and therefore they fit nicely into the behavior-modeling approach to training.

- For multiple sessions, videos help ensure that your message is consistent for all groups.

- Videos are an efficient and cost-effective means of dealing with multiple sessions and locations.

- Videos often provide the opportunity to bring well-known experts into your session.

If you are not receiving video producers' catalogues as yet, contact those listed in Appendix B; they will be more than happy to put you on their mailing lists. Spend time looking through the catalogues and reading the descriptions. If you find any videos that you think might meet your needs, simply contact the producer and ask to preview. The preview charge is minimal, and sometimes even free; in this case all you have to do is pay for traceable return postage.

Another option is to contact a distributor who represents several producers. The advantage of dealing with a distributor is that you do not have to spend hours poring over catalogues. Just call the distributor and tell the service representative your topic, the intended audience, and your objective in using the video. The distributor will recommend one or more and will also be happy to send you preview copies for your review. After you have made your selection, the distributor will handle the arrangements for you to buy or rent the video. If you are lucky enough to live in a city where one of these distributors is located, you can even arrange to preview videos at their site. Many even provide free popcorn!

Whatever route you choose, be sure to preview several videos for each topic and choose the one best suited to your purpose. It's a good idea to keep records of the videos you preview to help you make your selection and for future reference. See the sample form in Exhibit 7.1 and use it the next time you preview some videos.

## Instrumentation

An instrument is any paper-and-pencil device used to gather information about an individual, group, or organization. Types of instruments include surveys, checklists, inventories, questionnaires, tests, and reactionaries. An instrument can be used to provide feedback or self-reflection and examination, identify areas for improvement, or establish a baseline or starting point for future growth.

**Selecting and Developing Instruments.** As was mentioned earlier, assessment instruments can be purchased for a variety of purposes. For example, when addressing personality and style differences, use a personality-style profile to enable people to identify their own styles. Use this as a basis of exploring and adapting to style differences. The Instructional Styles Diagnosis Inventory from Chapter 3 is an example of this type of instrument and is also an example of one that does not have to be purchased individually, as it was published in one of the Pfeiffer *Annuals* and can be copied for internal use. Others can be purchased individually.

Instruments can be used to help people gain a deeper understanding of themselves and their approach to something. For example, the Coaching Skills Inventory (Phillips, 2004) can be used to identify respondents' behaviors in various coaching situations.

Questionnaires, checklists, and even some surveys are fairly easy to develop. Make them very specific to your situation. Techniques for using instruments will be introduced in Chapter 8.

When selecting an assessment instrument, consider the following guidelines:

**Selection Guidelines**

Validity

• Does the instrument measure what you want it to measure?

**EXHIBIT 7.1.   Video Preview Form**

Video Title:

Distributor/Producer:

Topic:

Length:

Synopsis:

Uses:

Value:

Additional Comments:

---

Reliability

- How accurate is the scoring?
- Does it yield the same results each time it's administered?

Theoretical Basis

- What is the theory behind the instrument?
- Does the instrument have a sound theoretical framework?

Language

- Is the reading level appropriate for the audience?

Accessibility

- How easy is it to acquire the instrument?
- Can it be purchased directly from the publisher or does a distributor have to be found?

Fear Factor

- Could the questions or items or the reported results be intimidating or embarrassing for participants?

Ease of Scoring

- Is the scoring process easy?
- How much help will the participants need?

Ease of Administration

- How complex is the entire process?

Interpretation of Data

- How meaningful is the interpretation of the data for participants?

Norms/Comparative Data

- Are norms comparative data available?

Time

- How long does it take to complete, score, and discuss the outcomes?

Cost

- How expensive is the instrument?

- Is it worth the investment?
- Can the instrument be used again for other training events, or is it designed for one-time use?

Copyright

- What are the restrictions on its use?

Facilitator's Guide

- How complete and easy to understand is the facilitator's guide or instruction manual?

## Lectures

Unfortunately, many people, trainers included, believe that training is nothing more than standing in front of a group of people with a series of PowerPoint® slides or a stack of transparencies and delivering what amounts to an information dump. People seem to know intuitively from their own experience as students that lecture is not only boring but that retention is limited. So why do these same people continue to lecture?

1. For one thing, a lecture is relatively easy to prepare. Of course, a lot of time has to be spent in advance putting your lecture or presentation together, but once that is done, it's done, and it can used over and over.

2. Another reason is that lectures save time. For those who believe that their goal is to cover vast amounts of content in a short period of time, lecture is the only way to go, with the trainer talking and the participants listening and taking notes.

3. The third reason is control. It is much easier to remain in control of the situation through lecture. There is no danger of getting off-track unintentionally.

Pure lecture does have its place, but a very small place in the overall training design. Sometimes lectures are needed due to time constraints or to provide certain background information. If you absolutely must lecture, deliver "lecturettes" in segments of no more than ten minutes each. One of the biggest challenges facing trainers is how to communicate cognitive material (content) without lecture. There are some very effective ways, however, of making the lecture more interesting and even interactive. Interactive lecture incorporates activities and involves the participants physically, mentally, or emotionally. Many of the techniques are advocated and used by professional speakers and taught in presentation skills courses, such as:

- Question-and-answer periods
- Interesting visual aids
- Stories and anecdotes
- Case problems
- Examples and analogies

## Alternatives to Lecture

You may be wondering, "How do I cover all this material without lecturing? They need so much information!" Believe it or not, there are many ways to present straight and even dull and boring information in an interesting and active way. Remember the principles and concepts from Chapters 2 and 3, particularly the concept that "people learn by doing, not by being told." Cognitive information can be taught actively, using cooperative-learning techniques. Cooperative-learning designs have been used formally for decades, primarily in academic settings. Training experts Mel Silberman, Bob Pike, and Sivasailam "Thiagi" Thiagarajan have adapted, refined, and pioneered their use for a corporate training setting.

Many of these active-training or cooperative-learning methods can be used in combination. Rather than being designed for use with a specific topic, most active-training techniques are "frames" that can be adapted to any content. As you design your program, look at the content and think about the different techniques that could be used to put across the information without taking an active role. There is no one right answer; it is a matter of judgment and personal preference in many cases.

The following designs can be used to present content without lecturing. For more specific examples of the following training designs as well as ideas on presenting cognitive material in an active way, see *101 Ways to Make Training Active* (Silberman, 2005).

**Group Inquiry.** Put participants in pairs to study information directly related to the course content. Ask them to study a handout containing broad information, then discuss the piece with a partner, trying to understand as much as they can, placing question marks and making notes on those things they do not understand. After a period of time, reconvene the entire group and begin answering questions the participants have generated. The purpose of this design is to arouse interest and stimulate questions. Learners raise questions as a result of their innate curiosity.

### CASE EXAMPLE

When I conduct a train-the-trainer session, I refer participants to the "Experiential Learning Cycle" included in Chapter 8. I explain that the Experiential Learning Cycle applies to individual activities. Then I ask people to work in pairs for five to eight minutes, studying and discussing the graphic, trying to make sense of it. I ask them to jot down questions they may have. At the end of the time period, I begin the discussion by asking, "Who has a question?" Generally, the first question posed by the participants is, "Where does the cycle begin?" I then ask, "Who has an answer?" Without exception, someone answers, "I believe it starts with the *experiencing* phase." I then confirm the answer and solicit other questions. This process continues until I am satisfied that the key points have been addressed. I clarify and fill in gaps as necessary throughout the discussion.

**Information Search.** Rather than giving information to participants, make them find it themselves. For example, you might create a worksheet listing a number of questions related to the information you want them to learn. Provide resource materials such as brochures, manuals, job aids, journals, or books. Put people into pairs or small groups, give them the study sheets and resource materials, and put them to work searching for information. At the end of the designated time period, reconvene the entire group, ask the small groups to report, and discuss what they have found.

### CASE EXAMPLE

In a new employee orientation session, you want to familiarize the employees with the employee handbook. Rather than simply "going over" the material page by page as many people do, you would develop an information search. In addition to distributing the employee handbook, you would also give each participant a worksheet with key questions such as the following:

- What is our standard work week?
- When do you get paid?
- How is overtime handled?
- What is the policy on sexual harassment?
- How many sick days (or paid time off) days do you receive?
- What is the procedure for calling in sick?

The participants then work in pairs to search out the answers in the handbook. After the designated time period, you would reconvene the group and discuss their answers.

**Guided Discussion.** Guided discussion or guided teaching is also known as the Socratic method. Socrates guided his students in the learning process by asking them a series of questions. With this approach, the trainer poses questions that draw on the participants' knowledge and experience and require them to think about concepts and ideas. Following cooperative-learning guidelines, pose a somewhat-broad question and ask participants to work in pairs or small groups to come up with answers.

### CASE EXAMPLE

In a session on "Coaching for Improved Performance," the trainer asked the participants to arrange themselves in small groups or clusters of four or five people and discuss the following questions: "What is the difference between coaching and counseling?" "How do you know when coaching is required?" "How do you know when counseling is required?" After a designated period of discussion, the trainer reconvened the entire group and asked for a representative from each group to present their points.

**Active Knowledge Sharing.** When trainers cite some interesting facts or statistical information about a subject, participants' reactions can range from genuine interest to polite attention to glazed eyes. Rather than giving participants the facts and figures, use an activity called "Active Knowledge Sharing" (Silberman & Lawson, 1995). Ask participants to work together in twos or threes and make an educated guess about the facts or statistics. Then show a prepared slide, transparency, or computer screen on which you have provided the factual statement with the number or percentage to be filled in by the participants. For example, in sessions dealing with listening skills, present the information using the following format (correct answers can be found in Appendix A):

- A speaker can speak at a rate of _____ words per minute; we can hear at a rate of _____ words per minute.

- On the average, we spend _____ percent of our waking hours communicating; _____ percent of that time is spent listening.

- People learn _____ percent by sight; _____ percent by listening; and _____ percent by all other senses combined.

If the participant group is small (twenty to twenty-five), I go around the room and ask people to quickly give me their figures, which I write on a flip chart or on the overhead transparency. If the group is large, ask a few people at random to share their figures. Then show the correct information. Participants really enjoy this activity. It takes very little time, yet it piques their interest and curiosity. They are motivated to listen because they want to find out whether they were correct. It is important to have them work together so that no individual is put on the spot and to create a safe environment for the audience members. People are much more likely to remember these facts and figures because they were directly involved.

**Peer Lessons.** Choose learning material that can be broken into several parts, such as an article with several sections. Divide the participants into small groups according to the number of segments and ask each group to master one section of the text. Have each group study its material, with group members reading, discussing, and deciding how to teach the information to others. They may communicate the information any way they choose. They could select one person from the group to present the information or they could have several people involved. Some groups may even choose to act out their segment. At the end of the designated study period, reconvene the entire group and ask each group to present its content segment to the rest of the group.

### CASE EXAMPLE

During a session on "How to Develop a Winning Team," the trainer wanted to convey the four stages of team development: forming, storming, norming, performing. The trainer prepared a handout that described each stage in detail. After dividing the group into four subgroups, the trainer assigned each group one of the stages to study and explain.

When the entire group reconvened, the "forming" subgroup conveyed their information by asking the rest of the participants to think about any experience they may have had during which they were part of a newly formed group and to describe what is was like and how people behaved. As the participants gave their input, one of the subgroup members captured the points on a flip-chart page. Key points included being confused, feeling uncomfortable, waiting to be told what to do, and making judgments about other team members. The subgroup then compared the newly generated list to the one the subgroup had developed, pointing out similarities and differences.

The "storming" subgroup chose to present a "skit" or demo role play in which they acted out what a team might do in that stage of development. Behaviors included people talking over each other, arguing, challenging the team leader, openly criticizing each other, and struggling for control.

The "norming" subgroup created a short true-false quiz that reflected the key characteristics of a team in the norming stage. The following are a few sample questions:

- Team members no longer argue. (F; conflicts continue, but team members deal with them in a more constructive way.)
- Member satisfaction increases. (T)
- There is more sharing of ideas as well as giving and receiving feedback. (T)
- Team leader is still very much in control. (F; leader's role becomes more consultative.)

Finally, the "performing" group chose a spokesperson to simply explain the characteristics of that stage:

- Group has open communication structure.
- Subgroups work on important tasks.
- Members develop rapport and closeness.
- Members try to minimize criticism from outside the group.
- Work is performed at a high rate of efficiency.

**Jigsaw Design.** This activity is very similar to Peer Teaching, except for one variation. After the adequate study and preparation period, form cooperative or "jigsaw" learning groups by taking one representative from each study group to become part of a new group. Each new group then has a person who has studied each segment. Have each member of the new group teach his or her particular assigned segment to the other group members. Reconvene the large group to review and answer questions, thus ensuring accuracy and uniform understanding. An example of synergetic learning, the jigsaw design creates interdependence among group members who are responsible for combining separate pieces of information to create a single, coherent body of knowledge.

### CASE EXAMPLE

Another way of presenting the four stages of team development would be to create a handout describing each stage (just as in the example of Peer Teaching). Form four subgroups and assign each subgroup one of the stages to study and be ready to teach that stage to someone else. The groups may decide among themselves how best to "teach" or convey the material assigned to them. After the study period, form new subgroups, each containing a representative from each of the four original study groups. The newly formed groups now have an "expert" on each of the four phases, with each person teaching the others what he or she knows about the assigned stage.

**Learning Tournament.** Divide the group into teams of five to seven people each. Give the teams time to study, discuss, and coach one another using material they have been given during the session. At the end of the study period, reconvene the entire group and distribute a handout with quiz items to each participant. Have participants complete and score the quiz individually; then have each team compute a team average. Post team scores and repeat the process. Decide how many rounds to conduct; three rounds work well. At the end of the designated number of rounds, total each team's score and award prizes to the winning team. With this design, there is individual accountability (individual quiz scores), cooperative learning (team coaching sessions), and interdependence (average team score).

### CASE EXAMPLE

In a session on leadership in which the participants learned about Situational Leadership, the trainer divided the participants into teams of four to six members. The trainer asked the teams to study the material and class notes dealing with leadership styles, the Situational Leadership Model, and stages of group development. The trainer explained that they would be participating in a learning tournament consisting of three rounds. They were told that they would have ten minutes before each round to study the material and coach each other.

After the study period, the trainer distributed five scenarios and asked the participants individually to indicate which leadership style they would use in each situation. After the participants completed the scenarios, the trainer shared the correct answers and explained the rationale for each correct choice. The participants counted the number of items they answered correctly and pooled their scores to obtain a team score.

The process (study, coach, quiz, score) was repeated for the next two rounds. At the end of the third round, the trainer totaled the scores for all three rounds for each team and rewarded the team with the highest overall score.

# Experiential Learning Activities

Experiential learning means that the participants are directly involved in the learning process. They learn by actually experiencing the activity. Experiential activities include role plays, case studies, in-basket activities, simulations, and games. Each is addressed separately below.

## Role Plays

The term "role play" often strikes a note of fear in the minds of even the most confident people. Role play conjures up all types of negative images and reactions, and the wall of resistance immediately goes up. Unfortunately, more than a few participants have had horrible experiences with role playing, being forced to act out or perform in front of their peers and subjected to criticism and ridicule. Embarrassed and humiliated, they vow to do everything in their power to avoid participating in role plays ever again. Others have only heard of these experiences, but the horror stories have been enough to convince them that they don't want any part of it.

The cause of bad role-play experiences is not the method but the trainer. Most problems can be traced to poor preparation and planning, as well as a lack of sensitivity on the trainer's part. To ensure that your use of role play is a positive learning experience, consider the benefits and then follow the tips for risk-free role-play experiences discussed below.

**Why Use Role Play?** An effective role play promotes affective, cognitive, and behavioral learning. Participants practice the skills taught, demonstrating their knowledge and understanding of the content through their application in the role-play situation. They also have an opportunity to gain insight into their own behavior.

**Types of Role Plays.** Several role-play options are available. The first decision is what type of role play to conduct and how to do it. Do you want to write scripts and have participants read their parts? Or do you want to create a general scenario and give each role player specific instructions that include facts about the role and how each should behave? Or you might decide to give the participants extensive detail and information about the situation, but not tell them how to behave. A fourth possibility is that the role players can create their own scenarios. The choice is yours.

Other decisions involve how you want the role play to be performed. Will role players act out the scenario in front of the room with the rest of the group observing and giving feedback? Will people in pairs or trios role play simultaneously while some participants observe each role play? Will there be one role-play situation or several? To reduce the risk during role play, try the four-part approach described below.

This approach assumes a training session that is six hours or more. It can be used with any topic to build skills or change behavior. For maximum success, design the program to include the following four types of role plays in the order presented here. Notice that the sequence starts with a type of role play that is fairly easy to do and doesn't really put anyone on the spot and then moves incrementally to more difficult and challenging activities.

*Scripted Role Play.* A scripted role play is one in which the trainer writes (or buys) a prepared script and asks for volunteer participants to read their lines in front of the entire group while the rest observe. The trainer then conducts a general discussion with the entire group. This type of role play should be used fairly early in the session to demonstrate desired behavior, or if you prefer, to illustrate undesired behavior. In either case, participants should be able to identify either what they should or should not do.

*Coaching Role Play.* A coaching role play involves both the trainer and the participants. It gives participants an opportunity to draw on the information already presented and demonstrate how well they understand the concepts and principles. In this type of role play, the trainer asks for a volunteer participant to come to the front of the group. The trainer creates the scenario and explains it to both the volunteer and the entire group. The trainer plays the role of the person whose skills are to be developed, and the volunteer will play the foil. The trainer begins the role play, stops periodically, and asks the group to tell the trainer what to say next. The trainer then takes the group's suggestions and continues the role play. The trainer repeats this stop-action technique several times and then conducts a discussion about what skills or principles were applied in the activity.

*Spontaneous Role Play.* A spontaneous role play is used during a general group discussion. For example, the trainer may want to communicate ways of dealing with an employee who is defensive and resistant. Instead of telling the group how to handle the situation, he or she engages in a spontaneous role play to demonstrate the appropriate approach, asking one of the participants to pretend to disagree and argue. Because this role play seems to spring from nowhere and appears to be spontaneous, the participant playing the other role does not even realize he or she is role playing. A variation of this would be for the trainer to reverse roles and play the person who disagrees.

*Rotating Trio Role Play.* The rotating trio role play gives each participant an opportunity to try out his or her skills. This type of role play should be used near the end of the session as a means of bringing it all together. The trainer breaks the group into groups of three. The role play consists of three rounds with three different scenarios. The participants in each trio take turns playing the primary character, who is to demonstrate the skills; the secondary character, who is on the receiving end; and the observer. Each person assumes a different role for each round. The trainer can either create the scenarios and roles or have the participants come up with their own three scenarios. If the participants come up with their own, additional time must be allowed.

## Case Studies

A case study is a written account of a problem, generally a real situation, and how it was handled. In one approach, participants are asked to analyze and discuss how the case illustrates the learning points from the training session. In another type of case study, participants are given a written description of a situation or problem, real or fictional, confronting an individual or organization and asked to analyze the situation, evaluate alternatives, and recommend an appropriate approach or solution.

Case studies, like other experiential activities, enhance retention, recall, and application of knowledge in actual work situations. The sense of realism and the participation required in small groups to discuss the case create a satisfying and fulfilling experience for the participants. Case studies are used in training on management, customer service, sales, and many other human relations topics.

Case studies are more complicated than they first appear. Many participants read the case and arrive at a solution or recommendation quickly. They fail to address the most critical part of case analysis: identification of the underlying problem. Therefore, be sure to provide specific directions when introducing the activity.

As with role plays, case studies can be purchased and used as is or customized for the specific situation and organization. They can also be written, either from your own experience and knowledge of the organization and industry or by interviewing people within the organization to gather more specific details and a deeper understanding of the problems represented in the cases. Although the latter approach is time-consuming, it is well worth the effort. When participants know they are working with real-life cases, the training program has instant credibility.

Because the cases are realistic and relevant, participants are more interested and eager to contribute. Cases can range in length from one paragraph to several pages, and they can also be used as the basis for role plays.

**Guidelines for Writing Cases Studies.** The beauty of writing cases is that you are completely in charge. Create any scenario you choose, and make the case simple or complex. The following are some guidelines for writing a case study for any topic or situation:

- *Write it in story form.* Create the scenario, and then just start writing what you imagine. Make it as realistic as possible.

- *Create characters.* To avoid potential problems with diversity issues, give the characters humorous names. For example, for a financial-services organization, name the characters Penny Less and Mort Gage.

- *Create some realistic dialogue.* It does not have to be much, but it makes the story more interesting and adds a sense of realism.

- *Provide specific details as appropriate.* You may or may not want to provide background information. If the details enhance the case study or provide essential information that could impact the outcome, them include it. Be careful not to include extraneous information that might detract from the main task or confuse the participants.

- *Be descriptive.* Create a picture in the minds of the participants. If appropriate, describe the physical environment or a character's emotional state.

- *Make the story easy to follow.* A lengthy or complicated case study needs subheadings. With shorter cases, the most easily read and understood are those that follow a logical sequence of events.

- *Provide discussion questions or guidelines for participants to follow as they analyze the case.* Many people, unfamiliar with this type of activity, could easily become confused and discouraged. Make the case challenging but not overwhelming.

## In-Basket Activities

An in-basket activity is another type of experiential activity that re-creates as closely as possible situations that participants would encounter on the job. These situations also include representative materials. The most common in-basket activities are used in time-management training to help participants learn how to delegate or set priorities. The trainer provides the hypothetical scenario. For example, participants may be told that they are about to leave on a two-week vacation and that all the work on their desks must be cleaned up before they go. An emergency has kept them from dealing with their in-baskets, and they now have only thirty minutes to go through the items and decide what to do with each one.

The trainer can have the participants work on the task individually, in pairs, or in small groups. Using pairs or small groups makes the activity more interesting and adds the dynamic of discussion and joint decision making. The trainer distributes to each person or small group an envelope containing ten to twelve items that would typically be in someone's in-basket: phone messages, memos, letters, reports, minutes from meetings, and so forth. At the end of the designated time period—generally thirty minutes—the trainer conducts a discussion about what the participants did and why. Again, use an in-basket activity already developed or create your own.

## Simulations

For our purposes, the term "simulation" refers to lengthy, case-like scenarios that simulate problems in the work environment. The design is complicated, often requiring participants to make decisions at various points during the activity. The most well-known simulations are the consensus-seeking survival simulations used in sessions dealing with teamwork.

Business simulations also fall into this category. Generally, business simulations are tied to management or financial disciplines and address a specific skill within that discipline such as problem solving, delegation, coaching and counseling, or planning. Unlike the survival simulations, the business game presents realistic management situations that test participants' knowledge and skill.

Survival simulations and business simulations are generally lengthy, requiring anywhere from one to three hours to complete and process. They are a great way to sharpen analytical thinking and task and people skills, and they help participants gain insight into their own behavior as they interact with others. More and more organizations are using computer simulations, but mostly for individual rather than group training. Simulations are available from several publishers listed in Appendix B.

## Instructional Games

To distinguish games from simulations, "game" is defined here as a rule-based, competitive activity based on a defined set of goals. Instructional games are often elaborate, professionally prepared packages related to a specific topic such as customer service, diversity, or communication. Another type of instructional game is a "frame game" that is designed generically so that different content can be inserted and the game adapted for many different topics. Frame games based on game shows such as "Jeopardy®" or the ever-popular BINGO are often used to review or reinforce content. Games are addressed in more detail in Chapter 12.

# Action Learning

Action learning is a real-time learning experience that occurs on the job and with the dual—and equally important—purposes in mind of (1) addressing a business need and (2) further developing individuals by exposing them to important, challenging, and useful learning experiences. Participants meet together in groups to solve organizational problems.

In action learning, the problem or project becomes the central learning experience. Participants are encouraged to learn from their attempts to solve a problem and then reflect on their decisions and behaviors during the process. Often the work on these projects continues long after the training program has been completed.

The following is a list of potential projects for a range of action-learning groups:

- Career-development process
- Succession planning
- Improvement of various processes
- Developing benchmarks for performance
- Strategic planning

## KEY POINTS

- People understand concepts better and retain information longer when they are actively involved with the learning process.

- The trainer's role is to create the environment and to facilitate the learning process.

- All instructional methods, including lecture and video, can be redesigned to involve participants more actively.

- Deliver "lecturettes" in segments of no more than ten minutes each.

- Use various ways to present cognitive material without lecturing.

Now that you have selected active-training techniques you would like to use and incorporated them into your design, the next step is to learn how to use them.

# Chapter 8

# Delivering Training

**LEARNING OUTCOMES**

In this chapter, you will learn

- To create a positive learning environment

- To use active-techniques to gain 100 percent participation

- To set up, conduct, and process an activity for maximum learning

- To fine-tune your platform skills and stage presence

## Creating a Positive Learning Environment

The success or failure of your training session is often determined long before the first participant sets foot in your training room. The trainer's job is to create and maintain an environment conducive to learning and to create opportunities for participants to experience personal growth, a sense of achievement and accomplishment, and recognition and rewards.

Much of the difference between success and failure has to do with one simple word: preparation. This includes preparing yourself and the learning environment, preparing the participants, and preparing the participants' managers.

## Active from the Start or Before

Participant preparation is critical to the success of the training session. Some ways to involve participants prior to the session are covered below.

**Pre-Session Questionnaire.** Several weeks before the session, send a letter and questionnaire to the participants. Use a letter similar to the one in Exhibit 8.1 to welcome them to the session, provide them with an outline of the session and logistical information, and explain anything that should be done prior to the session, such as reading assignments, self-assessment instruments, or the questionnaire.

The purpose of the pre-session questionnaire is to find out about participants' expectations and perceived needs as well as gather information to create customized role plays, case studies, and other activities. The questionnaire helps to prepare them mentally for the learning experience. A tip sheet can be included to help participants get the most out of the training program. This is particularly helpful for those who may be attending a training session for the first time or when the participants are coming from different locations or organizations and are unlikely to know each other. Exhibit 8.2 is a sample of a tip sheet. It is sent to participants from different organizations attending a three-day residential program at a conference center.

**Pre-Session Assignments.** Pre-session assignments are a good way to save valuable workshop time and get participants ready for the learning experience. Keep the pre-work minimal—a one- or two-page reading assignment and perhaps a self-assessment instrument. Participants overwhelmed with too much will be turned off before they begin. Also, keep in mind that there will always be some people who don't complete the pre-work assignments. Have a plan to deal with that situation. Ask them to work on the assignment during a break, or ask participants to work on the assignment while the group is involved in an activity.

**Manager Involvement and Support.** Ideally, managers of those attending training programs should sit down with their employees and tell them how the training relates to their jobs, explain what the program is about, tell employees why they are going and what the managers expect the participants to gain from the program, and find out what the employees hope to learn. The reality is that this scenario does not play out very often. Although managers cannot be forced to prepare their employees for the training experience, they can be prodded a little. Send the managers a memo such as Exhibit 8.3, suggesting how they can help prepare their employees for training.

| **EXHIBIT 8.1.   Sample Participant Cover Letter** |
| --- |

Dear Program Participant:

Welcome to the "Managing Conflict" workshop! I am looking forward to meeting and working with you as we explore ways to resolve conflict and prevent it from negatively impacting your business results.

In preparation for this session, I am asking you to complete the following pre-session assignments:

(1) Confidential Pre-Session Questionnaire: Please fax your completed questionnaire to me by [date]. My fax number is XXX–393–0000.

(2) Pre-Session Assessment: Please bring your completed assessment to the session on [date].

(3) Thomas-Kilmann Conflict Mode Instrument: Please complete pages 1 through 4 prior to the workshop session and bring the instrument with you on [date].

It is imperative that you complete these pre-session assignments. We do not want to take valuable class time to complete this work. It should take you about one hour to complete all three assignments.

This session will be highly interactive, and you will have several opportunities to apply concepts and skills to "real-life" scenarios.

See you on [date]!

Sincerely,

Karen Lawson, Ph.D.
Program Facilitator

**EXHIBIT 8.2.    Sample Tips for Participants**

## Tips to Help Participants Get the Most Out of "Management Skills and Techniques"

We are committed to making this the most rewarding learning experience you have ever had. For some of you, this will be your first professional-development program; others may be attending as part of an ongoing program. In either case, we want to help you get the most from your learning experience. To that end, we are offering the following tips to help you reap both personal and professional rewards.

1. This program is demanding in both time and energy. Not only will you be spending a full and active day in class, you will also be required to complete evening assignments. To minimize your stress, we strongly suggest that you make every effort to limit personal commitments while you are attending this program.

2. Because this is an intense, concentrated program, you won't want to miss a minute of exciting activities and exhilarating class discussions. Try to arrange your travel plans so that you can take advantage of every learning moment.

3. One of the greatest benefits of a program such as this is the opportunity to share with and learn from others, so come prepared to share your needs and concerns about the challenge of managing others.

4. Take advantage of the wealth of resources in the class. Spend your time during meals, breaks, and after class networking with others—both trainers and fellow participants. Take the opportunity to talk with others about common problems and possible solutions. Your goal is to learn as much outside class as in the class itself.

5. One of the major benefits of a residential program is meeting new and interesting people. Make a real effort to avoid "chumming" with people from your own organization or with your roommate exclusively.

6. You'll discover many new ideas and techniques that you will want to apply "back home." You'll be so excited you'll want to try everything! To prevent personal frustration, plan to return from the program with a "personal-development plan" of one or two new ideas that will help improve your performance on the job.

### EXHIBIT 8.2. Sample Tips for Participants, Cont'd.

7. Jump right in and get involved as much as possible when there are participative activities. You'll not only learn more, but have more fun, too.

8. Because there are so many new things to learn, you may sometimes feel overwhelmed. To maintain focus for yourself, continually refer to the objectives of the program and ask yourself, "What am I learning?" "How can I use this on the job?"

9. Use your time well to make friends, stimulate thinking, get new ideas, and strengthen your own thoughts. This is what makes an enriching learning experience. You'll leave the program "pumped up" and ready for action!

### EXHIBIT 8.3. Sample Memo to Manager

To:  Participant's Manager

From:  Trainer

Date:

Subject:  Title of Training Program

Your employee, _____, is scheduled to attend the training program entitled _____ on _____.

During the program, the following topics will be addressed:

The overall goal(s) of the session(s) is/are to _____

In order for the participants to be successful in transferring learning from the classroom to the job, the manager must be actively involved. Please take a few minutes and identify areas or skills you would like the participant to work on in this program. Be as specific as possible. Please share this information and discuss your expectations with the employee before the session.

Be sure to include an outline of the program and send a separate tip sheet, such as How to Prepare Your Employees for Training, shown in Exhibit 8.4.

**EXHIBIT 8.4.   How to Prepare Your Employees for Training**

**Before the Training Session**

- Well in advance of the training session, sit down with your employees and explain your reasons for sending them to the program.

- Explain what the program is all about, including objectives and content.

- If the employees are attending a program out of town in an unfamiliar setting, explain what they can expect. This should include a discussion of travel arrangements, lodging, and appropriate attire, along with travel-reimbursement policies and procedures.

- Tell them what you expect them to get out of the program and how the program relates to their jobs.

- Ask them what they would like to gain from the program. Encourage them to identify specific skills they would like to develop, information they want to learn, or problems they would like help in solving.

- Indicate that you will expect them to discuss the program with you when they return. You might even suggest that they write brief summaries of their learning experiences, including what they learned, how they are going to use the training back on the job, and how the training will benefit them, the organization, and if applicable, their customers. You may even want them to share what they learned with their co-workers at a staff meeting.

- Employees often worry about being away from the job because of work piling up. Assure them that the work will be there when they get back and not to worry about it. Emphasize that you want them to get as much out of the program as possible.

**After the Training Session**

- Shortly after they have returned from the training, meet with the employees to debrief.

| EXHIBIT 8.4.   How to Prepare Your Employees for Training, Cont'd. |
|---|

- Ask them what they learned and whether or not it met their expectations. Ask if they would recommend that others attend.

- The discussion should center on how they are going to apply what they learned. Press them to be specific, and ask how you can support them as they try to use what they learned.

- If appropriate, ask them to share their experience, key learning points, materials, etc., with their co-workers.

- Follow up with the employees over the next few months to make sure they are applying what they learned. After they have had adequate time to use what they learned on the job, you might ask them what they still want or need to learn.

*The Trainer's Handbook, Updated Ed.* Copyright © 2009 by Karen Lawson. Reproduced by permission of Pfeiffer, an imprint of John Wiley & Sons, Inc.

For multi-session training programs, involve the participants' managers in another way. Create "homework" assignments or projects that the participants must complete outside the sessions, discuss with their managers, and have the managers sign off on them. For example, with one or two weeks between sessions, participants can be asked to apply what they learned in the session, write a summary, discuss it with their managers, and be prepared to discuss it during the next session. Exhibit 8.5 is an example of an assignment following a session on delegation.

The more supportive and involved participants' managers are, the more positive and participative the participants are in the training session. Studies also find that the more voluntary the training, the higher the motivation and involvement of the participants.

## Rehearsal

Now that the up-front work to prepare your participants is over, do not overlook or short-shrift your self-preparation. You must be completely comfortable and proficient with the content and the activities. Take nothing for granted. Spend plenty of time practicing. Make sure to plan transitions or bridges from one activity to another. Anticipate questions and problems and think about how you would handle them.

**EXHIBIT 8.5.  Delegation Assignment**

You have now learned the skill of delegation. In using this skill, make sure that you:

1. Select an employee who has the capability of handling the responsibility.

2. Provide the employee with adequate training to handle the responsibility.

3. Specify the performance standards for the new responsibility.

In the space below, outline a responsibility that you can delegate to one of your employees. Discuss it with your manager and be prepared to share it in class on [date].

Name of Responsibility: _____

Person to Whom You Are Delegating: _____

Specific Tasks to Be Done:




Performance Standards:




Your Signature: _____ Date: _____

Your Manager's Signature: _____ Date: _____

## Seating Arrangements

In many cases, you will not have any control over the room in which you are assigned to train or even the seating arrangements. You could be in a boardroom with a huge oval mahogany table and overstuffed chairs, or you might find yourself in an amphitheater with the seats bolted to the floor. Even in situations in which the chairs cannot be moved, keep in mind that people can be moved.

Different room set-ups result in different group dynamics. Part of the planning process is deciding how much interaction you want and how much control you want as the trainer. Then you choose the seating configuration conducive to creating the desired outcome. Careful thought and planning of the seating arrangements will help facilitate participation and minimize problems.

Figures 8.1 through 8.7 illustrate common seating arrangements. Read the following seven lists indicating the trainer's intent and desired outcome. Then, referring to the figures, write down which setup will most likely achieve the desired results. Answers are given in Appendix A.

---

**Figure 8.1. Classroom Style**

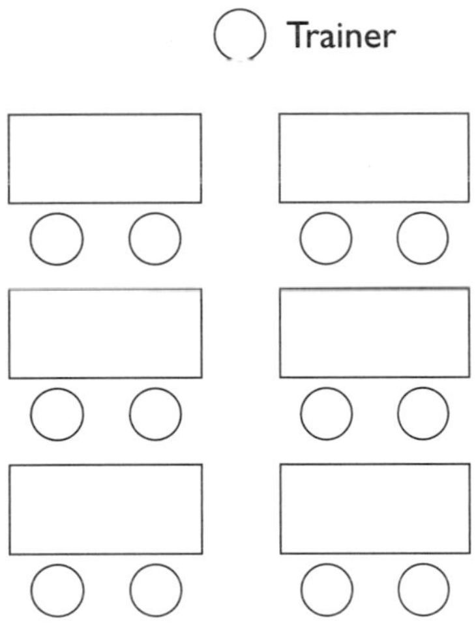

---

**Figure 8.2.   Horseshoe**

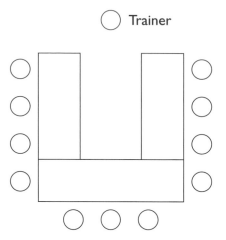

**Figure 8.3.   Single Square or Round**

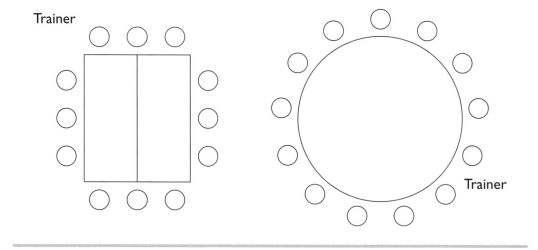

**Figure 8.4.  Cluster**

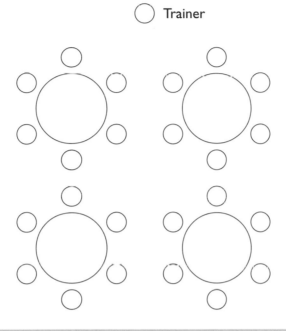

**Figure 8.5.  Conference**

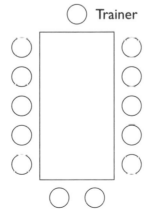

**Figure 8.6.    Semicircle and Full Circle**

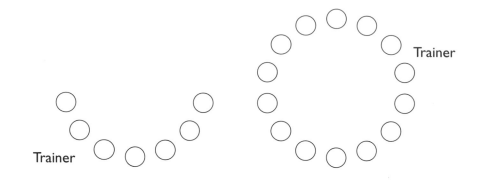

**Figure 8.7.    Chevron**

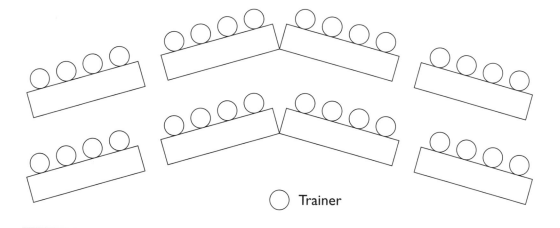

### Trainer's Intent/Desired Interaction 1

- Formal atmosphere
- Low group involvement
- High degree of trainer control
- Primarily one-way communication

### Preferred Setup 1

Seating arrangement: _____

### Trainer's Intent/Desired Interaction 2

- Trainer serves as facilitator
- Emphasis on small-group work
- High participant involvement
- Freedom of movement for both trainer and participants
- Room for flip chart and work table

### Preferred Setup 2

Seating arrangement: _____

### Trainer's Intent/Desired Interaction 3

- Moderate group involvement
- Trainer in control; focal point
- Allows for some participant movement
- Some two-way communication

### Preferred Setup 3

Seating arrangement: _____

### Trainer's Intent/Desired Interaction 4

- Trainer becomes part of the group
- High participant involvement and interaction

- Informal, relaxed atmosphere
- Facilitates problem solving and promotes open discussion

**Preferred Setup 4**

Seating arrangement: _____

**Trainer's Intent/Desired Interaction 5**

- High participant involvement
- Very informal
- Allows for changing configurations
- Conducive to a variety of activities and interactions

**Preferred Setup 5**

Seating arrangement: _____

**Trainer's Intent/Desired Interaction 6**

- Formal environment
- Low to moderate group involvement
- Some two-way communication
- High degree of control on part of trainer

**Preferred Setup 6**

Seating arrangement: _____

**Trainer's Intent/Desired Interaction 7**

- Formal atmosphere
- Moderate participant involvement
- Trainer clearly in control

**Preferred Setup 7**

Seating arrangement: _____

## It's Show Time

The importance of getting off to a good start cannot be overstated. What you say and what you do in the first few minutes can make the difference between a fabulous learning experience and a dismal failure. It is your job to (1) create a safe environment in which learning can take place; (2) stimulate participants' thinking; (3) involve the participants in the learning process; (4) manage the learning process; and (5) ensure individual participant accountability.

At the beginning and throughout the training session, you may be challenged, perplexed, and even stymied by participants' lack of motivation and sometimes outright resistance. You have, of course, taken participant motivation into account, using it as a driving force behind the design and development of your program. However, continue to be diligent and vigilant about motivational strategies throughout the delivery.

To guide you in those strategies, consider the ARCS model introduced by J.M. Keller (1983). The ARCS (attention, relevance, confidence, satisfaction) model offers an approach that ensures participant "buy-in" and participation. Use Keller's four-part model as a quality check on your design. An effective training program will reflect the following:

- *Attention.* From the very beginning, grab and hold the participants' attention, using a variety of techniques.

- *Relevance.* Design the program to meet the real-world needs and experiences of the participants, and clearly point out the tangible benefits. Throughout the program, provide a framework, helping participants link content with what they already know.

- *Confidence.* Design the training and facilitate the learning process in such a way that the participants gain confidence to apply new knowledge, behavior, and skills back on the job.

- *Satisfaction.* The artful design of the training program, coupled with skillful facilitation of the process, results in a high degree of participant satisfaction with the learning experience. Additionally, the participants' ability and motivation to apply the learning results in personal satisfaction.

## Grab Their Attention

The technique of grabbing participants' attention and creating a readiness for learning is called "set induction."

### EXAMPLE OF SET INDUCTION

I learned (quite by accident) about set induction and the powerful attention-getting impact of a simple visual aid many years ago when I was a high-school English teacher. I was part of a three-person team teaching American literature to high-school juniors. We used a large-group, small-group approach to teaching. Two days a week one of us lectured to all our combined classes. Imagine 150 sixteen-year-olds in a lecture hall.

This was my first experience lecturing a large group of teenagers, and my topic was Nathaniel Hawthorne and *The Scarlet Letter*. I knew this was not exactly a hot topic for a group of sixteen-year-olds. Furthermore, having observed the behavior of the group when the other two teachers lectured, I knew I needed to come up with some way to get their attention fast.

I decided to trace a stencil of an Old English style letter "A" on a transparency and hand-color it in red. I arrived at the lecture hall twenty minutes early and put the transparency on the overhead projector, and dimmed the lights.

When the bell rang and the students came rushing and screaming into the lecture room, they stepped through the door and immediately became very quiet because all they could see was a huge red letter "A" on the screen. They began taking their seats with hushed exchanges such as "cool," "heavy, man," "far out," and so forth. I had their attention immediately, and as a result I was able to conduct my lecture without the usual antics and disruptions the other teachers had experienced.

## Using Icebreakers and Openers

Techniques that immediately involve participants are very effective in piquing their interest and curiosity and preparing them for the learning experience. Many trainers start with an icebreaker, an activity designed to put people at ease and help them become acquainted. Typically, icebreakers are not necessarily related to the content. Their purpose is to help reduce tension and anxieties, energize the group, set a tone for the program, and involve everyone. Openers, on the other hand, are subject-matter-oriented activities that accomplish all the above and also introduce the participants to the session content. It is far better if the opening activity serves several purposes, including setting a tone or mindset, and does not seem frivolous and a waste of time.

Many trainers use the tried-and-true (albeit boring) method of having people introduce themselves and say what they want to get from the training. A variation of this method, and just as boring, is to have people pair up, interview each other, then introduce each other to the rest of the group. These two openers are not only unimaginative, but create an outcome quite the opposite from what the trainer intends. Rather than being at ease, participants are uncomfortable at having to speak up in a room full of strangers. Furthermore, with the partner introductions, many people are embarrassed because they forget the other person's name or fumble with the information.

Although it is true that people should be active from the very beginning, it is also true that the activity must have a purpose beyond introducing people to each other. To find ideas for icebreakers, browse through the dozens of books on the market that offer icebreakers, openers, and warm-up activities for every purpose. (Check those listed in Appendix A for specific titles.) Write down the ones that appeal to you and how they could be used, that is, with what topic and audience. File them for use in another session or to spruce up an existing design.

A few basic openers are included on the next few pages that can be adapted to any topic.

**Human Scavenger Hunt.** In programs of three hours or more, you may want participants to get to know each other quickly so you can establish a safe environment in which people will feel comfortable participating. One of the most popular get-acquainted activities that also guarantees instant involvement is the Get-Acquainted Scavenger Hunt made popular by Ed Scannell and John Newstrom (1983).

*Instructions:* Prepare a sheet on which you ask participants to "find someone in the room who. . ." and then list a number of descriptive statements. Ask participants to circulate around the room and find people who fit those criteria. When a person fits a particular criterion, ask that person to sign his or her name. Any individual can sign another person's sheet only once.

The following scavenger hunt, adapted from Scannell and Newstrom's (1983) activity, could be used for a session on time management.

*Find someone in this group who. . .*

- Has been told he/she is a good cook
- Uses a daily planner or "to-do" list
- Schedules his/her day the night before
- Was born in the same month as you

- Maintains a neat desk or work area
- Listens to educational tapes
- Has more than two pets

Notice that the statements are both content-related and personal. Content questions include those that address having a daily "to-do" list, maintaining a neat work area, listening to educational tapes, and scheduling the night before. Personal items include cooking, pets, and birthdays. The two types of questions give participants an opportunity to relate on a personal level, while preparing them mentally for the session content.

**The Party.** This activity is great for networking and becoming acquainted. It creates movement and enables people to meet a number of fellow participants, regardless of the group size. The topics discussed can be adapted to any content.

*Instructions:* (1) Prior to the activity, hang or display posters on the wall or on easels around the room related to both the theme of your session and your topic. For example, use movie posters for a movie theme in a session on conflict, leadership, communication, or almost any subject. To make the theme more specific, use any type or category of movies such as Disney films, science fiction, horror, westerns, musicals, comedies—the possibilities are endless. For a zoo theme in a diversity program, post large pictures of different zoo animals. Posters representing different sports (football, tennis, golf, basketball, soccer, hockey, skating, and so forth) or perhaps teams within a particular sport would be great for a sports theme and team building.

(2) Also prepare instruction sheets for each person (or list on a flip-chart page) with the following assignments for each round:

**Round One**

- Introduce yourself to other members of your group by stating your name, where you live, and your position and responsibilities.
- Explain briefly why you selected this particular [movie, animal, sport, etc.] as your favorite.

**Round Two**

- Identify something you have in common with the other members in your group. Some possible topics might include hobbies, sports activities, family, pets, or job.

**Round Three**

- What are your concerns or expectations for this session?

(3) Tell participants to look around at the posters and select their three favorites. Explain that there will be three rounds of groupings or gatherings. During round one, they are to go to the designated area for their first choice; round two, their second choice; round three, their third choice. Tell them how long they will have for each round.

(4) After the subgroups are formed for the first round, ask the participants to discuss the questions or topics that appear on their instruction sheets or flip-chart sheets for that round. At the end of the designated time period, stop the discussion and ask for volunteers to answer the following questions:

**Round One**

- Who in your group traveled the farthest to attend this session?
- Why did you choose this [movie, sport, team. . .]?

(5) Repeat the process for the next two rounds:

**Round Two**

- What did you find you have in common?

**Round Three**

- What were the major concerns or expectations in your group?
- What was the most interesting thing you learned through this activity?

This activity can also be used at any time during the session by making the questions content specific. For example, in a change-management program, you might ask the following:

**Round One**

- What changes are you experiencing in your organization?

**Round Two**

- What is the impact of change on employees?

**Round Three**

- What is the impact of change on you as a manager?

**Getting Around.** Another popular activity is conducted in the following way:

*Instructions:* Put four content-related questions (or unfinished statements) on a flip chart or transparency. Show only one at a time. For example, for a workshop entitled, "Managing Change and Stress," post these four items:

- It's important to manage stress effectively because. . .

- Some reasons people resist change are. . .

- Some of my strengths in managing stress are. . .

- I know I'd be healthier if I. . .

1. Ask participants to stand up, pair with someone they don't know (or don't know very well), and discuss the first statement or question for a few minutes. (Be specific about how much time they have.)

2. Call time. Then ask participants to pair up with someone different (again, someone they don't know well) and discuss the item.

3. Continue until all four items (four rounds) have been discussed. If time is short, use only three rounds.

4. Discuss in the total group what the participants learned from this activity.

**Instant Assessment.** Another activity that gets people involved from the beginning is called an "Instant Assessment" (Silberman, 2005).

*Instructions:* Prior to the session, prepare sets of different colored 3-by-5 cards. Each card set consists of four different colors each with a different letter (A, B, C, and D) on it. Give each participant a set of cards. Begin by telling the participants that you would like to find out a little more about them so that you can address their specific needs. Tell them to indicate their answers to some questions by holding up the card that corresponds to the chosen response. Display the questions one at a time on the overhead projector, giving the participants time to respond to each item. Ask a few people to explain their choices.

For example, for a session on influencing others you might use the following items:

A. My main motivation for attending this session is. . . .

- To escape from the office

- To learn how increase my personal effectiveness

- Because my boss made me

- I have no idea why I'm here

B. When giving feedback, I believe you should. . . .

- Be blunt and to the point

- Cushion the negative between positive statements

- Describe specific behavior

- Address the person's attitude

C. When faced with a conflict situation, I. . . .

- Ignore it and hope it will go away

- Hold firmly to my position

- Give in with little resistance

- Beat the other person into submission verbally

D. Which of the following words do you most closely associate with the word *influence*?

- Power

- Authority

- Compel

- Persuade

People really enjoy this activity. It takes little time, yet gets people immediately involved in the content of the session. Notice that the items have an element of fun to them, yet also have a serious content-related component. This activity also appeals to those people who are tactile because they have an opportunity to touch and pick up the cards. From the trainer's point of view, the responses reveal some interesting information that can be referred to throughout the session.

**What Do You Want to Know?** Another activity you might like to try follows.

*Instructions:* Prior to the start of the session, prepare flip-chart pages with the major subtopics as headings, one subtopic per sheet. Post the pages on the wall. At the beginning of the session, give each participant a pad of Post-it® Notes. Ask them to look at the topics and write down any questions they have about any or all of the topics. They may write as many questions as time permits (you set time limit), but may put only one question per Post-it Note.

After they have written their questions, they are to stand up and place the Post-it Notes on the appropriate flip-chart pages. Rearrange and group similar questions, followed by comments linking their questions to the session content. Occasionally participants will post questions unrelated to the session. This is a good opportunity to clarify expectations by pointing out what will and will not be addressed.

**Pretest.** Also try the following activity for a quick start.

*Instructions:* At the beginning of a session, have participants complete a quiz related to the content. This technique not only raises the participants' interest level but also establishes the purpose of the training session. For example, the following are questions you might ask about writing business letters (correct answers can be found in Appendix A):

### True or False

1. It is acceptable to abbreviate the month when typing the date on a business letter.

2. In business letters, when the salutation consists of only a first name, it is acceptable to use a comma, for example, "Dear John,".

3. When using full block style, the complimentary close should be flush with the left-hand margin.

4. When writing a letter to a company, if you do not know the names of the people to whom you are writing, you may use "To Whom It May Concern."

5. When addressing more than one individual, place names on separate lines in alphabetical order.

This type of quiz creates awareness among participants that they may not know as much as they may think they do about the topic, and that recognition motivates people to "buy" what the trainer is "selling." You might make it even more interesting by asking participants to estimate how many correct responses they expect to get on the quiz.

A quiz or self-evaluation can be handled two ways. One approach is to have people complete it and score the quiz individually. Another is to ask participants to work on it with partners. Working in pairs is less threatening and serves to generate interest and enthusiasm as the pairs discuss and debate their answers.

You can make this activity more complex and fun by turning it into a game called "Test Match" (Sugar, 1998), which is designed as a team competition.

## What's in It for Them

Participants attend a training session for a variety of reasons. Some really are excited and cannot wait to get started; others view the experience as something worse than a trip to the dentist. Some cannot imagine why they are there. After all, they have "been there, done that."

Although it is true that people come to sessions with a lot of "baggage" you do not know anything about and cannot do anything about, you can lessen their resistance and improve their general mindset by pointing out "what's in it for them." Tell them how this session will benefit them by enhancing their skills, providing them with additional information, or helping them overcome any barriers that might be preventing them from doing their best—how the training will improve their lives.

## Preview of Coming Attractions

After explaining the benefits to them and providing any background as to why and how this program came about, review the objectives by comparing intended outcomes with their needs and expectations. Several of the opening activities mentioned earlier, such as "What Do You Want to Know?" are very effective in making sure both trainer and participants are on the same page from the very beginning.

Be sure to provide an overview of the program, including your expectations, time frames, break times, and logistics. Let the participants know, for example, how often and how long the breaks will be, as well as how you are going to monitor and signal when breaks are over. This is also the perfect opportunity to explain the interactive format, particularly for those who have only experienced teacher-centered, passive learning.

# Experiential and Active-Training Techniques

After the opening activities are over, it is time to move to the meat of the program. Introduce the first activity. If you follow your carefully crafted design, you should have no problem. Not necessarily! The design may look great on paper, but how it plays out is what is important. Many trainers design and develop what appears to be a dynamite session, with plenty of participant interaction. If the session fails, they blame the participants ("What a bunch of losers!"); others denounce the use of participant-centered, active-learning methods and revert to the comfortable and less-risky trainer-centered approach.

## Using Small Groups

Participants will be in small groups for most of the activities you will be conducting, such as those described in Chapter 7. The ideal size for a subgroup is five to seven people. The minimum is three, with eight as the maximum. Sometimes, however, participants will be working in pairs. Small groups, by definition, include pairs and trios. Pairs provide intimacy and thus instant interaction. Trios have the advantage of offering multiple views on the problem being discussed. "Buzz group" is another term for small group, from the "buzzing" sound of multiple groups engaged in lively discussion.

If possible, arrange for breakout rooms for small-group activities. Putting subgroups in separate rooms saves time, is less noisy, and preserves a collective spirit. Unfortunately, it is not always possible to have separate rooms. If that is the case, carve out areas within the main room and form small-group clusters with as much space between them as possible.

Assignments to small groups typically assume the form of a question or problem. Or ask small groups to develop a list, share personal incidents, or produce a definition.

## The Power of Two

So far we have addressed methods and activities that involve the entire group or a number of small groups, but do not overlook the power of pairs to promote active learning. Asking participants to work with learning partners is an efficient and effective cooperative-learning technique. It guarantees 100 percent participation; as Mel Silberman puts it, "People can't hide or be left out in a pair." Pairing not only promotes interaction, but also creates a safe environment in that no individual feels pressured to come up with the right answer.

## Experiential Learning Cycle

For activities to do what they are designed to do, the trainer must make sure each activity completes the steps in the Experiential Learning Cycle.

Experiential learning is a process by which participants learn inductively, that is, discover for themselves the intended learnings through direct experience during an activity. The Experiential Learning Cycle is a model of the five-step process that enables the participants to learn or derive meaning from what they experienced. This model is represented in Figure 8.8.

**Figure 8.8.   The Experiential Learning Cycle**

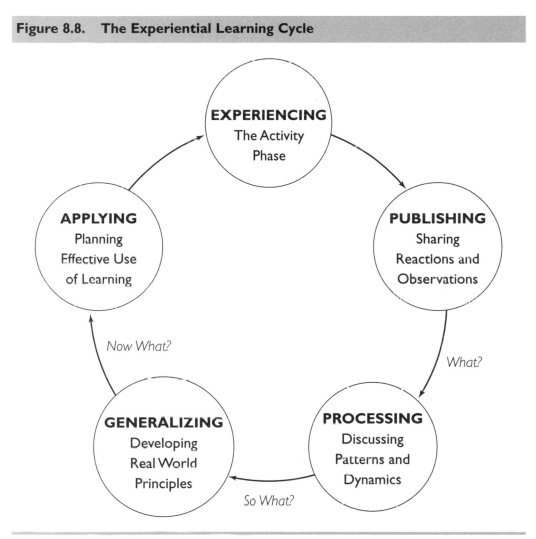

*Source:* Introduction to *Reference Guide to Handbooks and Annuals* (1999 ed.). San Francisco: Pfeiffer.

- *Experiencing.* The process starts with participants experiencing or becoming involved in the activity. The basis for the entire process, the experience itself requires participants to do, say, hear, observe, etc.

- *Publishing or Sharing.* Following the actual experience, participants share their reactions to and observations about the activity.

- *Processing or Interpreting.* In this part of the cycle, the trainer helps participants address the dynamics of the group interaction. During this critical stage, the facilitator helps the group explore and analyze what happened to them during the experience.

- *Generalizing.* After processing, participants make a connection between the activity and their real-world situations. They explore the meaning of the activity and how it relates to them. This is where most experience an "AHA!" The light bulb goes on. The participants reach a deeper level of understanding and insight.

- *Applying.* The final step requires participants to think about what they are going to do with this new learning, how they are going to apply it.

If any part of the cycle is omitted or inadequately addressed, there is a high probability that the structured experience will not produce the desired results. In fact, the processing and subsequent parts of the cycle are where the real learning takes place. Therefore, plan carefully and allow sufficient time for the complete processing of the activity. As a rule of thumb, spend as much time on processing—that is, discussing the activity—as you spend on the activity itself.

With that in mind, take a look at a systematic process for managing each experiential learning activity.

## Introducing the Activity

All training activities, including role plays, case studies, assessment instruments, small-group discussion, and other structured experiences, must be introduced or positioned within the context of the overall session. Here are some guidelines for introducing any learning activity:

- Give a purpose and objectives for the activity. Be careful not to give out too much information. If you are focusing on discovery learning, then do not tell the participants what they are supposed to learn from doing the activity. That would defeat the purpose of inductive or discovery learning.

- Rearrange the furniture and regroup the participants as appropriate for the activity. The goal is to group people as quickly and as efficiently as possible.

- Provide specific instructions as to what the participants are to do both during and after the activity. Define terms and distribute materials, carefully going over printed material. It's a good idea to write and display on a flip chart a brief, step-by-step outline of the activity including times associated with each step. For example, the time line for a survival simulation might look like this:

| | | |
|------|------------------------|------------|
| 2:00 | Individual reading | 10 minutes |
| 2:10 | Individual ranking | 15 minutes |
| 2:25 | Group discussion | 25 minutes |
| 2:50 | Group ranking | 15 minutes |
| 3:05 | Scoring and posting | 10 minutes |
| 3:15 | Discussion of activity | 40 minutes |

Make sure all participants are settled in their small groups *before* you give them any instructions or explanations. People have a hard time concentrating on two things at once.

- Make appropriate role assignments. To help pace the group on longer assignments, have each small group appoint a timekeeper. If small groups must write something on flip-chart pages, they will need a scribe or recorder. If each small group must report back to the large group, tell each to appoint a spokesperson. Make it clear that you do not want the same people assuming the same roles each time.

- Solicit questions and make sure everyone understands what they are to do before you continue.

- If necessary, demonstrate any rules or procedures.

- Begin the activity and circulate around the room to each small group to determine whether everyone knows what to do. Clarify as needed.

## Conducting the Activity

Even though the participants are engaged in the activity, the trainer still has work to do. The following are some guidelines for keeping the activity on track:

- In the first few minutes of the activity, expect some confusion and/or frustration. It's okay. Some of this helps encourage problem solving and learning. Remember that the participants are learning by doing.

- Continue to move about the room from group to group to make sure the participants are on track.

- Remain in your role as the facilitator. Resist giving participants the answers or becoming directly involved in the activity. Give suggestions or ask guided questions, if you find that participants are way off the mark.

- Constantly observe how individuals and small groups are working on the task or problem as well as how the members work together. Intervene only when absolutely necessary!

- Remind the participants of time passing, giving them signals half-way through a particular stage and also two-minute warnings for each deadline.

- Use your judgment about calling time. In some cases, you may have to allot extra time; in other situations, the small groups may finish earlier than anticipated and be ready to move on to the processing stage.

## Processing the Activity

What happens after the actual activity is over is critical. For our purposes, "processing" the activity refers to the entire discussion of the activity and includes the four stages of the Experiential Learning Cycle: publishing, processing, generalizing, and applying.

- Remember that this is where the real learning takes place. Plan to use about as much time to process an experiential activity as it took to conduct it.

- If you used only some participants to do a demonstration or role play, elicit feedback from them first before eliciting it from others.

- To make sure you address each part of the Experiential Learning Cycle, prepare questions using the following format: What? So what? Now what?

- Begin by asking participants WHAT they experienced during the activity. "What" questions are designed to elicit how the participants *feel* about the activity.
  - What went on during the activity?
  - What was your reaction?
  - What did you observe?
  - How did you feel?
- Next ask questions that address SO WHAT? "So what" questions relate to what the participants *think* or have learned from the activity.
  - What did you learn about yourself?
  - What did you learn from the experience?
  - What similar experiences have you had? How does this relate to anything you have experienced on the job?
  - How did this experience help you?
  - What are the implications of the behaviors you experienced or observed?
- Finally, ask participants to answer questions dealing with NOW WHAT? "Now what" questions address what the participants are going to *do.*
  - How can you apply what you learned through this activity on the job?
  - What might you do differently?
  - How can this experience help you in the future?
- Record participants' feedback and points on the flip chart. Ask one participant to serve as a scribe so that you can concentrate on facilitating the discussion.
- Do not be alarmed if people have differences of opinion. That is quite healthy. Just make sure the discussion does not get out of control.
- Be sure you have completed the learning cycle and helped participants make the connection between the activity and their own situations.
- Wrap it up by asking a few general processing questions to elicit feedback and reactions to the activity itself.
  - What did you like about the activity?
  - What did you dislike about the activity?

- What changes would you make?
- What suggestions do you have to make this a more meaningful experience?

- Don't worry about getting some negative reactions. Every participant cannot be expected to like every activity. Negative reactions are prompted by many factors, including learning style. Do not agonize over one or two negative comments. However, if your entire group reacts negatively, do some real soul searching and take a careful look at the design as well as your facilitation.

## Creating Your Own Activity

Think about something you would like to communicate to participants. Then decide on an activity or specific method that will actively involve the participants in learning the material. Using the worksheet in Exhibit 8.6, think through and then outline the entire process for the activity, including specific processing questions.

# Tips for Using Specific Methods

Although the steps and guidelines just mentioned are appropriate for any method, it is important to address some special considerations and guidelines related to specific techniques.

## Assessment Instruments

Like other activities, assessment instruments need to be properly introduced and positioned. This is particularly important with self-assessment instruments that some participants might find threatening. Consider the following guidelines for the use of assessment instruments:

- Begin by explaining what the assessment is designed to do and why you have chosen this one in particular.

- Emphasize that this is an assessment, not a test. A test implies that there are "right" and "wrong" answers. Point out that there is no right or wrong.

- Explain thoroughly how participants are to respond to the assessment items. It is a good idea to read the instructions aloud and also demonstrate, using a transparency, how to mark the responses. This, of course, depends on the complexity of the instrument.

- Give participants adequate time to complete the instrument, but let them know how long it should take.

| **EXHIBIT 8.6.** **Creating an Activity** |

Name of Activity:

Participants:                                    Group Size:

Objectives/Purpose for Using This Activity:


Type of Training Method:

Time Needed:                                   Room Set-Up:

Supplies/Equipment:


Materials/Handouts:


Directions for Activity:


Introducing:


Conducting:


Processing (include specific questions):


Variations:


Resources:


Notes:

- After they have completed the instrument, ask them to put it aside until everyone has finished.

- At this point, you may want to present a lecturette or engage participants in an activity that introduces them to the theory behind the instrument and the topic.

- After participants have an understanding of how the instrument relates to the topic and what the assessment is designed to show, ask them to predict what their scores might be. For example, the Thomas-Kilmann Conflict Mode Instrument (Thomas & Kilmann, 1974) is designed to give participants insight into their approaches to dealing with conflict. After they complete the instrument and put it aside, introduce them to the five approaches using a card sort activity. Then ask them to write down which approach they tend to use most frequently. (Most people believe they primarily use collaboration, when, in fact, collaboration is the least-used approach.)

- After the participants have written down their predictions, ask them to score the instrument and read the interpretive material.

- Then conduct a discussion to clarify the participants' understanding of the assessment and what the scores mean. Ask for volunteers to share their scores and personal insights. Ask people to indicate whether or not their scores were consistent with what they expected. In other words, did the data confirm or refute their speculations? If people disagree with the results of the assessment, point out that they generated the data, and only they can verify it. Suggest that they revisit particular items that caused them concern and analyze their responses.

- The last step, of course, is to process the activity using the general suggestions and guidelines discussed earlier.

## Videos

Participants often regard videos as an opportunity to "take a snooze"—sometimes literally. How the video is used is critical to the success of this method. Follow these suggestions to ensure maximum impact:

- Introduce the video by explaining why you are showing it and what the video is about, including a brief description of the setting and characters. Also, prepare participants for anything unusual or unique in the video. For example, any of the videos produced by Video Arts reflect the British accent and dry wit of actor John Cleese.

- Tell the participants what to look for as they view the video. In fact, it is a good idea to prepare a list of specific questions related to the video and create a handout or post the questions on a flip chart. The entire group can address each question, or different questions can be assigned to specific individuals or groups of participants. This technique will make the participants much more attentive because they know they will have to report their observations to the entire group.

- Show the video in its entirety; then lead a discussion based on the questions or points the participants were to look for.

- Another method for making a video more interactive is the stop-action technique. This involves stopping the video at strategic places to discuss points or observations. Studies show that this stop-action technique results in significantly greater learning. Here are three ways to use film-stopping intervals:

  - Ask the group, "What would you do?" to give the participants an opportunity to speculate on what they believe is the most appropriate action or behavior.

  - Ask the participants to recap or review the key learning points they saw demonstrated in the segment just viewed.

  - Ask them how the video segment relates to their own situations on the job.

- Whichever viewing method you choose, make sure you devote adequate time to processing, just as you would with any other activity or technique.

## Role Plays

As discussed earlier, role plays are extremely effective if handled properly. Keep in mind the following guidelines when using any type of role-play activity:

- Be clear about your objectives and communicate them clearly to the participants. Be sure they understand that the purpose is to practice the skills they have learned in the session.

- A risk-free environment is critical to the success of a role play. The key is to introduce role plays incrementally and only after you have presented a model of desired behavior through a video or demonstration.

- Review the procedure, steps, or skills that have been presented throughout the session.

- Prepare an Observer Sheet that helps the observer focus on each role player's behavior. This sheet can also serve as a checklist for the participants to follow even after the session is over.

- Hear feedback first from those who participated as actors and then from observers before giving your input.

- During the discussion, maintain focus on the process, not the content.

## Simulations

Because of its length and complexity, a simulation requires more time and thought when preparing the participants for this activity.

In addition to following the general guidelines for introducing, conducting, and processing an activity discussed earlier, be sensitive to the potential risks. Since participants are in small groups, they will interact with a smaller number of people for a lengthy period. These factors coupled with the nature of the activity are likely to create more stress among individuals as they deal with both task and people skills. People tend to "show their true colors," sometimes resulting in intra-group conflict. Do not be surprised when it happens, and use it as a learning opportunity during the processing stage.

## Storytelling

Do not overlook the power of telling stories to illustrate points throughout your training session. Stories touch us in ways that no other medium can. Stories reach in and grab at the core of our existence. They help define who we are and what we believe. Storytelling is just as powerful, and perhaps even more so, today as it was a thousand years ago. Throughout the world, every culture has its own oral history. The ancient Greeks, Romans, and Vikings, as well as the American Indians had rich folklore. Explore the world of ancient storytelling and you will discover the reasons the best trainers use stories so extensively and successfully in their sessions. New trainers, in particular, often ask, "Where do I get my stories?" The answer is simple: from your own life experiences.

**Telling Personal Stories.** I discovered the power of storytelling quite by accident. I never planned on using stories—they just happened. I began using stories in my training sessions to illustrate or further explain my learning points. Several years ago, I began asking participants at the end of a session, "What did you like best about this program?" The response is always the same. Participants always say they like two things: the activities and the stories. One day I decided to ask what they liked about the stories. As one participant put it, "They made the ideas and points come alive. We could really relate to your experiences."

Storytelling engages the individual participants, allowing them to relate to or identify with the trainer's story. They have either had a similar experience or they are reminded of a similar situation that evoked the same thoughts, feelings, or reaction. Storytelling forms a psychological bond with the audience because it describes a common human experience.

People love to hear real-life accounts of events. Such accounts make the session come alive and lend credibility to the training. For example, when I tell my "red suit" story (described later in this chapter) in sessions dealing with perception and non-verbal communication, participants will often remark at the end of the session (orally or on the evaluation) that the story really made an impact. In fact, when I have encountered former participants months and even years after a session in which I told that story, they tell me they still remember my "red suit" story.

The following special types of stories are very effective for training:

**Parables.** Parables are short narratives from which a moral can be drawn. One of the most familiar sources of parables is the Bible. *Example:* The prodigal son who squanders all his money but returns home to a forgiving father.

**Fables.** Fables are brief tales from folklore, sometimes using animals that speak and act as humans. *Aesop's Fables* is probably the best-known collection of fables. These charming and simple tales teach valuable and timeless life lessons. For example, "The Crab and Its Mother" teaches a lesson about the power of example. In this fable, the mother crab chastises her son for walking one-sided instead of straight forward. The young crab agrees to do so if his mother can show him how. The mother tries and tries but cannot model the behavior she expects from her son. Great online sources of fables include www.fables.org and www.AesopFables.com.

Spend some time reading parables, fables, myths, and even fairy tales. Think about how you can use existing ones in your training to reinforce your message. In addition to the classic sources mentioned above, another great resource is *Tales for Trainers* by Margaret Parkin (1998). Better still, try your hand at making up your own tales to drive home a point.

# Improving Platform Presence

How you come across to your participants is just as important as your training design and content. In fact, because you are the medium through which the message is communicated, your demeanor, appearance, and behavior can make or break a program.

## Physical Appearance

People form an impression of you within the first few seconds—as soon as you enter the room. That impression is lasting and often determines how your participants react to you.

Three words should guide you in your selection of dress for your training sessions: professional, appropriate, comfortable. First and foremost, remember that you are a professional, and that is the image you want to project at all times.

A good rule of thumb is to dress equal to or above the level of your training group. If, for example, your participants are dressed in business casual, then you should dress accordingly, but go one step beyond a skirt or slacks and a sweater. Add a blazer or sport coat. Make sure your clothing is comfortable and fits well.

Avoid wearing anything distracting. This is a particular concern for women and their accessories: Do not wear bangle bracelets or dangling earrings; both become a distraction rather than an enhancement. Shoes are another consideration. Men's choices are pretty limited—slip-ons or tied. That choice is determined by the degree of casualness of the rest of your attire. Women, however, can choose flats or heels of varying height. This becomes a matter of personal preference and comfort. Particularly when conducting an all-day seminar or workshop, do not wear very high heels. They change your center of gravity, cause you to walk and stand differently, and do not provide you with the stability and balance you need in front of a training group.

### EXAMPLE OF CLOTHING'S EFFECT

Never underestimate the effect your clothing and appearance can have on a group. I experienced this firsthand when, at the end of a one-day session, a participant gave me extremely low marks on his evaluation sheet, noting that I had worn a red suit. He also complained to the program director about the red suit. The program director remarked that she had advised me to wear bright colors since I was training in a very large, tiered lecture hall and standing against a black background. The participant would not be swayed. He had learned somewhere that red is an aggressive color and was put off by it. In another session, a participant reacted negatively to my eye make-up and noted it on his evaluation. These examples also illustrate that sometimes, no matter how well you plan and think things through, you just can't anticipate some reactions.

## Body Language, Gestures, Movement, and Facial Expression

Your body language, gestures, movement, and facial expression all contribute to the impression your participants form of you. They can either encourage participants to listen or discourage them from paying attention to your message.

**Posture.** Always stand straight with your feet shoulder width apart to give you balance. If you stand with your feet close together, you will have a tendency to sway. Of course, in an all-day training session, you may find yourself becoming less formal and sit on a table or with the participants later in the day. So much depends on the group, the topic, the organization's culture, and the mood you are trying to create.

**Gestures.** Gestures are very effective means of emphasizing your points. They should be natural, meaningful, and controlled. Do not fling your arms wildly or use your hands and arms in a robotic manner. When you extend your arm and hand in a pointing gesture, be sure to keep your fingers together, using your entire hand to point rather than one finger. Remember that sharp, sudden gestures create negative emotions.

**Movement.** Although movement is a matter of style, be aware of the impact it can have on a group. At one extreme is the statue, the trainer who stays in one place and never moves. Although certainly not distracting, this posture is uninteresting. At the other extreme is the trainer who is in constant motion, who never stays in one place for more than a few seconds. Not only is this behavior distracting but participants will probably feel worn out or exhausted by the end of a session just from watching the trainer.

**Facial Expressions.** Do not overlook the importance of facial expressions. From the first moment the participants see you, they should feel your warmth. The most effective way of achieving this is to smile with both your mouth and your eyes. Throughout your session, your facial expressions can help or hinder your message. Make sure they are congruent with your words. Do not frown if you are saying something meant to be positive and upbeat.

*Remember:* What people see is more powerful than what they hear. Perception is reality, and how participants perceive you will impact not only how they react to you personally but how they react to the learning experience.

## KEY POINTS

- Involve participants in the learning process even before the actual training session.

- Spend a significant amount of time preparing for the program delivery.

- Using a variety of techniques, involve participants from the very beginning of the session.

- Make sure each activity completes the Experiential Learning Cycle.

- Spend as much time processing an activity as you spend on the activity itself.

- Real learning takes place during the discussion (processing) following the activity itself.

- Guide participants through the Experiential Learning Cycle by asking questions using the following format: What? So what? Now what?

- Use storytelling throughout your training session to illustrate your points and connect with the group.

- Be aware of your own demeanor, appearance, and behavior and their impact on the participants and the learning experience.

As you can see from this chapter, there is a lot involved in the actual delivery of the training program. There is, however, even more to consider, such as the use of visual aids, which we will explore in the next chapter.

# Chapter 9

# Using Visual Aids

---

**LEARNING OUTCOMES**

In this chapter, you will learn

- To use visual aids to enhance your training and improve retention

- To achieve maximum impact with visual aids

- To create various visual aids

---

## Retention Rate in Visual Learning

In a landmark paper entitled "The Magical Number Seven, Plus or Minus Two: Some Limits on Our Capacity for Processing Information" (still cited by today's educators), the author discusses his research and concludes that most people retain between five and nine bits of information in short-term memory (Miller, 1956). Because short-term memory decays in a matter of seconds, presenters, educators, and trainers must find ways to "fix" information presented in long-term memory and thus increase retention. One way of doing that is through the use of visual aids. Visual aids play an important role in helping participants retain information; however, they should never take the place of good training.

Before exploring other reasons for using them and specific examples, let's take a look at the classic research supporting the use of visual aids.

The 3M® Company sponsored the two most often quoted presentation-related research studies, one with the Wharton School's Applied Research Center (Oppenheim, 1981) and one with the University of Minnesota's Management Information Systems Research Center (Vogel, Dickson, & Lehman, 1986), to look at the impact of visuals (primarily overhead and computer-generated visuals) on business presentations and meetings. The results of these studies support the widely held belief that visuals do indeed increase retention and effectiveness.

The Wharton study found that presenters using overhead transparencies were perceived as more polished and professional. They came across as better prepared, more persuasive, more highly credible and more interesting (Oppenheim, 1981). Results from the University of Minnesota 3M® study showed that when visuals were added to an oral presentation, retention was increased by about 10 percent and the presentation became more than 43 percent more persuasive. Furthermore, presenters using computer-generated visuals were perceived as being more concise, more professional, clearer, more persuasive, more interesting, and more effective in the use of supporting data (Vogel, Dickson, & Lehman, 1986). David Peoples (1992) cites Harvard and Columbia studies that showed retention increased 38 percent when visuals were added to presentations. You will find more information about the effects of visual use on presentations in *Multimedia Learning* by Richard E. Mayer (2001).

Researcher Edgar Dale developed what is now known as "Dale's Cone of Experience" (Walters, 1993). His studies conclude that people will remember:

- 20 percent of what they hear

- 30 percent of what they see

- 50 percent of what they see and hear

- 80 percent of what they hear, see, and do

# Why Use Visual Aids?

The main purpose of visual aids is to enhance the training and to improve retention. The key word here is *aid*. Visuals should not take the place of the spoken word. After all, if the visual can stand alone, then the trainer is not necessary.

## To Capture Attention

Visual aids help capture and keep the participants' attention. The visual aid can be extremely simple and even somewhat primitive, or it can be slick and dramatic. It all depends on personal choice, cost, available resources, type of presentation, room size and set-up, audience, and purpose.

## To Reinforce Points

Visual aids also reinforce the points being made. With key words or graphics, the message is communicated both visually and verbally. As we noted earlier, the likelihood that the message will be retained increases from 20 percent to approximately 50 percent.

## To Organize Information

Visual aids help you to organize your material. They help keep you on track and ensure all the information is covered. Keep in mind, however, that the visual aids do not drive the training session. The trainer has already developed the program and the training materials, and the visual aids are placed strategically within that framework to enhance the program.

As a tool for organizing, visuals are also a way for the trainer to guide the participants. If the trainer uses a visual to present a key point, the participants are better able to follow the organization of the session. As a result, the trainer appears more professional, looks better prepared, and comes across as more competent.

## To Promote Understanding

The use of visual aids promotes understanding. They illustrate the spoken message with graphs, charts, pictures, or key words. This is particularly valuable if the trainer is explaining concepts or somewhat complex information. You can simplify the information by distilling it into understandable segments. For example, the trainer might be making a presentation involving a lot of figures and statistics. The information will be more interesting and meaningful if it is presented in charts and graphs, rather than in rows and columns of numbers.

## To Support the Spoken Message

Visual aids support the message by stimulating the participants' senses. Easy access to computer-generated graphics enables trainers to enhance their messages with interesting colors, pictures, motion, and sound.

## To Emphasize Key Points

Although various verbal techniques may be used to emphasize key points, many participants may not be attuned to the trainer's use of emphasis. For example, the trainer may say something like, "The first important point is . . ." or "I can't stress enough the importance of . . ." or "Now that we've addressed the causes, let's look at the effects." Keeping in mind that most people are not good listeners and that many people process information through different modes, putting the key points on a visual helps place the emphasis where the trainer intends it to be. There should be no doubt about the importance of information that is displayed visually.

# Guidelines for Using Visual Aids

The most commonly used visual aid is the PowerPoint® slide presentation. Computer-generated slides take the place of transparencies and 35 mm slides. The equipment requirements include a computer and an LCD projector. The flexibility of the medium enables you to modify information on a moment's notice to reflect late-breaking developments or audience input. Unfortunately, trainers with this capability often rely too heavily on using this medium and deliver passive rather than active training.

Other visual aids include flip charts and transparencies. A summary of advantages, disadvantages, and usage of various visual aids is shown in Table 9.1.

Regardless of which visual aid you use, the following guidelines will help you to create visuals that achieve the results you want.

### Limit Their Use

First of all, do not use too many visuals. Some so-called training sessions are nothing but one screen, slide, or transparency after another. Keep in mind that the visual is an aid, not the entire presentation.

### Keep It Simple

Nothing is more annoying than looking at a slide or transparency made directly from a page of text crammed with uninterrupted lines of information. Put only one idea on each visual and no more than one illustration. There should be only six or seven words per line and six or seven lines per slide. If you have a great deal of data, divide it among several slides. Some trainers who have discovered the myriad of options available through computer software programs tend to go overboard by doing too much, such as adding animation and sound effects, both of which are distracting. Remember that less is much more effective.

**Table 9.1. Using Visual Aids**

| Aid | Advantages | Disadvantages | When to Use |
|---|---|---|---|
| Chalkboards | Spontaneous<br>Easy to use<br>Inexpensive<br>Erasable<br>Attention-getter<br>Breaks lecture monotony | Slow<br>Temporary<br>Poor readability<br>Limited to chalk<br>Turn back to audience<br>Association with school days<br>Messy | Small, informal meetings<br>Spontaneous idea development<br>Brainstorming sessions |
| Flip Charts | Spontaneous<br>Advance preparation<br>Better contrast<br>Permanent<br>Easy to use<br>Portable<br>Allows you to present ideas in sequence<br>Inexpensive<br>Colorful (depending on range of colors in your set of markers) | Dependable<br>Bulky<br>Limited to writing<br>No flexibility in size or sequence<br>Expensive if prepared professionally<br>Tendency for trainer to write small to get all ideas on one page<br>Paper tears easily | Small groups<br>Lectures with spontaneous highlighting<br>Brainstorming<br>Lists, procedural steps |
| PowerPoint® Slides | High quality<br>Photographic detail<br>Very portable<br>Easy to operate<br>Can accommodate any size group<br>With remote control, trainer can move around | Dark room<br>Can appear "canned"<br>Slides become focal point, not speaker<br>Long sequences encourage mental absenteeism | Repetitive programs where photographic detail and professional look are important |

*The Trainer's Handbook, Updated Ed.* Copyright © 2009 by Karen Lawson. Reproduced by permission of Pfeiffer, an imprint of John Wiley & Sons, Inc.

**Table 9.1. Using Visual Aids, Cont'd.**

| Aid | Advantages | Disadvantages | When to Use |
|---|---|---|---|
| Overhead Projector | Fast, simple preparation of transparencies (any copier)<br>Lights on<br>Speaker faces audience<br>Any size group<br>Spontaneous or advance preparation<br>Very flexible<br>Optional quality<br>Inexpensive<br>Exact illustrations can be portrayed<br>Easily updated | Projector can block view unless positioned carefully<br>Less portable than 35 mm<br>Transparency preparation so simple that people tend to use items that are too busy<br>Tendency to overuse<br>Focus on overhead projectors sometimes difficult to control | Financial and technical presentations<br>Group sales presentations<br>Seminars, workshops where speaker wants to maintain rapport |
| Videos | Professional<br>Good discussion generator<br>Immediate feedback<br>Any size group<br>Effective for demonstrating how not to do something<br>Most effective for learner-centered training<br>Both sight and hearing are utilized in learning<br>"Expert" on tape can reinforce what the trainer has been saying | Dark room<br>Expensive<br>Used as substitute for lesson or presentation | Supplement to a training program<br>Visual feedback of trainee performance<br>Create mood or feeling as prelude to speaker's presentation |

*The Trainer's Handbook, Updated Ed.* Copyright © 2009 by Karen Lawson. Reproduced by permission of Pfeiffer, an imprint of John Wiley & Sons, Inc.

## Make It Easy to Read

Each visual should be seen clearly by the entire audience. Use type no smaller than twenty-four point for text and larger for titles. Use *sans serif* type such as Arial or Helvetica. Also use a combination of upper-case and lower-case letters.

## Use Color

Color is more effective than black and white for a variety of reasons. First, it has better cognitive impact. People simply remember color. As a result, a color visual is more interesting, has more impact, and makes a greater impression. With the availability of color printers and other pieces of technology, using color is easy.

Another important consideration is that audiences expect color. Even classic black-and-white films have been "colorized." Why? Because people are put off by black and white.

Use a solid background color. Medium blue is good for a background with the text in white, bright yellow, or pink. Do not use dark red, dark green, or dark blue. They do not project well.

Keep in mind, however, that many people are colorblind. It has been estimated that 20 percent of men cannot distinguish colors of the spectrum, causing colored objects or words to appear as shades of gray, black, and white, varying only in degree of lightness and darkness. The more distinction you can create among colors, the easier those with colorblindness will be able to see.

If you have lists, design your slides so that items come up one at a time and the previous items change to a different color. This technique not only helps the audience see what has led up to the item being discussed but also directs their concentration.

## Use It, Then Lose It

Because the visual is an aid, it should be visible only when it is relevant to the point being made. When you are finished with the slide, hit the "B" key on your computer to go to a blank screen. (If you are using a remote, it will have the capability to create a blank screen as well.) Otherwise, the participants may continue to focus on the visual aid and will pay little or no attention to what you are saying. People are easily distracted as it is, so do not give them anything that might divert them from your important message.

### Do a Dry Run

Slides that look great on your computer monitor may not look as good projected on a screen. Test your slide presentation in a semi-dark room with the projector as far back as you expect it to be in your actual room. What you see on your computer monitor is not what you will see in a semi-dark room, for example, colors may be washed out.

## Other Commonly Used Visual Aids

### Flip-Chart Pad and Easel

The flip chart has two different applications: (1) prepared pages and (2) blank pages on which to capture information spontaneously throughout the session. Let's start with prepared pages.

**Guidelines for Using Flip Charts.**  Prepared pages are used the same way as slides or transparencies, but they tend to communicate a more casual approach or atmosphere. A major advantage of prepared pages is that you can take the time to make sure the printing is neat and legible. This is particularly important if you have a problem writing legibly. Another advantage is that valuable session time is not spent at the easel; you are able to show the information quickly and move on. As with other forms of visual aids, the pages double as notes for the presenter.

For blank pages used to present or capture information as you move through the session, consider these important do's and don'ts. First, if you have asked for input from participants and you are capturing their responses, write down exactly what is said. Do not translate the information into your own words.

What if the person responding has a difficult time making his or her point succinctly? Some people do. Two different approaches can used: (1) After listening intently to the person's response, ask the individual to summarize his or her point in a few words so you can capture it on the flip chart or (2) if the person is not able to condense his or her point, paraphrase what you heard and ask permission to write down your interpretation of the contribution. As training guru Bob Pike says, "People don't argue with their own data." But they may argue with yours, so make sure you are respectful of their words and intent.

In full-day or half-day sessions, it is a good idea to tear off the pages and tape them to the wall. Before doing so, however, put a brief descriptive title at the top of each sheet. To save time, cut one-inch masking tape into several two- to three-inch strips before the session begins. That will enable you to post the sheets quickly.

Depending on the wall covering, you might be able to use push pins. If you are not permitted to use tape or pins, a safe alternative is to use a magnetic dry-erase easel pad that clings to most wall surfaces and can be positioned and repositioned on the wall. The sheets are erasable and reusable as long as you use dry-erase markers. Do not write on a sheet after it is posted on the wall, since many markers have a tendency to bleed through! Be sure to use washable markers just in case.

**Guidelines for Writing on Flip Charts.** Whichever method you choose, the following guidelines will help you create a polished, professional image for your participants:

- Use flip charts with relatively small groups of no more than twenty-five or thirty participants.

- Print in block letters two to three inches high so that everyone in the room can see the information.

- Do not put more than about six lines of information on a page.

- Do not fill the page to the bottom. People are sitting; their vertical range of vision is somewhat limited.

- Do not talk to the easel while you are writing.

- Wait at least twenty to thirty seconds after you finish writing before flipping the page so that people can copy the information if they wish.

- Do not stand in front of the easel after you have finished writing. Once again, give people an opportunity to capture the information.

- Consider using two or more easels across the front of the room to develop a continuous, uninterrupted flow of ideas or if you cannot post pages on the wall.

- If possible, choose easel pads of white paper with perforated sheet tops for easy tearing. Do not use flip chart paper with dark lines on it; it looks unprofessional.

- Use a wide, felt-tipped watercolor marker that will not bleed through the paper.

- Leave blank pages in between, particularly if you have prepared some pages ahead of time. Unless paper is quite opaque, the writing on the page underneath the blank page will show through.

- Be mindful of the impact of color. Use blue, green, brown, and black to add variety and interest. Save red for emphasis. Also, do not use red and green on the same page. Those who are color blind will not be able to distinguish the two colors.

- Alternate colors by lines to make reading easier.

- Use colors systematically: one for page headings, one for primary points, another for subpoints.

- When you are not writing, put the marker down.

## Overhead Projector and Transparencies

Transparencies are great for medium-sized and small audiences. They are easy to make and to use, but as with any other visual aid, they can be misused easily.

**Preparing Transparencies.** There are several ways of creating transparencies—a method for every pocketbook. At the low end, you can buy a box of clear transparencies and write in colored markers right on the acetate.

As a step up, purchase a box of clear or colored transparencies made especially for either a laser printer or a photo copier. If using a laser printer, generate text from your computer, loading the transparency film into your printer. If you have a piece of printed material and would like to make a transparency, substitute transparency film for paper in your copier.

Some people prefer colored lettering. If that is the case, you will need to purchase a colored printer for your computer to generate the document.

**Guidelines for Using Transparencies.** In addition to the basic guidelines for all visual aids in terms of type size, simplicity, and use of color, the transparency presents some unique advantages as well as important considerations.

*Creativity.* The transparency lends itself to creativity with the use of a little imagination. In addition to the different types of film mentioned earlier, you can create an "active" transparency resulting from a layering effect. For example, you would create a transparency with your key words and then cut the film apart so you have several "mini-transparencies." Then you would create a hinge effect by laying each word on the projector as you announce or refer to it.

*Framing.* Professionals' transparencies are framed. Framing a transparency blocks unnecessary light, provides rigidity, makes it easier to handle, and creates a more polished appearance. Once again, there are options, depending on cost and personal preference. One way is to purchase a box of cardboard frames on which you mount the transparency with transparent tape.

Another option is to purchase an Instaframe®, a plastic frame with a glass insert. Simply place the frame on the overhead projector and put the individual transparencies on and take them off as you use them. This enables you to store your transparencies any way you choose—in a box, folder, notebook, envelope—without purchasing more frames.

A third framing option is to purchase the 3M® Company's FlipFrame®, a transparent sleeve in which you insert the transparency. It has hinged flaps that when "flipped out" form a frame around the transparency and provide room for notes that no one else can see. FlipFrames are hole-punched along the left side so you can put them in a binder for better organization and protection.

*Control.* We have all been in sessions in which the overhead projector became an annoyance because the trainer did not control its use properly. For example, the participants should never have to look at a blank screen with a blinding light. Put the transparency on the platform, then turn on the projector. Turn off the projector before you remove the transparency.

Some people believe that the process of turning the screen on and off for many transparencies is a nuisance to both the presenter and the audience. There are ways around this annoyance and inconvenience. Cut a square of heavy paper or cardboard the size of the lens aperture; attach it with masking tape in hinge-like fashion to the top of the lens casing. Instead of turning off the projector between transparencies, you simply bring down the hinged cover, creating a black screen. Note: Turning the projector off and on in a quick series is often more distracting.

Similarly, you can lay a sheet of paper or cardboard on the platform to block the light. A remote device can be purchased from an electronics store that enables the projector to be turned on and off from several feet away. This is particularly effective when you are going to talk at some length before showing the next transparency or if you have moved into the audience and do not want to break the mood by returning to the front of the room to turn off the projector.

Another aspect of control involves the way in which you use the overhead projector. The purpose of the overhead projector is to allow you to show the visual while interacting with the participants. You can call attention to specific points on the transparency without ever turning your back on the group.

The group's attention can be directed in several ways by using the transparency. One way is to cover the transparency with a sheet of paper; as you make your point, uncover each word or line on the transparency. That way, the participants will read only what you want them to read and when. Another way is to use a pointer or pen to direct participants' attention to key words on the transparency. Any standard or retractable pointer will do, but you might want to make things more interesting by purchasing specialty pointers, such as the one sold by Creative Training Techniques or that are available in novelty stores.

Still another method of calling attention to specific information on the transparency is to use a transparency marker to underline or circle key points as you go. One word of advice: absolutely never point at the screen itself! Your arm will create a shadow on the screen, which is not only distracting, but it also obstructs the full view of the screen. Another reason for not pointing to the screen is that it causes you to turn away from the group, taking away the advantage of maintaining direct contact with the group. The final reason for not pointing to the screen is to avoid damaging the screen with your pointer.

The last small piece of advice about using an overhead projector is to dim the lights near the screen to create a sharp contrast and make it easier for the audience to see the visual.

## Videos and Video Clips

Video clips can be used in much the same way as demonstrations or scripted role plays. As with other media and methods, you have several options. Use a small portion from a movie or television show to illustrate a point. This is very effective, but be sure to obtain written permission. Copyright laws are not to be taken lightly. However, there are libraries of copyright-free video clips for use in presentations. Also, news clips and other events captured on film are often in the public domain.

One way around the cost and inconvenience of dealing with copyrighted material is to create your own video clips. The quality largely depends on the amount of money you are willing or able to spend. Use a video camera or hire a professional videographer to help produce the video, keeping in mind that the greatest expense is associated with the editing process.

You could write your own script and use your friends, colleagues, or acting students from a local college or university to illustrate the points, skills, or concepts through short vignettes. It is a great opportunity for aspiring or nonprofessional actors to gain both experience and exposure.

**KEY POINTS**

- Visual aids increase participants' ability to retain information.

- Since the purpose of visual aids is to enhance the training, not to replace it, use them sparingly.

- Create high-quality, yet simple, professional slides to capture the group's attention, reinforce points, organize information, and promote understanding.

- When writing on flip-chart pages, be sure to use large lettering that everyone can see.

- Although visual aids can be a powerful enhancement to your training program, a good trainer will not rely on them solely as the basis for the training program. In fact, you should plan on a worst-case scenario, that is, what you would do if something happened and you were unable to use your visual aids. Would you still be able to conduct your session? If you can't answer with a positive "yes," you need to rethink the way in which you are using them.

Of course, visuals play a very large role in the delivery of distance learning, which we will discuss in Chapter 10.

# Chapter 10

# Distance Learning

**LEARNING OUTCOMES**

In this chapter, you will learn

- To adapt traditional classroom activities to distance-learning methods

- To explore the key elements of distance learning design and delivery

- To define the different types of distance learning

- To distinguish between asynchronous and synchronous methods

- To identify the pro's and con's of distance learning methods

## Workplace Trends

More and more organizations are supplementing or even converting many of their classroom-based courses and training sessions to distance learning venues. For our purposes, distance learning in its purest sense is when the instructor and learners are separated by time and/or location. According to the American Council on Education, "All distance learning is characterized by (1) separation of place and/or time between instructor and learner, among learners, and/or between learners and learning resources and (2) interaction between the learner and the instructor, among learners, and/or between learners and learning resources conducted through one or more media; use of electronic media is not necessarily required" (1996, p. 10).

Several trends are driving this departure to non-traditional methods of conducting training:

1. Today's workplace offers a variety of employment options, including a growing number of contract and temporary employees as well as telecommuters. These non-traditional employment arrangements require a different approach to learning.

2. Sometimes it just is not cost-effective or practical to bring employees to a central location for a training session. People are often spread out among remote sites and locations. Bringing them to the corporate headquarters can be very costly. Some organizations, particularly small to mid-size, have few new employees and, therefore, it could be a long time before there are enough new employees to hold a group session. Although situations such as these may prevent you from conducting the traditional-style group session, you can still develop and administer an interesting and interactive program.

3. Younger workers entering the workforce have grown up using electronic media and expect to have it available to them for learning purposes.

The discussion of various distance learning venues in this chapter is by no means an attempt to provide detail on distance learning implementation. The purpose of this chapter is simply to present an overview of distance learning, including terminology, benefits, drawbacks, and resources, should you choose (or be directed) to implement distance learning in your organization.

# Advantages/Benefits of Distance Learning

The use of distance learning can be very helpful to organizations that seek to bridge the learning-delivery gaps caused by multiple geographic locations, time constraints, and other barriers to learning. The following is an overview of the many benefits of distance learning:

**Easy Access.** Learners can access the course material at their convenience, when and where they need it. This is particularly important for people who work at remote locations, are "on the road" a great deal, or just have busy, jam-packed schedules, both at work and at home.

**Cost Savings.** Traditional classroom-based courses are expensive. In addition to the cost involved with the training room and its associated overhead costs, distance learning saves travel costs. Think about how much it costs to bring people from various geographic areas to a central location. The organization pays heavily for hotel accommodations, transportation, and meals, not to mention the cost of lost productivity as a result of the time it takes to get to the training site. Granted, today's technology enables employees to conduct business while "on the road," but because of the "hassle factor" created by increased security (particularly when traveling by air), more and more companies as well as their employees are looking for ways to decrease any type of business travel.

**More Efficient.** In addition to being economical, distance learning allows you to deliver training to a large number of people at multiple sites at the same time. This is particularly important when an organization with multiple sites is rolling out a new product or process that needs to be introduced to all employees at the same time. Think about how long it would take (and how costly) to train several hundred people on a new product.

**Timeliness.** For training to be effective, it must take place as close as possible to when the learner is actually going to use the knowledge and/or skills. For example, banks are frequently faced with systems conversions resulting from mergers and acquisitions. Without distance learning options, the schedule for training tellers might have to start months before the actual conversion takes place. People might be trained in May but would not have an opportunity to apply what they learned until the new system went "live" in October. By then, they would have forgotten much of what they learned. Distance learning can be delivered "just in time," that is, when the person actually needs it.

**Learner-Centered.** In many cases, distance learning puts learners in control of their own learning, particularly web-based training. They can access the material or segments of material they really need and bypass or review those that they already know. They can spend more time on or revisit content without feeling rushed or pressured. Learners can also start and stop when they need to in order to accommodate their schedules.

**Simplified Distribution of Material.** Traditional training materials are costly. Think about a recent traditional classroom-based training session you have conducted or attended and add up the cost of participant binders, assessment instruments, job aids, and other ancillary materials. Electronic distribution of materials not only saves printing and postage but it also enables efficient and cost-effective updates to the existing material.

**Links Employees.** With growing globalization, technology-based distance learning enables people from different locations throughout the world to connect and learn from each other.

**Consistency.** Because the content is being delivered from a central source, there is consistency in what the learners see and hear.

**Better Use of Experts.** Subject-matter experts' time can be used more effectively and efficiently, particularly when they can choose when and how their expertise will be made available to learners, rather than be at the mercy of a specific classroom-based time and location.

# Disadvantages/Drawbacks to Distance Learning

No delivery mode is perfect, and distance learning has its drawbacks as well. The following list describes the most frequently cited disadvantages to distance learning:

**Learner's Experience with Technology.** One of the first obstacles one needs to overcome in implementing technology-based distance learning is the technophobic learner. Some people may be unfamiliar with the technology and require extra time and training to bring them up-to-speed. Still others may be resistant because their overwhelming workload prevents them from spending the time to complete self-directed courses or participate in real-time seminars.

**Available Technology.** Although technology and its capabilities are advancing rapidly, not all people and organizations are keeping up with it. Some organizations may be on the cutting edge, while others may be several iterations behind in software and/or hardware capabilities. Existing technology may be inadequate. For example, the system may not have enough bandwidth to run some graphics programs or the new software needed to deliver a program may not be compatible with the hardware. Not all employees may have access to the Internet.

**Reduced Social and Cultural Interaction.** What is often missing in the technology-based sessions is the peer-to-peer interaction and learning opportunities that contribute to team building and relationship building. However, as communication technologies continue to advance, this perceived barrier will diminish somewhat.

**Does Not Appeal to All Learning Styles.**  If designed properly, a technology-based course will incorporate most of the perceptual modalities discussed in Chapter 2. We know, however, that learning styles are also important to consider, and technology-based learning does not fit the needs of those whose learning preferences lean heavily on group interaction.

**Up-Front Investment.**  While distance learning may be cost-effective in the long run, it requires a substantial up-front investment in development costs, hardware, and software.

**Not All Subjects Are Appropriate.**  Technology-based courses that are heavily focused on cognitive learning are the best candidates for the various modes of e-learning. Skills (behavioral learning domain) can be taught through simulations and other interactive designs. Affective learning is much more difficult to address in technology-based learning because of the need for human interaction.

**More Cumbersome.**  More collaboration and teamwork are needed for distance learning because more people are involved. Traditional classroom training primarily involves an instructional designer, course developer, and facilitator/trainer. In many cases, these roles may be assigned to one person. In developing distance learning, you need to include technology experts, distance site facilitators, and facilities support.

Only one thing is certain: All delivery methods (including traditional classroom) will change and evolve with the growing development of technology.

# Types of Distance Learning

As one researches the topic of distance learning, one discovers a plethora of terminology that adds to the confusion and, for some, the mystery, of distance learning. Not only are various words and terms used interchangeably but often they are in conflict, depending on the author.

The following glossary of terms is an attempt to establish a common vocabulary for the discussion of distance learning in this book.

For starters, distance learning delivery methods fall into one of two categories: synchronous and asynchronous.

## Synchronous

Synchronous means that all learners and the instructor access the same information at the same time. They may or may not see each other, but they can communicate through various means such as audio or video transmission, e-mail, or chat rooms.

**Video Teleconferencing.** Learners and instructor can hear, see, and interact with one another through a conference call via two-way video and speaker phone or bridge line.

**Audio Teletraining.** A type of audioconferencing in which learners and the instructor can hear and interact with one another through a conference call via speaker phone or bridge line.

**Audiographics.** A type of audioconferencing involving audio interactions coupled with the ability for learners and the instructor to share computer-generated slides with one another.

**Web-Based Training (WBT).** Often referred to as e-learning or online learning via the Internet or an intranet. Instruction is delivered via learners' personal computers, all connected at the same time. Learners can respond to the instructor using the keyboard or a mouse click, and they can raise their hands electronically to ask questions or make comments. WBT can also be asynchronous.

## Asynchronous

Asynchronous delivery falls into two categories: facilitated and self-paced. Facilitated asynchronous delivery involves the instructor and a group of learners, but not in real time. The instructor posts assignments on a Web page, and the learners communicate through threaded discussion (also known as bulletin boards or forums) and submit "homework" via e-mail. This type of delivery is found mostly in academic environments.

The asynchronous mode used in corporations tends to be self-paced, that is, the material can be accessed and completed without learner interaction with the instructor or other learners.

**Computer-Based Training.** The term "computer-based" is used widely to include delivery via CD-ROM (compact disc, read-only memory), intranet, or Internet. CD-ROM training is primarily self-paced. The advantage of a CD-ROM is that it can hold large amounts of information, is lightweight, portable, durable, and "speedy."

It is an easy and inexpensive way to distribute large files and programs, including audio, video, and complex information. The increasingly popular DVD-ROM (digital video disc, read-only memory) is larger and faster than the CD-ROM. The biggest disadvantage with both is that it is time-consuming and costly to make changes.

Although asynchronous delivery is primarily one-way communication, it can be interactive through the use of e-mail, voice mail, listservs, chat rooms, computer conferencing, and audio or video teleconferencing.

**E-courses.** E-courses or e-seminars are text-based lessons delivered to the participants via an auto-responder. The instructor uploads the content to a service provider. Participants sign up for the course and then receive a lesson at regular, prescribed intervals (for example, every week).

## Technology-Based and Computer-Based Programs

Organizations with videoconferencing or teleconferencing capabilities may choose that venue to deliver their training programs. Before you get excited about these state-of-the-art approaches, carefully consider the costs involved with the development as well as the resources necessary. Make sure that employees have access to a computer with the appropriate bandwidth.

Another consideration of any computer-based approach is the issue of updates. You need a program administrator to monitor the program and make sure the information is up-to-date and accurate. It is also important to select a delivery platform that lends itself to easy and cost-effective updates.

# Guidelines for Designing Distance Learning

When designing distance learning programs, follow the same basic principles of instructional design discussed throughout this book.

## Objectives and Content

No matter what the format or venue, the subject content does not change, nor do the learning objectives or outcomes. Employees at remote sites still need the same information as those located at corporate headquarters. So the place to start in designing a distance training program is to determine the objectives and content. Refer to Chapters 5 and 6 for objectives and content ideas.

Cognitive objectives are the most easily adaptable to asynchronous learning.

## Basic Considerations

When you design web-based training and other distance learning programs, follow the same principles of good instructional design that you would for classroom learning, including perceptual modalities, learning styles, participant ages, and other issues discussed in Chapter 2.

One of the important elements of learning lost in many of the distance learning delivery modes, web-based training in particular, is the loss of non-verbal communication and interaction. Because many people have a need to exchange ideas, opinions, and viewpoints, the designer needs to build in opportunities for learners to interact with the instructor and with each other. There are many ways to add the human touch: bulletin boards, threaded discussions, chat rooms, e-mail, and audio or videoconferencing.

Even with synchronous learning methods, it is difficult to gauge participants' reactions when you cannot see them. Digital cameras at each work station help only somewhat. It also takes participants longer to form questions and for replies to be digested. Thus, facilitators must pause more often. Sessions should be around sixty minutes, but certainly not more than ninety.

To compensate for the lack of "the human touch," designers need to create situations in which people can work together online.

## Discussion Groups

Asynchronous discussion groups can be created through the use of e-mail, whereby participants broadcast messages to all other members of the list. These are known as e-mail lists, list servers, listservs, or mailing lists. Participants can also visit sites where people post messages relevant to the subject of the group. With this approach, referred to as bulletin boards or newsgroups, participants can thread messages, that is, replies are indented under the original message so that everyone can follow the conversation.

Synchronous online methods of discussion include the following:

- *Chat Rooms.* Participants engage in real-time conversations conducted over a low-speed Internet connection. This is also called text-conferencing.

- *Response Pads.* Participants can use this tool to make real-time choices or vote.

- *Audioconferencing.* Participants use the network as a telephone.

- *Videoconferencing.* This method lets participants see a small image of the presenter in real time.

## Types of Interaction

As noted in Chapter 7, the more interaction, the more effective the learning experience. This is true for both classroom and distance learning. Basically, participants can interact in three ways:

1. They can interact with the materials through simulations, tests, multiple-choice activities, or case studies.

2. They can interact with the instructor and subject-matter experts through audio or videoconferencing, e-mail, or threaded discussions.

3. They can interact with other participants through class projects and other out-of-class assignments and activities, including bulletin boards and chat rooms.

## Delivery Methods

After deciding on content, the next step in design is to determine how to deliver the content, that is, what distance learning technology you want to use. Keep in mind, however, that the technology should not be the driving force. Choose the appropriate delivery method based on a number of factors, including cost, the number of people to be trained, course content, type of learning (cognitive, affective, behavioral), and available resources, just to name a few.

# Designing and Developing Activities

Follow the basic rule in designing activities: make it easy. Be sure to write simple, easy-to-follow instructions. Then make it easy to download materials, find resources, and respond to questions, activities, assignments, and so forth. Break content into chunks of information. Keep in mind that text and images will vary depending on the quality of the user's screen, browser, and the access speed of the computer. Because of these potential limitations, limit your use of charts, graphs, and pictures. If you use video, keep it to less than one minute. You also need to remember that web-based asynchronous content is non-linear, allowing participants to jump in where they need to depending on what they already know. They can move ahead or they can go back to fill in knowledge gaps.

Classroom activities can be adapted, but just as in the classroom, they must be carefully thought out and developed.

The following is a sampling of the types of classroom activities that can be adapted for distance learning:

## Activities Involving Others

**Case Problems.**  In a module on Managing Conflict, post the following case problem:

> Joan is a member of a twelve-person department. Because of the overwhelming volume of work and her strong work ethic and sense of responsibility, she often stays late to do her work. Several others stay late also. For some time Joan has been quite annoyed because others in the department apparently do not share her dedication to the job. One person in particular, Betty, never stays late but frequently wants Joan's help. So far Joan has made excuses or passively resisted helping Betty in any way. This situation has been going on over a period of several months, and Joan's irritation has steadily increased. During the most recent incident, Betty approached Joan and asked her for some information she desperately needed in order to complete an assignment. This time Joan decided not to hide her irritation. When Betty asked for her help, Joan snapped, "I don't have time to help you because I'm busy doing your work already." Betty replied, "I don't know what you mean. I didn't know you needed any help."

Ask participants to respond to the following questions:

- What do you think is the cause of the conflict?
- What advice or coaching would you give to Joan to help her resolve the conflict?

Participants could respond by posting their answers on a bulletin board or sending them via e-mail to fellow participants and the instructor. If the session is an audioconference or teleconference, they would share their answers, just as they would in a classroom discussion.

**Point-Counterpoint.**  The facilitator of a module on customer service presents the following statement: "Customer service is everybody's responsibility—even those who are not in a direct customer contact position." The facilitator requests that half of the participants prepare arguments in support of the statement and the other half prepare arguments disagreeing with the statement. Then the participants are asked to present their positions in a chat room interaction.

**Group Assignments.**  In a new employee orientation program, the facilitator wants participants to identify the organization's core values and to reflect the organization's values in their own workplace behavior. The facilitator creates subgroups and assigns each subgroup one or two values and asks them to submit examples of specific behaviors that illustrate the value(s) assigned. These examples should focus on specific employee behaviors. For example:

| | |
|---|---|
| Honesty | Admitting when you make a mistake |
| Respect | Talking to people in a polite, civilized manner |
| Teamwork | Pitching in to help even when it's not in your job description |
| Professionalism | Answering the telephone in a business-like manner |

The subgroups work on the assignment outside the online session. At the next session, the subgroups could share their examples by posting them on a bulletin board. They could also e-mail their answers to their fellow participants prior to the actual session.

**Peer Teaching.** The facilitator gives each participant sections or parts of a larger topic to research and then report back to the group during the next online session. For example, in a session on business development, participants would be assigned various legal structures for a business: S Corporation, C Corporation, Partnership, Sole Proprietorship, or Limited Partnership. Each participant submits his or her assigned topic to the group as a whole.

**Group Critique.** Participants in a business writing class would be asked to write a particular piece of business communication, such as a letter or memo, and submit their piece to the entire group. The facilitator would then assign each participant to critique another participant's letter or memo using a set of guidelines or a checklist the group had already discussed or studied.

**Action Learning Projects.** In action learning, the problem or project becomes the central learning experience. Participants are encouraged to learn from their attempts to solve a problem and then reflect on their decisions and behaviors during the process. The facilitator would create subgroups and assign each group a different real-life project that would span several weeks or months. The following is a list of potential action learning projects:

- Develop a mentoring program
- Develop performance benchmarks for various positions
- Improve a particular process
- Create an employee recognition system
- Develop a new employee orientation program

The subgroups would meet via e-mail or chat rooms and then would pull their various pieces together and present their projects at the end of the class.

## Individual Activities

For individual activities, the participants could complete the assignments in much the same way they would respond to an online test. Although the facilitator would indicate a particular timeframe for completion, the participants could work on the activities on their own time.

**Matching.**  To help new employees identify who to contact or where to go when they have questions or need information, the facilitator could create a matching activity. The facilitator would provide a list of types of information new employees would want or need to know during their first few weeks and months on the job. The participant would be instructed to match the information needed with the appropriate resource from a list provided. The following is a specific example:

> If you wanted to find out about. . . , you would go to. . . . (Match the numbered items [1 through 12] with the information sources [A through E] below.)

| | |
|---|---|
| 1.  Tuition reimbursement | A.  Immediate supervisor |
| 2.  Time off without pay | B.  Benefits administrator |
| 3.  Medical coverage | C.  Human resources |
| 4.  Problem with a co-worker | D.  Payroll |
| 5.  Leaving early | E.  Employee handbook |
| 6.  Vacation schedule | |
| 7.  Getting a raise | |
| 8.  Payroll problems | |
| 9.  Sick days | |
| 10.  Overtime | |
| 11.  Dress code | |
| 12.  Taking breaks | |

**Guided Analysis.**  The facilitator presents a graphic, chart, report, or other item and participants are asked to analyze or explain the item. The facilitator can also present data that the participants must plot or engage in a compare-and-contrast assignment.

**Making Lists.** This type of activity has many applications. Instead of the facilitator presenting lists such as characteristics of effective coaches, benefits of delivering quality service, or product features and benefits, the facilitator solicits such lists from the participants and then presents the facilitator's list for comparison.

**Information Search.** The facilitator would refer participants to the employee handbook and/or other sources on the intranet where they would find the requested information regarding the organization's policies and procedures. The facilitator would provide a list of questions for which the participants would have to search online. Examples of questions are as follows:

1. When are you eligible for sick days? How many sick days do you have?
2. What constitutes sexual harassment?
3. What is the policy regarding family and medical leave?
4. When and where are employees permitted to smoke?
5. What are the differences between exempt and non-exempt employees?
6. When can you apply for another job in the organization?
7. What is the standard work week?
8. How is overtime handled?
9. When do you get paid?
10. What is considered excessive absenteeism?

**Mini Cases.** To help participants distinguish between ethical and unethical behavior in the workplace, the facilitator would present a list of scenarios such as those listed below. Referring to the organization's ethics policy, the participant would indicate to which section each scenario relates.

1. Making personal long-distance calls
2. Taking pens, paper, or paper clips home to your teenager
3. Sending an e-mail to your friend to confirm your weekend party plans
4. Working at night and on weekends for one of the company's competitors
5. Sharing personal information about one of your customers with friends
6. Coming in thirty minutes late and not noting it on your time card

7. Submitting all expenses for an evening out with a client in which you included other members of your family

8. Accepting a set of golf clubs from a vendor

9. Telling friends and family members about a potential merger between your company and a competitor you overheard two managers discussing

10. Promising to deliver a product to a customer by a certain date, even though you know the deadline cannot be met

You will find other outstanding specific examples of instructional interactivity in Michael Allen's *Guide to e-Learning: Building Interactive, Fun, and Effective Learning Programs for Any Company* (2003). Another excellent source for designing interactive web-based training is *Designing Web-Based Training* by William Horton (2000).

# Delivering Content and Activities

As a facilitator of synchronous training, you will need to modify the way in which you have been accustomed to delivering your programs. First and foremost, be sure to receive proper training on how to use the technology. It is important that you be comfortable in this new environment. Also keep in mind that, because of delayed responses, you may not be able to include as much interaction and/or content as in a traditional setting. To compensate, build in several question-and-answer periods and ask very specific and directed questions. Also create ways to give timely feedback, and include plenty of projects, tests, discussion opportunities, and other out-of-class assignments.

# Blended Learning

Non-traditional methods such as computer-based training and other distance learning should be part of an overall training strategy and one of several delivery strategies.

Even non-interactive methods such as tapes, CDs, CD-ROMs, videos, and cable TV can all be made interactive with the addition of a site facilitator or combined with other approaches.

The key to meeting the training needs of an increasingly diverse audience is to offer a variety of delivery options and methods.

---

**KEY POINTS**

- Distance learning is not appropriate for all situations.

- Many traditional classroom activities can be adapted to distance learning.

- Learners can access material at their own convenience and when they actually need it.

- Distance learning is often more efficient and cost-effective.

- Technology-based sessions often overlook the "human touch."

- Synchronous learning means that learners and the instructor access the same information at the same time.

- Facilitated asynchronous learning involves the instructor and learners, but not at the same time.

- With self-paced asynchronous learning, the learner can access the information without interaction with the instructor or fellow learners.

- Designers of technology-based learning need to create situations in which people can interact and work together online.

---

As we have learned in this chapter, distance learning is both exciting and challenging. Because participant interaction is somewhat limited, it is easier to manage the "human element." For this reason, many trainers (and learners, too) prefer distance learning venues. As we shall discover in the next chapter, face-to-face contact between trainer and participants, as well as group interactions, require knowledge of and skill in dealing with group dynamics.

# Chapter 11

# Working with Groups

**LEARNING OUTCOMES**

In this chapter, you will learn

- To stimulate discussion among participants

- To master the art of asking and answering questions

- To deal with difficult people and situations

## The Trainer as Facilitator

Standing up in front of a group and presenting information is one thing; facilitating discussion and interaction is another. Each requires a different set of skills. If you accept the changing role of the trainer—from "teacher" to "facilitator"—then you will have to understand and develop facilitation skills.

Any time you work *with* a group in a participant-centered environment instead of talking *at* that group, you are facilitating the learning process. Facilitation skills are particularly critical for processing activities, as discussed in Chapter 8.

The most important thing to remember about your responsibilities as a trainer is that you are a *role model*. How you conduct yourself verbally and nonverbally determines how participants conduct themselves.

# Ways to Encourage Participation

Your behavior throughout the session sends a message that either encourages or discourages participation. Sometimes these messages are pretty straightforward; sometimes they are much more subtle. Not only are these subtle messages communicated without our awareness, but their impact can be quite powerful.

## Nonverbal Communication

What you do often speaks more loudly than what you say. Use the power of these nonverbal communication techniques to encourage participation:

- *Eye contact.* Be attentive by making eye contact with all participants.
- *Head nodding.* Nod your head to show understanding and encourage the participants to continue.
- *Posture.* Avoid defensive posture such as folded arms.
- *Body movement.* Avoid distracting movements such as too much walking and pacing. Move toward people to draw them into the discussion.
- *Smile.* Concentrate on smiling with both mouth and eyes to encourage and relax the group.

## Verbal Communication

What you say and how you say it can either shut down or encourage participation. Be mindful of the difference between intent and perception. Frequently conduct your own reality check by asking yourself this question: "What is my intent, and how am I being perceived?" Practice using the following techniques to create an exciting and positive learning environment.

**Praise or Encourage.** Use simple, but powerful, words of encouragement to prod the participant to continue:

- "I'm glad you brought that up."
- "Tell me more."
- "Okay, let's build on that."
- "Good point. Who else has an idea?"
- "I would like to hear your thoughts about. . . ."

**Accept or Use Ideas.** Clarify, build on, and further develop ideas suggested by another participant:

- "To piggyback on your point, Juan, . . ."
- "As Salina mentioned earlier, . . ."

**Accept Feelings.** Use statements that communicate acceptance and clarification of feelings:

- "I sense that you are upset by what I just said."
- "You seem to feel very strongly about this issue."
- "I know it's hard to maintain a positive outlook when you are at risk of being a downsizing casualty."
- "I can imagine that you feel. . . ."

# The Art of Questioning

The art of asking questions is central to your success as a facilitator of adult learning. The key is to ask questions that stimulate discussion and interaction, rather than questions that elicit simple factual responses reminiscent of grade school. To stimulate discussion, be sure your questions are open-ended.

People often think they are asking open-ended questions when they are not. An open-ended question is one that begins with *who, what, where, when, why,* or *how.* Questions that begin with these words will elicit a more detailed and meaningful response from participants. Closed-ended questions, on the other hand, are questions that someone could answer with a simple "yes" or "no" and certainly do not encourage participation. To make it easy, try to ask questions that begin with *how* or *what.* If you can get into the habit of asking these kinds of questions, your group discussions and processing segments will be very effective.

Avoid using questions that begin with *why. Why* questions tend to put people on the defensive. They feel that they have to explain and justify their responses.

Different types of questions obtain different results. Practice using questions that match your desired outcome. For example, if you want to start the discussion, ask a general question of the entire group. In a customer service program, you might ask, "How do you think your organization is doing in terms of delivering quality service?" This type of question prompts people to express an opinion.

Because there are likely to be a variety of opinions offered, interest is generated in the topic and the discussion is underway. You may next want to uncover the reasons behind the opinions just expressed, so ask a specific question such as, "What are some examples of situations that lead you to believe that your organization's level of customer service is [outstanding, needs improvement]?"

After you have asked the question, be quiet. Trainers have a tendency to ask a question, and then when no one responds immediately, they answer the question themselves. Silence, of course, is uncomfortable, and you may feel that you have to speak up and fill the void. Let silence happen. Learn to ask the question and then be silent for ten to twelve seconds to give people time to think of their responses. If you keep answering your own questions, there is no reason for participants to offer their ideas.

# Responding to Questions

In a lively, risk-free, and dynamic environment, participants will be stimulated to ask questions as well as answer them. Although this is certainly what we want to happen, this type of participant interaction can be quite challenging.

## Reasons People Ask Questions

Before addressing some of the do's and don'ts of fielding questions from the group, let's look at the reasons people want the opportunity to ask questions. Understanding their motivation will help you better prepare for both the expected and unexpected.

**To Obtain Information or to Clarify.** No matter how clear you were in delivering a message, the participants will not all process and understand the information in the same way or at the same time. Some will want and need additional information to help them understand points more clearly or to satisfy their desire for more detail. They may want further assurance that you know what you are talking about.

Something you said earlier may have ignited a spark of curiosity or may provoke an interest in finding out more about a topic. In the latter case, they will ask questions about other resources and will expect you to point them in the right direction. Even if you have provided a bibliography or recommended reading list, some will want you to recommend or identify sources for specific interests and pursuits.

**To Impress Others.** Every group has one or more people who like to ask questions as an opportunity to be noticed either by peers or someone at a higher level. Being in the spotlight may satisfy some people's ego needs. For others, it affords them the chance to demonstrate qualities such as assertiveness and risk taking or to showcase their knowledge of the subject as a means to career advancement.

**To "Get" the Trainer.** For various reasons, some participants will not like the trainer or what he or she has to say. They take every opportunity to make the trainer look bad or see him or her squirm for their own amusement. They may see this as a chance to "get even" or undermine a trainer's credibility.

**To Help the Trainer.** At the other end of the scale are participants who really like the trainer and want to help him or her look good. If they agree with the trainer's position on a particular topic, they will want to help increase the persuasive impact even more.

**To Keep from Going Back to Work.** Some people may ask questions as a way to prolong the session, thus avoid returning to work, particularly if the session is due to be over near the end of the day. They may reason that the more questions they ask and the more time they can take up, there will not be enough time to get anything accomplished back on the job and so they will be dismissed early.

## Guidelines for Handling Questions

To master the art of responding to questions, consider the following guidelines:

**Set the Ground Rules in the Beginning.** At the beginning of the session, tell the participants how questions will be handled: throughout the session; at intervals; or at the end. If you encourage people to ask questions as they think of them, you may need to limit the number of questions or the time spent addressing them in order to stay on schedule. The important thing is to communicate clearly when you will and will not take questions. If you plan to wait until the end of a section to take questions, suggest that they write their questions down so they do not forget them.

**Repeat the Question.** Sometimes a trainer's answer to a question will be totally off the mark, probably as a result of not taking the time to clarify and confirm what he or she thought the participant actually asked. Sometimes, the person asking the question is not very articulate and may have a difficult time stating the question concisely and succinctly.

Repeat or paraphrase the question before answering it. Repeating the question accomplishes three things:

1. It ensures that the rest of the group has heard the question.
2. It ensures that you have heard the question correctly.
3. It buys a little time to organize your thoughts before answering.

To ensure that the question is the same as intended, paraphrase the question by saying, "If I heard you correctly, your question is. . . . Is that right?" If the question is long, ask if you may reword it; then restate it concisely and check to see that you indeed captured the essence of the question. Do not, however, paraphrase by using any of these phrases:

- "What you mean is. . . ."
- "What you're saying is. . . ."
- "What you're trying to say is. . . ."

These phrases are insulting and condescending. The subtle message is: "You're obviously not articulate in expressing yourself, so let me help you out."

**Use Eye Contact.** Look at the person who asked the question while you are paraphrasing to make sure you understood the question. When you deliver your response, direct it to the entire group, not just to the person who asked the question.

**Choose Words Carefully.** Choose your words carefully and think about the impact they may have on individual participants. Avoid using words like "obviously." This implies that the person asking the question should already know the answer. Along the same line, phrases such as "You have to understand. . ." come across as ordering and directing. "You should. . ." sounds like preaching or moralizing.

**Respect the Group.** Never belittle or embarrass a participant. This means that sometimes you have to exercise a little patience, particularly when someone asks a question that you have already addressed in the session. Absolutely never say, "As I already mentioned. . . ." Instead, answer the question by carefully rewording your point so that you are not repeating the remark exactly as you said it earlier.

**Responding to Individual Concerns.** Sometimes a participant will ask a question that is extremely narrowly focused and pertains only to himself or herself. If that happens, give a brief response and then suggest that the two of you talk about it after the session. Use this same strategy with those who ask questions unrelated to the topic. Always indicate your openness and willingness to talk further one-on-one. Above all else, project compassion and concern.

**Cover All Parts of the Room.** Trainers sometimes have a tendency to look only to the right or to their left, and as a result, entertain questions from only one side of the room. Although unintentional, people on the side being ignored will become anxious and annoyed. Similarly, some trainers will acknowledge participants who are in the front because it's easy to both see and hear them. Make a concerted effort to take questions from all parts of the audience.

**Do Not Bluff.** Sometimes people may ask questions that you cannot answer. Be honest. Do not be afraid to say, "I don't know." However, do not leave it at that. Offer to check further and get back to them by phone or e-mail or at a later session or tell them where they can find the additional information themselves.

**Things Not to Say.** In an effort to be supportive and encouraging, trainers will often respond to a participant by saying, "That's a good question." The danger here is that you may come across as patronizing or insincere. Also, others who do not receive the same feedback or reinforcement may feel their questions were not as "good." Instead, comment by saying, "That's an interesting question" or "That's an intriguing question." Similarly, a response such as "I'm glad you asked that question" may be understood by others to mean that you are not glad that they asked a question.

After you have responded, do not say, "Does that answer your question?" What happens if the participant responds that you did not answer the question? Worse still, the participant may not have had his or her question answered but does not want to embarrass you or himself/herself and just lets it go. By asking whether you answered the question, you give up some control and you suggest a lack of confidence in your answer. A better response would be, "What other questions do you have?" or "Would you like me to go into more detail?"

This is a much more gracious and face-saving approach for both the trainer and the participant. It also gives the participant an opportunity to clarify his or her question or probe a little further, if necessary, so that he or she is satisfied.

# Scaling the Wall of Resistance

It's quite probable that you will experience some resistance from individuals, or even entire groups. Unless you can overcome that resistance, you will have a very difficult time achieving your learning objectives. The first step in scaling the wall of resistance is to recognize it so you can deal with it before it undermines the learning process.

## Recognizing Resistance

Resistance among participants takes many forms. Some people bring work to the session and busy themselves with that rather than pay attention. Others might bring in a newspaper and start reading it. Some ask antagonistic questions, while others won't open their mouths or even crack a smile. Because symptoms of resistance are so varied, you must be observant and look for various behaviors that may indicate a potential problem. Pay particular attention to facial expressions and other nonverbal communication. If participants look angry, confused, or bored, be ready to acknowledge it and deal with it.

## Causes of Resistance

In order to deal with resistance and prevent dysfunctional behavior, you must first understand it. In many cases, you will have to address the underlying psychological climate. Some possible reasons for resistance are covered below.

**Do Not Want to Be There.** Sometimes participants just do not want to be there. Often people resent attending a session. Perhaps they feel they are being punished, or they may feel overwhelmed by their workload and do not believe they can afford to take time away from the job.

### CASE OF RESISTANCE TO TRAINING

I was asked to conduct a session on performance appraisal for first-line supervisors in a manufacturing setting. During my assessment meeting with the vice president of operations, I sensed that there might be some resistance to the training, so I discussed the importance of explaining to the supervisors why the company was investing time and money in this program and how they could benefit from attending. The vice president agreed to communicate that message. The morning of the session, I met briefly with the vice president, who assured me that he had prepared the participants as I had suggested. Breathing a sigh of relief, I walked into the room only to be confronted by nineteen frowning men with their arms folded seated in a horseshoe configuration. Although the situation did not look good, I was confident that I could bring them around. I started with an appropriate icebreaker and opening activities. The supervisors absolutely refused to participate. After several failed attempts to break through the stone wall of resistance, I stopped and said, "Guys, it's clear to me that something's going on here, and I think we need to talk about it. Let me ask you a question. Why do you think the company is offering this session?" With that, the flood gates opened, and I was bombarded with comments such as "Beats the [expletive] out of me" and "I guess we must be doing a pretty [expletive] job and now we're being punished." I spent the next forty-five minutes just talking with the group and helping them see how this session could help them do their jobs better. Clearly, the vice president had not done his job.

**Do Not Know Why They Are There.** Believe it or not, some people walk into a session and have no idea why they were asked to attend. Sometimes, they do not even know what the topic is.

### CASE OF NOT KNOWING WHY

I had been engaged to do a two-hour session on communication for line employees at a packaging plant. As I frequently do, I asked the participants why they were there and what they hoped to learn. I was surprised to learn that they thought they were attending a safety-training session. I used the situation as an opportunity to stress the importance of communication in the workplace. I even managed to tie communication to safety issues and how good communication could prevent accidents and safety violations. Because I was able to adjust my design on the spot to meet the needs of my participants, the session was a success.

**Personal Issues.** Session participants are human beings, and human beings have personal lives and problems that sometimes get in the way of learning new things. Some may simply not feel well. Others may be preoccupied with a personal problem.

### CASE OF PERSONAL ISSUES

I was delivering a three-day management development program, and a woman in her late forties or early fifties told me during a break that her husband of twenty-five years had just left her for a much younger woman. It was obvious from her demeanor and tone of voice that she was miserable, which was reflected in her behavior during the session. She was argumentative and confrontational, challenging and contradicting everything I said and being downright difficult and unpleasant. Every time I said something, she attacked. I tried every technique I knew, but nothing worked. I decided to take our mid-morning break early and went into a private office to calm down and regain my composure. When we reconvened, she had toned down. One of the participants later told me that several of her fellow participants had talked to her during break and told her that her behavior was inappropriate. In situations like this one, quite often others in the group will deal directly with the difficult person.

**Attitude Toward Boss or Organization.** If a participant has negative feelings about the organization or his or her manager, the individual will bring that negativity into the session. The resentment is transferred to the trainer. Whether you are internal or external, the "boss" or the organization hired you. You are guilty by association and automatically you are viewed as "one of them." This is further amplified when the participants do not see a real commitment to training on the part of the organization. Participants will often remark, "My boss should be attending this training, too."

Sessions dealing with change present a particular problem. For many, the session only serves to magnify the change or changes they are experiencing, and in many cases, the participants are not happy about these changes.

### CASE OF PROBLEMS WITH A BOSS

At the beginning of a program on managing change and stress, I asked participants to share the most difficult or troublesome change they were currently experiencing. One man was quite emotional when he related that he was moving his office from the suburbs to the city. As the day progressed, we learned that he had been with the company thirty years, enjoyed six weeks' vacation and a very comfortable salary. In our discussion about values, he was quite clear that money, material possessions, and vacation time were very important to him.

At one point in the program, I emphasized that, in dealing with change, we all have choices and that those choices are based on many things, including our values, personality type, family situations, and so forth. As I finished my statement about having a choice, this man started yelling at me, "You don't understand! I don't have a choice in moving my office! I'm sick of you high-priced consultants coming in here and telling us what we should do. You have no idea what you're talking about. . . ." He continued his tirade, and I sat down and allowed him to run out of steam. After he was finished, I told him that I could see his point and that I was sorry this change was causing him such distress.

Very likely his feeling of powerlessness and the resulting anger and frustration had been smoldering for some time. The discussion triggered an intense emotional response that was really directed toward the company. Although he may have seen me as a representative of the "enemy," I was not in a position of power and therefore was a safe target on which to unleash his pent-up hostility.

**Attitude Toward Topic.** Not every participant will be happy with the topic, particularly if his or her attendance has been mandated. This is particularly true when presenting controversial topics such as diversity or sexual harassment. Some participants have been quite open and candid about their perception that the topic is "being shoved down their throats."

---

### CASE OF DISLIKE OF TOPIC

In a session I conducted on sexual harassment for a group of bank managers, one man expressed his disapproval of the entire subject by saying, "If women don't like the way they're treated, let them go work elsewhere." I pointed out to him that, although he was certainly entitled to his personal feelings, in his role as a manager, he had a responsibility to support his organization's policy as well as the law of the land.

**Pushed Out of Their Comfort Zones.** Particularly in human relations training, participants are challenged to look at themselves, situations, and beliefs in a different way. Managers who have been used to a very traditional and autocratic style of managing may be required to learn new approaches and philosophies that are more democratic and participatory. People who have been used to working on their own as individual contributors may be expected to learn how to work in a team environment. New organizational expectations require employees to learn new skills and assume new roles. For example, a bank customer service representative may be expected to sell banking services. Many people are uncomfortable and unsure of themselves in these new roles, and that insecurity creates a barrier to learning. As a trainer, you not only must help them develop new skills but also to see how they might personally benefit from these new roles and responsibilities.

**Literacy Problems.** If people have a difficult time reading, they will be resistant to attending a session that requires them to do anything that involves reading, such as case studies, written exercises, and assessment instruments. Trainers must be observant of behavior that suggests a literacy problem and make every effort to work with people so that they succeed.

**Language Problems.** For those who are not fluent in the language in which the session is being delivered, the experience can be frustrating and unpleasant. Because of their frustration and difficulty in understanding what the trainer is saying, they may act out their frustration by being difficult and uncooperative, either intentionally or unintentionally. As the workplace becomes more diverse, this issue will become an even greater challenge for trainers.

Past Experiences. Some participants may have had unpleasant learning experiences either in school or as adults attending other work-sponsored programs. Often they come to the session expecting it to be much of the same, and they are braced to expect the worst. Sometimes this comes out at the end of a session.

### CASE OF COMPARING PAST EXPERIENCES

Depending on the group, and particularly if I sense some resistance early on, I ask the group during the feedback portion of the session: "Was this program different from what you expected?" The answer is always "yes." When I probe further, participants usually tell me that they expected it to be dull and boring. Some will say that they thought I would just lecture or talk "at" them. They will often add that my approach was a pleasant surprise and made the experience both meaningful and enjoyable.

## Effects of Resistance

Now that we have looked at the causes of participant resistance, let's take a look at the effects. Left unchecked, this resistance can divide the group into various factions, polarizing them against you or one another. These negative behaviors interfere with learning. No one can learn in an environment dominated by disruptive behavior. Additionally, undesirable behaviors cause emotional stress and anxiety for the trainer as well as for those who are witnessing the shenanigans.

# Problem Situations

No matter how well you have planned and prepared for your workshop or seminar, more often than not, something unexpected will happen. Sometimes what started out as a terrific session turns into your worst nightmare. Some human behavior, attitudes, or reactions are predictable. It is your job as a trainer to anticipate these behaviors, prevent them if you can, and if not, deal with them effectively.

## Prevention Strategies

Often problems in a training session can be avoided through proper planning, preparation, anticipation, and communication.

**Planning.** When designing your training session, consider the various learning styles and perceptual modalities discussed in Chapter 2. Be sure to use interactive techniques and do not be afraid to be creative, even outrageous. Also use a variety of methods and media to appeal to various styles.

Planning also involves having a back-up plan for equipment problems, materials that do not arrive, schedule changes, and activities that might not work with your group of participants.

**Preparation.** The importance of finding out as much as possible about participants through the use of questionnaires and surveys, interviews, and discussions with their managers has already been covered in Chapter 8. It is also a good idea to send something to the participants ahead of time: an interesting, attention-getting flyer, a short article to read, or anything that will pique their interest and prepare them for the session. You might assign readings or other pre-work.

**Anticipation.** For full-day or half-day sessions, make sure you request (or bring) the accoutrements that help create a professional environment. These include tent cards, pads and pencils, water, quality participant materials, and dishes with wrapped candies. This communicates an important message to the participants: this session is important. A professional touch will help set the tone and make it more difficult for people to act up. For sessions of three hours or more, make sure there are refreshments available during breaks. Not only is this reflective of a professional touch, it shows consideration for the participants.

### CASE OF MEETING NEEDS

During an all-day session for a trade association, the meeting planner and I learned a valuable lesson about the importance of meeting participants' basic needs. The meeting planner had arranged for coffee and tea to be available when participants arrived for the workshop. The participants, however, noted on their evaluation sheets the conspicuous absence of donuts, muffins, or bagels; their disappointment impacted the overall rating of the session.

Also keep in mind that many people today forego the traditional coffee and tea in favor of soft drinks, juices, and bottled water. Health-conscious and calorie-conscious participants also prefer fresh fruit to pastries.

## Communication

It is helpful to set the tone for the session at the beginning by clearly communicating your expectations or "ground rules." For example, remind participants to turn off (or set on mute) their cell phones and pagers. Tell them when you have scheduled breaks and tell them they will be able to make calls at that time. You need to consider your policy regarding participants' use of PDAs and other electronic devices as well as other behaviors such as reading the newspaper, doing other work during the session, and coming back late from breaks.

Sometimes no matter how well you plan, prepare, anticipate, and even communicate up-front, you may find yourself faced with a particularly difficult group. Sometimes groups as a whole behave as a single entity. The key to dealing with these situations is to be able to size up your audience and quickly adapt your style accordingly.

If you sense you have a difficult or even hostile group, consider addressing the issue up-front. Ask questions such as, "What concerns do you have about today's session?" or "Why do you think the company is offering this program?" This brings issues out on the table so that you can address them. As participants are expressing their issues and feelings, capture the information on flip-chart pages. Remain objective, non-judgmental, and empathetic. Facilitate a discussion or an activity that forces the group to come up with solutions or recommendations. Do not take responsibility for solving the problem yourself.

If a group is particularly disruptive or, at the other extreme, shuts down completely and will not participate, use the "divide-and-conquer" technique. Break the group into pairs or subgroups and give each a specific assignment. Pose questions similar to the ones in the previous paragraph or have them come up with a list of suggestions related to the topic.

Another effective tool is the "parking lot." Post a flip-chart page with the words *"Parking Lot"* at the top. Give participants Post-it® Notes and explain that if issues come up throughout the session unrelated to the topic, to jot them on the Post-its Notes and put them in the "parking lot." This technique allows the participants to acknowledge their issues and concerns and get them out of the way. Say, "Your point is well taken, although it's not relevant to what we're talking about now. Write it down and put it in the 'parking lot,' and we'll be sure to address it before the end of the session."

Remember: An ounce of prevention is worth a pound of cure. Refer to Exhibit 11.1 for tips on preventing dysfunctional behavior.

| EXHIBIT 11.1. **Preventing Dysfunctional Behavior** |
|---|

- Send pre-session questionnaires/interviews
- Send pre-session letters and outlines
- Make pre-session assignments
- Encourage pre-session manager-participant discussion
- Involve participant/manager in session design
- Use a variety of training methods/activities
- Select appropriate seating configurations
- Create comfortable, non-threatening environment
- Get them active from the start
- Make learning relevant
- Use participants' knowledge and experience
- Give assignments between sessions

*The Trainer's Handbook, Updated Ed.* Copyright © 2009 by Karen Lawson. Reproduced by permission of Pfeiffer, an imprint of John Wiley & Sons, Inc.

## Personal Attacks

Personal attacks may be triggered by something you say that strikes a nerve with a participant, or the attacks could come from a "professional heckler" who just enjoys the challenge of putting you on the spot and making you squirm.

Far less annoying but offering a different challenge is the person who begins attacking you because he or she disagrees with something you said.

### CASE OF PERSONAL ATTACK

For example, I was conducting an all-day workshop for a group of managers, talking about the importance of managers communicating clearly their standards of performance and expectations to their employees. I also emphasized the need to include guidelines or parameters as part of those expectations.

I decided to use a personal parenting example to illustrate my point. I had learned through earlier questioning that 95 percent of the audience members were parents. I related an incident involving my fourteen-year-old stepson many years earlier. I created the appropriate backdrop for the story by explaining that fourteen-year-olds go through a "black period" during which everything they wear is black. So when my stepson wanted to redecorate his room, I thought it would be prudent to tell him that he could decorate his room any way he wanted except for two things: he could not paint his walls black, and he could not put up posters of nude women. The audience laughed as always when I tell that story.

Before I could go on to draw a parallel between parents setting parameters and managers doing the same, I was interrupted by a man yelling at me from the back of the room: "How could you do such a thing? That was your son's room, and you have no right telling him what he can and cannot do with his own space!" As he continued his ranting, I interrupted by saying, "I can certainly understand your point of view. However, we're not here to debate parenting philosophy. I was making a point that, just as parents have the right to set standards and expectations for their children, managers have the right to set standards and expectations for their employees. And in both cases, one person's standards may be quite different from another's. The important thing is that you clearly communicate them and hold people accountable."

**Keep Your Cool.**  When faced with the unexpected, the most important thing to remember is to maintain your composure. You must remain calm and in control. Several techniques will help in these situations:

- *Lower the pitch of your voice.* When we get nervous or upset, the pitch of our voices tends to get higher, particularly with women.

- *Breathe deeply.* Shallow breathing is a sign of nervousness and will affect the quality of the voice.

- *Control your speed.* Many people have a tendency to speak faster when they are under stress, so concentrate on maintaining a moderate rate when responding.

- *Control your volume.* Although you want to project your voice, do not shout. Maintain a reasonable volume level, loud enough to make sure you are heard but not so loud that you sound angry or out of control.

- *Attend to nonverbals.* Avoid nervous gestures such as fiddling with clothes, jewelry, paper clips, or pointer. Those are a dead giveaway that you are losing control. Also, be careful not to appear in a counterattack mode. If you gesture, keep your palms open and do not point.

**Handle Challenges with Grace and Professionalism.**  Accept the fact that you are not always correct. If someone points out an error, thank the individual. Do not be defensive. Sometimes an individual may challenge you by offering a different opinion or point of view. When that happens, acknowledge the difference of opinion and thank the person for offering a different point of view. Do not, however, get into an argument or a debate.

People automatically ask questions that start with "why." Quite naturally, you may have a tendency to react defensively. To avoid delivering a defensive-sounding response, reframe the "why" into a "how" or "what" question when you restate it. For example, if someone poses the following question, "Why did you. . .?, reframe it by saying, "If I understand you correctly, you're asking me *how* I . . . " or "As I understand it, you want to know *what* I. . . ." When responding to these challenging questions, begin with "In my experience . . ." or present facts or quote experts as appropriate.

More specifically, sometimes a participant (especially one who doesn't want to be there) complains about having to participate in activities and may challenge you by asking, "Why did you waste our time with this activity instead of just telling us the information?" You would reframe the question by saying, "If I understand you correctly, you're asking me how this activity relates to the topic" or "As I understand it, you want to know what my reason is for spending time on this activity." You would then follow this clarification with an explanation such as, "Based on my experience as well as hundreds of studies on retention of learning, people learn best by doing, not by being told."

## Participant Behavior

More often than not, the group as a whole is not a problem, but there may be a few difficult people in the session. Here are some coping strategies on dealing with specific character types.

**Talkative.** The talkative participant has something to say about everything. This person always volunteers to be a group leader, answer questions, or offer suggestions. He or she seems to want to be the center of attention. To deal with the talkative type, you might say something like, "I appreciate your contribution, but let's hear from some other people." Suggest further discussion at break or lunch by saying, "In order to stay on schedule and on track, let's discuss this further during the break or after the session."

**Clueless.** This person seems to have no idea what's going on. He or she totally misunderstands the question or the topic being discussed. As a result, this person's answers or remarks do not even remotely relate to the subject under discussion. For this person, say, "Something I said must have led you off track. What I was trying to say was. . . ."

**Rambling.** This person goes on and on about nothing. He or she digresses frequently and uses examples and analogies that do not relate to the topic being discussed. This person is different from the "clueless" individual in that the rambler knows what is going on but prefers to follow his or her own agenda. To get this person back on track, try asking, "I don't understand. How does this relate to what we're talking about?" This is a good opportunity to use the "parking lot."

**Belligerent.** The belligerent person is openly hostile, challenging and arguing every point. This person questions the trainer's knowledge and credibility and may even accuse the trainer of being "out of touch" with the real world. Do not engage in any verbal sparring. Say to this person, "I understand and appreciate your point of view. What do some of the rest of you think?" By turning to the rest of the group, you get yourself off the hook and give others an opportunity to exert some peer pressure to change this person's behavior. You might also offer to discuss the issue further during break.

**Stubborn.** This individual refuses to see anyone else's point of view and is particularly difficult to deal with in a group environment. His or her refusal to give in on a point will thwart group decision-making or consensus-seeking activities. Sometimes you can take the direct approach and say, "I appreciate your position [or point of view], but for the sake of the activity [discussion, etc.], I'm going to insist that we move on. I'll be happy to discuss this with you later."

**Silent.** Every group has one or more silent types who seem attentive and alert but will not volunteer comments or answer questions. He or she may be naturally shy or uncomfortable speaking up in a group and seems content just to listen.

You might ask yourself, "So what's wrong with that?" The problem is that often these quiet people have some wonderful comments and contributions to make, and if we don't make an effort to involve them, their ideas never surface and the group misses the opportunity to learn from another of its members. The participant himself or herself misses an opportunity to be heard and receive validation. Try prompting the reluctant or shy participant by saying, "[Person's Name], I know you have some experience in this area. It would be helpful if you would share your thoughts with the group." Another approach is to break the group into pairs or trios. The shy person is much more likely to participate in these smaller groups.

**Know-It-All.** The know-it-all individual often tries to upstage or overshadow the trainer. Often viewing himself or herself as an authority on every subject, this person assumes a superior role with both the group and the trainer. This person relishes the opportunity to flaunt his or her knowledge, often using big words, quoting facts and figures, and dropping names. Although it may be difficult, do not let your annoyance show. Acknowledge his or her contribution by saying, "That's one point of view. However, there are other ways of looking at it." Depending on the situation, ask other participants for their opinions or move on.

**Class Clown.** The class clown is relatively harmless unless you allow him or her to get out of control. This person makes a joke out of everything and goes out of his or her way to get attention, often at the expense of others. Do not give in to this person's attempt to control the situation. Simply say, "We all enjoy a little levity. But right now, let's get serious and concentrate on the topic at hand."

**Negative.** This individual complains about the organization, his or her boss, co-workers, you name it. In addition to the negative verbal remarks, he or she displays negative non-verbal behavior such as frowning or assuming a defensive posture. Often this person is a chronic complainer who has nothing positive to contribute. Say something like, "I understand your point. What suggestions do you have to change the situation?" Or you might say, "For the sake of discussion, what might be some arguments for the opposite point of view?"

**Indifferent.** It is pretty clear to everyone that this person does not want to be there. He or she makes no attempt to participate or contribute. Because he or she has been forced to attend, not only will this person show no interest, but he or she may even resort to engaging in activities separate from the group. Use a tactic similar to the one you might use with the silent type: "I know you have some experience in this area. Please tell us about it."

**Personality Clashes.** Some people in a group may not get along. They may engage in verbal battles, either directly or indirectly, often with remarks becoming very personal and hurtful. When a situation like this occurs, it is important to address it early by invoking ground rules or saying, "I suggest that we keep personalities out of the discussion. Let's get back to the topic at hand."

**Side Conversations.** Side conversations are a frequent and annoying occurrence. Far too often, two or more members of the group engage in their own conversation while a fellow participant or the trainer is talking. More than one strategy may be needed to bring them back. Sometimes just walking over to the individuals will cause them to stop their conversation. If that does not work, try saying, "[Persons' names], we were just talking about. . . . What are your thoughts?"

## General Guidelines

When dealing with any of these situations, keep in mind four important goals:

1. *Stop the dysfunctional behavior.* Your first objective is to stop the disruptive behavior.

2. *Keep the individual(s) engaged.* Your second objective is to prevent the person from "shutting down" and not participating at all.

3. *Keep the rest of the group involved.* Your third objective is to prevent others in the group from "shutting down." Keep in mind that others will judge you by the way you handle these difficult situations.

4. *Respect the individual.* Your fourth objective, and perhaps the most important, is to respect the individual and help maintain his or her dignity. Do not embarrass or belittle the person.

After you have addressed a behavior or responded to a hostile participant, look toward another person or section of the room. Continued eye contact will only encourage the participant and may result in a continued debate or argument. Remember that you can never win an argument with a participant. Even if the group is annoyed with their fellow participant's behavior, if you attack that person, the others may turn against you. After all, he or she is one of them.

When participants demonstrate intense negative emotions, it is important to acknowledge those feelings and emotions with a statement such as, "I can tell you feel strongly about this" or "I'm sorry you feel that way." Be careful not to make judgmental statements such as, "You're being negative" or "You're not listening."

## Learning to Live with It

One of the biggest challenges a trainer faces is to accept the fact that some people and some situations are beyond his or her control. When, despite all your efforts, the session still does not go according to plan, assess the situation as objectively as possible. Ask yourself what you could have done differently. If you conclude that you did everything you could to prevent or handle the situation, then do not fret about it. Accept the fact that people bring a lot of "baggage" to your sessions that you have no way of knowing about or controlling. On the other hand, if you think you could have handled the situation better, then learn from your mistakes and move on.

### KEY POINTS

- The role of the active trainer is to facilitate discussion and group interaction.

- The art of asking open-ended questions that begin with "what" and "how" is central to your success as a facilitator of adult learning.

- The use of silence is very effective in eliciting participant responses to your questions.

- Be prepared for the expected as well as the unexpected: proper planning, preparation, anticipation, and communication are great prevention strategies.

- Answer questions directly and honestly.

- When dealing with difficult people and/or situations, remain calm and in control; handle challenges with grace and professionalism.

- Setting ground rules at the beginning of a session can be very effective in preventing dysfunctional behavior.

- Your goal in dealing with dysfunctional behavior is to stop the behavior, yet at the same time, to respect the individual and to prevent that person from shutting down.

Now that you have "mastered" the basics of design, development, and delivery, it's time to add some spice to your programs. Chapter 12 presents a number of topics and techniques for being more creative in your training sessions.

# Chapter 12

# Using Creativity

**LEARNING OUTCOMES**

In this chapter, you will learn

- To develop creative ways to form subgroups
- To use creative approaches to motivate and energize the group
- To incorporate games into the instructional design
- To create and maintain structure for small-group assignments
- To use games to increase learning and improve retention
- To adapt games to specific content and learning objectives
- To design closing activities that reinforce the learning

## Creativity with Small Groups

The use of small groups is a very effective learning technique and the cornerstone of cooperative learning. Sometimes, however, when you announce that you are going to break into subgroups, you might hear, "Oh, no! Not again!" To maintain a high level of interest and enthusiasm throughout the session, draw on your creative muse even when dealing with small groups.

### Grouping Techniques

Many learning activities require you to break a large group into subgroups. The most frequently used method of creating subgroups is to ask participants to count off by however many groups you want to create. However, this method is boring and people often forget their numbers or where they are supposed to relocate. Instead of the old "ho-hum" approach, let's look at some other more creative ways to create small groups.

- *Puzzles.* Make or buy six-piece jigsaw puzzles and give each person a puzzle piece. To form subgroups, the participants have to find those who have pieces to the same puzzle.

- *Candy.* Different flavors of wrapped candy can be distributed to participants just before breaking into groups. (Be sure to tell them not to eat the candy just yet.) Ask the peppermints to go to one spot; butterscotch pieces, another; Hershey Kisses®, still another.

- *Participant Materials.* Give your participants pens or folders of different colors to indicate their groups.

- *Grouping Cards.* Another way to move people quickly and efficiently into different group configurations throughout the day is to create grouping cards. Each person receives a 3-by-5-inch card on which is a colored dot, a number, and a colorful sticker. The numbers, dots, and stickers are placed on the cards so that they will form random groups of varying sizes, depending on the purpose of the activity and required subgroup size. For example, say there are twelve people in a workshop and you will need to create four groups of three (red, blue, green, yellow dots), three groups of four (zoo animal stickers: lions, giraffes, zebras), and two groups of six (numbers 1 and 2). When you are ready to put people into subgroups, tell them how to group and where.

- *Finding Famous Fictional Friends and Families.* Another excellent way to group people is called "Finding Famous Fictional Friends and Families." First, depending on the number of groups you need, create groups of four or five fictional characters in the same "family" such as Robin Hood, Maid Marian, Friar Tuck, Little John, Sheriff of Nottingham; Tin Man, Cowardly Lion, Dorothy, Scarecrow, Toto; Peter Pan, Captain Hook, Wendy, Tinkerbell, Crocodile; Hawkeye, Hot Lips, Trapper John, Radar, Klinger. Put the names of characters on separate index cards (one card per person in the workshop), shuffle the cards, and give each participant a card. Next ask the participants to find the other members of their "families." Suggest to participants that if they do not recognize the name of a character they drew, to ask their fellow participants for help.

When the subgroups have been formed, ask them to discuss a particular topic or come up with a list related to the topic. For example, for a customer service program, ask the groups to share the best or the worst experience they ever had as a customer. In a program on managing change, ask subgroups to list the changes they are experiencing in their organizations and the industry.

## Assigning Roles

Roles can also be assigned in creative ways, rather than leaving the decision to the groups themselves. Suggest that the spokesperson, scribe, or discussion leader be the person whose birthday is closest to the day's date or who lives the closest to the training location.

Bob Pike of Creative Training Techniques in Minneapolis uses a fun finger-pointing technique. He asks people in their small groups to point their index fingers in the air, and when he gives the signal, they are to point to someone in their group. The person who has the most fingers pointing at him or her is the spokesperson. To add a little more fun, variety, and surprise, the trainer can then tell the person who was just chosen to choose someone else.

Come up with your own creative ideas. Let your imagination run wild!

## Regaining Control

Sometimes trainers are afraid to have participants interacting with one another or moving into small groups because they are afraid of losing control and not being able to get the group's attention again. This is no problem with a little planning and communicating up-front. First, be very clear and specific when telling participants what you want them to do; give them a timeframe and tell them what signal you are going to use to let them know when time is up. There are many ways of regaining the audience's attention—both auditory and visual.

**Auditory Signals.** Try Bob Pike's multiple clapping method. When he wants to call the group back to order, he asks them to clap once if they can hear his voice, and then he claps once. Then he asks them to clap twice if they can hear his voice, and he claps twice. Finally, he asks them to clap three times if they can hear him, and he claps three times. By that time, people have quieted down and refocused their attention on the trainer.

Use a variety of other sounds (a train whistle, cow bell, siren, police whistle, sleigh bells, horn, wind chimes, or kazoo) to regain the group's attention. When participants do not know what sound to expect, they love the surprise.

**Visual Signals.** Some trainers use visual signals such as turning the lights on and off or holding up a sign or object. Use any other idea you choose.

# Props and Other Theatrical Techniques

The use of props is becoming increasingly more popular. Although props are visual aids and are used for a purpose similar to those discussed in Chapter 9, they are included in this chapter because of their unique relationship to the theater and show business. Props can include hats, objects, magic tricks—any object that enhances the message.

Using props is an easy and economical theatrical technique that will capture the audience's attention and help you communicate your message. Props appeal especially to the visual modality. They help reinforce a message by relating the visual image to the spoken word. The image will last long after the words are forgotten.

**EXAMPLE OF USING PROPS**

When I do a session on professional image, I begin by holding up two boxes of the same shape and size. One box is professionally wrapped with attractive paper and coordinating ribbon and bow; the other is wrapped in haphazard fashion in aluminum foil and tied with white curling ribbon. I ask the audience to indicate with a show of hands which package they would like to receive. Almost everyone chooses the attractive package. (Of course, there are always a few who choose the other.) I then ask one or two people to explain their preference for the professionally wrapped box to the others. They mention, of course, that it is more aesthetically appealing. This provides the segue into my points about professional image:

- Image is a matter of perception.
- Successful people first decide how they want to be perceived.
- Then they determine what to do to create that perception.

## Props and Points

Coming up with ideas for props is not difficult. The key is to sit down and think about your learning points and brainstorm what objects might relate to or represent that particular message.

---

### SAMPLE PROPS

For my session on coaching to improve workplace performance, I use a teddy bear dressed as an athletic coach in baseball cap and polo shirt with a whistle around his neck. I use my "coach" bear to introduce the concept of coaching and how coaches in the work environment are similar to coaches in the world of sports.

During management development programs, I speak about employee motivation. To make my point about the different approaches to motivating employees, I bring in three props: a whip, a carrot dangling at the end of a stick, and a flowering plant. I show the whip to illustrate threats managers often make; the carrot represents incentive programs or promises of rewards as a motivational tool; the flowering plant is a metaphor for an environment in which people are motivated. A plant needs the right amount of water, light, heat, and fertilizer, and each plant requires different kind of care. The same is true for people. Successful managers will understand the different "care" required by each of employee and create an appropriate environment accordingly. My "motivation" props are always a big hit. The participants frequently refer to the props throughout the session.

I also use a Slinky® magic spring to illustrate the importance of remaining flexible and adapting to change and a kaleidoscope to represent the changing environment. I use puzzle pieces for team building, giving each team member a puzzle piece that they hold until the end of the session, when I ask all of the team members to get up and put their pieces together to complete the puzzle. I remind them that they are individuals, but they must all come together to form the whole.

I often use a magic wand, "magic dust" [glitter], or a crystal ball. In a management development session, I might mention that people are promoted to management positions and someone sprinkles "magic dust" or waves a magic wand and "abracadabra!," they now know how to manage.

The crystal ball can be used in a career development program to make the point that many people expect to look into a crystal ball and see their future rather than taking control of their careers by developing plans and managing those plans.

## Posters

Display posters of quotations related to the topic around the room to create a mood and generate interest in the topic. Quotations work well at the beginning of a session. Ask participants to choose one of the quotations and explain how it relates to them. The following quotes are appropriate for a time-management session:

- "Money lost can be replaced, but time lost is gone forever."

- "People who have half an hour to spend usually spend it with someone who hasn't."

- "Everybody has the problem of time; of all resources, it is the scarcest, the most perishable, and the most elusive."

## Giveaways

A prop becomes even more effective and memorable if you use "giveaways" that coordinate with your theme. For example, you might give participants whistles in a coaching session; miniature Slinkies to remind people to be flexible, or kaleidoscopes to help them look at things differently.

Use cube puzzles to represent problem solving. Give out small compasses in a session on goal setting to emphasize the importance of staying on course.

Give away buttons and stickers with words or slogans as a reminder of your theme or key learning points. Steve Sugar distributes 2-inch by 2-inch "Koala T Idea" cartoon stickers to recognize unique ideas contributed by individuals or groups.

### EXAMPLES OF RECOGNITION AND REWARDS

For a session for managers on motivating employees, I had buttons made that read, "I'm the greatest. My boss told me so!" as an example of inexpensive ways to recognize and reward your employees. The managers were so excited about the button idea that they not only ordered those particular buttons to give to their employees, but came up with other button ideas and used them periodically to let their employees know how important they were to the success of the organization.

## Using Themes

Another way to add creativity to a workshop is to use a theme as a metaphor for the topic. Decorate the room and choose props and giveaways to support the theme. For example, the metaphor of a sailboat cruise to represent team building, with the meeting room decorated in a nautical theme. When participants arrive, place leis around their necks and give out compasses to help them "stay on course." Give each person an eraser shaped like a sea creature and a roll of LifeSavers®.

Use an outer space theme and have the room darkened and decorated with glow-in-the-dark stars and other celestial objects. If your session is about group problem solving or decision making, you might choose the NASA task simulation from Teleometrics.

## Using Imagination

Do not be afraid to take risks. Do something different. For example, use music. Have it playing as people come in the room and during breaks. Trainers often use recordings of currently popular songs used to set the mood for a training session and/or activity. Although the use of recordings for this type of usage requires no special agreements with the copyright owners for its use, you must pay a *performance royalty* to the publisher for these uses. For permission to play recorded music, contact the American Society of Composers, Authors, and Publishers (ASCAP) or Broadcast Music Incorporated (BMI). Even better, use royalty-free music produced especially for training venues. An excellent source is "Powerful Presentation Music" from the Bob Pike group.

Use balloons to show how managers can "celebrate" their employees' achievements. One word of caution: do not get carried away. Your creativity must not get in the way of your main purpose: a meaningful learning experience. Whatever you do should be an enhancement, not a distraction.

# Games

Unfortunately, in many instances, games have received a bad reputation because they have not been used properly. Games, like other activities, must have an instructional purpose. They are tools for learning.

It is important for the trainer to evaluate a game well and link to the "real world" through the skillful conduct of the game and the facilitation process that follows the actual play. Game master Steve Sugar, principal of the Game Group in Ellicott City, Maryland, refers to instructional games as HOT (High-Outcome Techniques) training. He believes success depends on the facilitator's ability to know what to do, how to do it, and when to do it.

## Instructional Games

To put it simply, an instructional game is an activity that involves rules and a repeating pattern of play. Reflecting a balance between knowledge and chance, an effective instructional game contains the following four C's:

- *Challenge.* By its very nature, a game is competitive and, therefore, has challenge, either built in or assumed.

- *Chance.* Unlike a simulation or other experiential activities, a game includes an element of chance created by the roll of the dice or the luck of the draw.

- *Complication.* Complication is a factor involving both rules of play and questions that "test" the players' knowledge or skills.

- *Closure.* A game has a clear ending determined by time or point factors, resulting in winners and losers.

A popular and versatile type of instructional game is known as a "frame game." A frame game involves selecting a well-known game structure and placing your instructional material within that structure. Think of a frame game as a template, designed generically so that you can "load" or plug in your own content into the game. The two most popular classroom frame games are paper-and-pencil (Bingo, Tic-Tac-Toe, Scavenger Hunt) and board and TV game shows (for example, Monopoly®, Trivial Pursuit®, "Jeopardy®"). The TV game show has spawned a series of templates from Learning Ware and other vendors. You do not have to limit your use to popular and well-known games. There are a number of sources available to you for frame games that are easy to use. Game guru Sivasailam "Thiagi" Thiagarajan has a number of frame games as well as simulation games available on the market, as noted in Appendix B.

## Advantages of Games

Like other experiential activities, instructional games can serve a number of purposes. Games serve two main purposes simultaneously: instruction and group development.

**Instruction.** As an instructional technique, games can be used:

- To assess the participants' knowledge or skill prior to the training

- To teach new content: new information, concepts, and skills

- To review or reinforce your learning points for a particular segment or as a summary and review of the entire program

- To assess how much the participants have learned

**Group Development.** The instructional purpose of the game should be of primary concern. At the same time, games can be used:

- To break the ice and help people become acquainted with one another

- To build rapport and create a comfortable learning climate

- To build group cohesiveness by having people work in teams, resulting in collaboration as well as competition

- To motivate participants and generate interest and enthusiasm for the topic

## Using Games

Results of a study conducted by James Kirk (1995) indicate that certain groups like games more than others. Kirk found that people under forty are more likely to enjoy the instructional use of games. Furthermore, supervisors or managers, those in sales and marketing positions, and professionals tend to respond favorably to games. Technicians, support staff, and operation workers are less likely to like games.

The following factors must be taken into consideration when deciding whether or not to use an instructional game.

### Factors to Consider

- *Time.* Steve Sugar estimates that it takes between seven and twelve minutes in development for every minute of playing time to create a game.

- *Cost.* Cost depends on a number of variables, including the complexity of the game, the number of game sets you have to produce, production costs, purchasing costs, and, of course, how much time you have to devote.

- *Audience.* You must consider the makeup of the group. Some games are more complex than others and will require some higher-order thinking and application.

- *Enjoyment.* Although a game is a vehicle for learning, it should also be fun.

- *Adaptability.* The best instructional games are those that can be adapted easily to audience, subject, and time constraints.

- *User-Friendliness.* An instructional game needs to be easy to use and understand for both the participants and the facilitator.

- *Safety.* The name must be non-threatening. In other words, participants need to feel that it's okay to make a mistake.

- *Learning Objectives.* The instructional purpose needs to be clearly understood. Like all other activities, the game must lead to a learning outcome.

## Adapting Games to Training Programs

After deciding to incorporate a game into the training design, you must then actually build the game. The "master of instructional games," Steve Sugar, suggests the following approach:

**Determine Your Objectives.**  Decide why you are using a game. Are you using it to involve the participants? Add variety to your design? Energize the group? Make the learning interactive?

**Select and Adapt a Frame.**  Choose a frame that is user-friendly, adaptable, flexible, and challenging. Particularly if this is your first experience with a game, choose a frame that is familiar to both you and the participants such as "Jeopardy," Bingo, or Trivial Pursuit. Participants from cultures outside the United States may not be familiar with these games, so be sure to learn about your audience before you choose a particular frame.

**Develop Your Rules.**  Be clear about what people can and cannot do, how you will keep track of who is winning and losing, and when the game is over. Write the rules so they are easy to understand and are non-threatening.

**Load the Frame.**  At this point, you will develop the questions specific to your content. This is time-consuming, so plan and manage your time accordingly.

**Produce or Construct the Game.**  This step involves creating the physical pieces of the game, including game board, sets of cards, game pieces, dice, and so forth. You can save yourself some time by purchasing frame games that have been created for instructional purposes. (See Appendix B for some sources of games.)

For example, Steve Sugar has developed a great frame game called QUIZO! available on www.thegamegroup.com. Participants use a Bingo-type game sheet that is "covered" (marked with an "X") for each correct response to a content question. The trainer decides on the content questions and controls the game flow by presenting each question and then informing participants which game space is awarded for a correct response.

**Pilot the Game.** Sometimes a game that looks good on paper fails miserably in the actual execution. Before going to great expense to produce slick materials, test it out on a small group of people representative of those who will actually play the game. As you observe and later debrief the game, ask yourself (and others) the following questions:

- Were the participants involved? Was there a high level of participation among all the players?

- Were they learning? How do you know they were learning?

- Did they have fun? Were they animated and smiling? Were they energized?

- Were the questions and situations realistic? Whether the content was cognitive, behavioral, or affective, did it reflect what they needed to know or do on the job?

- Was the environment non-threatening? Was there an atmosphere of trust? Could people make mistakes without feeling embarrassed?

**Revise the Game.** Based on the feedback you received from the pilot, you will probably need to make some revisions. Let the games begin!

## Writing Game Questions and Items

In writing game questions, keep in mind that you want variety. Consider the following types of questions and items:

- *Short Answer.* These questions include many types: direct question (elicits a simple factual response), partial listing (elicits a list of characteristics), multiple choice, identification, definitions, and fill-in-the-blank.

- *Case Study.* These questions present hypothetical situations requiring the participant to explain briefly what he or she would do.

- *Role Play.* A role play requires the participant to actually do something that relates to the topic. For example, in a class on interpersonal skills, a role play question might direct the participant to give feedback to one of his or her colleagues.

- *Discussion.* A discussion question requires the group to discuss the question among themselves. In a session on business etiquette, the participants might discuss a female taking a male client to lunch and how to handle the check.

- *Activity or Process.* Tasks are written on cards, such as "Complete [task] in thirty seconds," or "Without words, demonstrate how to greet a new customer."

## Facilitating a Game

The biggest contributing factor to a game's failure is what the trainer does (or does not do) after the game is played. In a survey conducted by James Kirk (1995), 80 percent of training providers responded that they have received no structured training in game facilitation.

Games require the same care in processing as do other activities. If you follow the *What? So What? Now What?* formula along with the other processing tips introduced in Chapter 8, your game will be successful. Be prepared, however, for mixed reactions. Because of the differences in learning styles, it's understandable and predictable that people will react differently. Some people may hate the game, while others think it is one of the best learning experiences they ever had.

So don't be concerned unless you receive a lot of negative reactions.

## Caveats

Trainers who have had little or no experience using an instructional game in training sessions are often very uncomfortable the first time. They are unnerved by the perceived loss of control, particularly if they have been delivering trainer-centered training. If the participants are really involved in the game, then the trainer is really not even needed, except to answer the few questions that may arise, to observe the process, and to monitor the flow of the activity.

# Creative Closings

The way in which you bring a session or program to a close is very important. Think of it as a package tied with a neat little bow. Make sure you allocate adequate time in your design to process the entire session or program. In a full-day session, I allot thirty to forty minutes for closing activities.

## Summarizing Techniques

Throughout the session, participants have been bombarded with information and activities. Before you send them on their way, help them pull it all together so that they leave the session with a clear understanding of your key learning points. Rather than taking on the responsibility of summarizing the session yourself, put the onus on the participants to think about what they have learned, synthesizing the content and experiences into key learning points. Remember that they will learn (and remember) better by doing rather than by being told.

**Small-Group Summaries.** Divide the participants into subgroups. Give each subgroup a flip-chart page and markers and ask them to come up with a list of the key learning points from the session. Make it as specific as you want. For example, for a customer service program, ask the small groups to pretend that they are going to be responsible for training new employees on the "do's and don'ts" of serving the customer. Ask them to develop a list of guidelines they would give new employees as a job aid and reminder of how to deliver quality service. After each group has developed its list, compare the lists, noting the similarities. They now have a summary checklist to take with them.

**Full Circle.** A technique mentioned in Chapter 8, "What Do You Want to Know?," uses Post-it Notes™ to keep track of questions participants have about subtopics that will be addressed in the session. They place their questions on flip-chart sheets on the walls around the room. Ask participants to retrieve questions that were answered or addressed during the training program. Ideally, the wall will be empty.

Sometimes a few remain, generally questions that had absolutely nothing to do with the topic of the session. Occasionally, questions may remain that were touched on, but the participant who wrote the question does not recall the discussion. Either ask whether anyone in the group remembers that question being addressed in some fashion or point it out for the participant yourself.

## Self-Assessment

Also give participants an opportunity to reflect on how much they have personally grown or learned during the session. A great technique is to create a human continuum. This activity is adapted from a design called "Physical Self-Assessment" in *101 Ways to Make Training Active* (Silberman, 2005).

For this activity, create two signs that represent the two extreme ends of a continuum and post them on opposite ends of a wall. For example, use "competent" and "clueless." Then ask participants to think about where they were at the beginning of the session or program relative to their knowledge, understanding, or skill level as it relates to the topic. Ask them to imagine the wall as a continuum and to get up and place themselves where they think they were.

After the participants are in position, ask two or three to explain why they placed themselves where they did. Next ask them to think about where they see themselves now, at the end of the program, and to place themselves accordingly. Once again, ask a few to explain their positions. In most cases, you will find participants moving in varying degrees from "clueless" to "competent." This activity is a graphic way for both you and the participants to see how they have benefited from the training session.

## Making Commitments

Mel Silberman tells trainers, "It's not what you give them, but what they take away that counts." Unless participants take what they learned and apply it to their own situations, the training will not be effective. To help ensure that the training is transferred to the work environment, ask participants to develop their own action plans. Ask them to write down two or three action items as a result of the training. Ask them to write down not only what they are going to do but how and when. Also ask them to consider what barriers they might anticipate and how they can overcome them. Exhibit 12.1 is an example of an action plan used at the end of a management-development program.

## Follow-Up Activities

Do not overlook the importance of building into your design follow-up activities to reinforce the training. Send various learning resources such as articles, tapes, and CDs to the participants at regular intervals for them to use individually or with others. You can also give them specific assignments to complete and submit to you. Remember that training is a process, not an event.

## Reflections

At the end of many training sessions, you can use a simple activity that combines self-assessment, action plan, and personal reaction all in one activity. I put the following statements on a transparency or flip chart:

- The most important thing I learned in this session is. . . .

- As a result of this training, one thing I am going to do is. . . .

- What I liked best about this training session was. . . .

Then ask a few volunteers to share their responses to the items. It is a great way to obtain feedback and to help participants focus on or clarify in their own minds what was the most meaningful learning for them. Aside from being great feedback for the trainer, this technique helps participants leave with a sense of enjoyment and satisfaction with the learning experience.

**EXHIBIT 12.1.    Sample Action Plan**

1.  What new thoughts, ideas, or insights have I gained from this program?

2.  As a result of these new ideas, what specific thing(s) do I want to do differently on the job?

3.  What within myself could keep me from doing these things?

4.  What outside barriers or obstacles could keep me from doing these things?

5.  What can I do to overcome these internal and external barriers?

6.  What help do I need from others in order to overcome these obstacles?

7.  How will I know that I have succeeded (what results do I anticipate from my new behavior)?

KEY POINTS

- Use a variety of creative techniques to form subgroups.

- Use both auditory and visual signals to regain control of the group.

- Use props and other theatrical techniques to increase participants' interest, keep their attention, and illustrate a point.

- Use instructional games to add fun and excitement (while having an instructional purpose) to your training sessions.

- Use a variety of creative techniques to bring your session to a close.

Although your training session is over, your work is far from done. Now it's time to focus on the program's success in meeting the business needs of the organization and the developmental needs of the participants. The next chapter addresses the various ways to evaluate training.

# Chapter 13

## Evaluating Training

**LEARNING OUTCOMES**

In this chapter, you will learn

- To use the four levels of evaluation
- To create evaluation tools
- To use the evaluation process to improve training effectiveness

## Why Evaluate?

How many times have you heard someone say, "It was a great training program but. . ."? Unfortunately, that statement (or a variation) is spoken far too often and reflects a growing concern by both line managers and senior management that training is costly and not always worth the investment of time and money. This attitude is also reflected in the actions of senior managers who cut training budgets first when times are tough.

### Purposes of Evaluation

Following are some of the main reasons to evaluate:

- To determine whether the training achieves its objectives
- To assess the value of training programs

- To identify areas of the program that need improvement
- To identify the appropriate audience for future programs
- To review and reinforce key program parts for participants
- To sell a program to management and participants

### Linking Evaluation to the Needs Assessment

Clearly, needs assessment is critical to the success of any training initiative. It provides the basis for program development and establishes the criteria for measuring the success of the program after its completion. For evaluation to have any meaning, it must be tied to the needs assessment process. Always remember that the evaluation process should reflect specific business-related or performance-related outcomes.

## When to Evaluate

Evaluation is an ongoing process, not just something that happens at the end of a session or program. Consider evaluation during the session, at the end, and after the participants return to the job.

**During the Session.**  As people participate in skill practice, case studies, exercises, simulations, and other activities, observe the degree to which they have mastered the content.

**At the End of the Session.**  Participants' evaluation questionnaires will indicate their personal reactions to the training session.

**After the Training.**  A few weeks to several months after the session, observe the participants' job performance to determine whether they are applying what they learned to their work situations.

## Whom to Involve

Any category or number of people can be involved in the evaluation process, depending on what you want to know and what level of evaluation you conduct. The participants are directly involved because they are the customers whose level of satisfaction you are trying to determine. The participants are the major source of information on how much they have actually learned in the training. In addition to the participants, involve others in the evaluation process. Survey or interview the participants' managers, their co-workers, peers, subordinates, or even customers or vendors. At some point, you may need to involve senior management.

## How to Evaluate

The methods used for evaluation are pretty much the same as those used to gather data during the needs assessment. Trainers will often ask, "Which method(s) should I use?" Unfortunately, there is no clear-cut answer. As Jane Holcomb (1994) says in her book *Make Training Worth Every Penny*, "Use any method that works for you—any method at all that gives you the information you need."

## What to Evaluate

Before developing an evaluation process, be clear about what you want to evaluate. This is not as easy as it might seem. Do you want to evaluate how much the participants have learned? Or do you want to know what the participants thought about the program and you? Do you want to find out whether the participants are applying what they learned on the job? If they are using the learned skills and information on the job, is their enhanced performance making a difference to the organization?

## Four-Level Model for Evaluation

The most widely known model for evaluating training programs was introduced by Donald Kirkpatrick in 1959. It is regarded as a classic by training practitioners. Although all four levels of the model (reaction, learning, behavior, results) are important, you may choose not to evaluate at all four levels. Studies show that a vast majority of organizations evaluate reaction. A significantly high percentage measure learning as well. The evaluation or measurement of behavior lags behind the first two levels; evaluation of results finishes last.

Today's organizations are much more cost-conscious, and the need to measure the effectiveness of training will continue to grow. Should you need to undertake a comprehensive approach to evaluation, you will be able to make appropriate recommendations or respond confidently when someone asks you to prove that training gets results.

Table 13.1 provides an overview of the four levels of evaluation.

**Table 13.1.** **Measuring Training Results**

| | What | Who | When | How | Why |
|---|------|-----|------|-----|-----|
| Level 1 | Reaction: Did they like it? | Participants | End of program | "Smile sheet" | Determine level of customer satis-faction; may indicate need for revision |
| Level 2 | Learning: What knowledge or skills did they retain? | Participants; trainer | During, before/after program | Pre-test/post-test; skills application through role plays, case studies, exercises | Identify whether trainer has been successful in delivery of course content and achieving program objectives |
| Level 3 | Behavior: How are they performing differently? | Participants; bosses; subordinates; peers | 3 to 6 months after program completion | Surveys; interviews; observation; performance appraisal | Determine extent to which participants have transferred what they learned in the session to the actual work situation |
| Level 4 | Results: What is the impact on the bottom line? | Participants; control group | After completion of Level 3 follow-up | Cost/benefit analysis; tracking; operational data | Determine whether benefits outweigh costs; ascertain degree of contribu-tion of program to organizational goals |

On the WEB

*The Trainer's Handbook, Updated Ed.* Copyright © 2009 by Karen Lawson. Reproduced by permission of Pfeiffer, an imprint of John Wiley & Sons, Inc.

## Level 1: Reaction

Level 1 deals with participants reactions, that is, "customer" satisfaction. Level 1 evaluations are often referred to as "smile sheets," implying that participants' reactions are based on how much "fun" they had in the training session. For that reason, trainers frequently dismiss Level 1 evaluations as a waste of time.

On the contrary, Level 1 is an important first step in determining the success of a training program. Participants' reactions can help you determine the effectiveness of a program and how it can be improved. Kirkpatrick believes that you cannot bypass this first level because, as he puts it, "If they [participants] do not react favorably, they will not be motivated to learn" (Kirkpatrick, 1994).

**What Level 1 Cannot Measure.** One of the problems with and the main cause of criticism of Level 1 evaluation is that it is too subjective and often becomes nothing more than a popularity contest. Before constructing a participant end-of-session evaluation form, understand what it cannot and is not intended to do: (1) it does not measure learning or the ability to apply learning on the job; (2) it also cannot measure changes in attitudes or beliefs; (3) because it deals only with participants' perceptions and reactions, a Level 1 instrument can in no way measure organizational impact; (4) also, although frequently asked, participants cannot measure the trainer's knowledge. Think about it. How could the participants have any way of knowing what the trainer does and does not know about the subject? Your ability to *communicate* or *demonstrate* your knowledge is an entirely different story.

**Deciding What to Measure.** Before you design a Level 1 instrument, you need to be clear about what you want to know, why you want to know it, and what you are going to do with the information. Do not ask for information about something you cannot change or have no intention of analyzing or reporting.

**Designing an End-of-Session Evaluation Form.** *Categories.* First decide what you want to measure and create questions or response items that address or fall into certain categories, including many, if not all, of the following:

- Content
- Materials
- Instructional methods
- Trainer
- Environment
- Logistics

It is also a good idea to provide an opportunity for respondents to make recommendations as to how the program can be improved and also to express their overall reactions to the session.

*Format.* To counteract people's tendency to respond the same way to every item on a questionnaire or survey, use a variety of response formats. Choose at least four from the following options:

- *Two-choice questions with room for explanation or comments.* These would include responses such as "yes" or "no" and "agree" or "disagree." *Example:* Did the course meet the stated objectives? Yes      No      Why or why not?

- *Short answers.* These items are written as open-ended questions and require the respondent to write down a brief response instead of just checking a box. *Example:* What parts of the workshop were most valuable/beneficial to you? Why?

- *Complete the sentence.* With this item, the respondent is asked to complete a sentence. *Example:* What I want/need to know more about is. . . .

- *Ratings.* Participants respond to a question or statement using some type of scale or rating such as a Likert scale. The Likert scale measures both the direction (positive to negative) and intensity (strongly positive to strongly negative) of an individual's opinion or attitude. *Example:* Today's session was an enjoyable and satisfying learning experience for me.

  | 1 | 2 | 3 | 4 | 5 | 6 | 7 | 8 |
  |---|---|---|---|---|---|---|---|
  | Strongly Disagree | | | Neutral | | | | Strongly Agree |

- *Rankings.* This item asks respondents to indicate priorities or preferences. *Example:* Please rank each topic in order of its importance or relevance to your job: 1 = most important to 5 = least important.

- *Checklist.* A checklist provides a "laundry list" from which participants can choose words that express their reactions. *Example:* Check the words that describe your reaction to today's session:

  _____ Exceeded my expectations

  _____ Met my expectations

  _____ Fell short of my expectations

A question could also be added focusing on the impact of the session on the participant, designed to obtain a deeper and more personal response, for example:

"Imagine that a co-worker(or friend) of yours is thinking about attending this program. He or she asks you: 'What was this program like for you?' How would you respond?"

**Evaluation Form Guidelines.**  Evaluation forms are more difficult to construct than you might imagine. Use the following guidelines:

- Keep the form brief. Participants should be able to complete it quickly.

- Create a balance among the various types of information you are collecting. For example, do not ask five questions about the instructor and only two about content.

- Obtain participants' immediate reactions. Have participants complete the evaluation before they leave the room. This will ensure that you receive a 100 percent response rate. It will also prevent "mob mentality" response, the possibility of several people getting together to discuss the class either before or while they are completing the evaluation.

**Interviews.**  In addition to the end-of-session questionnaires, you can use interviews to increase the reliability of the data collected from the questionnaires. This method of data collection is quite flexible, allowing the interviewer to probe for more specific answers and to clarify questions as needed. The method also allows the interviewer to record spontaneous answers and, therefore, get a more complete picture of the participants' reactions. The interviewer can explore in more detail the reactions gleaned from the questionnaires.

Plan on spending about thirty minutes per interview. You will not be able to interview every participant, so select a random sample. It is important to hold the interviews within one week of the session so that the experience is fresh in their minds. Through one-on-one interviews, you can further explore the reasons for participants' reactions and solicit suggestions for improvement. Either tape the interviews and have them transcribed, allowing you to analyze or interpret the responses more thoroughly, or simply take notes during the interviews.

When developing the interview questions, do not duplicate the questions on the written form. Instead, ask specific questions about the methods used or the content covered. For example, below are several questions about the methods used in a training session on leadership:

- What feelings did you have about the methods used in the program?

- What did you like about the jigsaw design?

- What did you like about the learning tournament?
- What didn't you like about the jigsaw design?
- What didn't you like about the learning tournament?

## Level 2: Learning

Level 2 evaluation deals with what the participants actually learned during the training session. Kirkpatrick defines learning as the "extent to which participants change attitudes, improve knowledge, and/or increase skill as a result of attending the program" (Kirkpatrick, 1994). It is far easier to determine what new knowledge or skills the participants acquired than to find the ways in which the training changed their opinions, values, and beliefs.

The three most appropriate methods used to evaluate learning are tests, observation, and interviews, with tests being the most frequent. See Table 13.2 for a summary of the advantages and disadvantages of each method.

**Tests.** Testing should be kept fairly simple. Many trainers give both a pre-test and a post-test to get an even more accurate picture of what the participants have learned.

*Types of tests.* First determine whether you want to construct subjective (short-answer or essay) or objective (multiple-choice or true-false) items or even a combination of the two types. When constructing test items, consider the time needed to grade the test as well as the validity and reliability of each item. Make sure the test assesses the learning as specified in the learning objectives. When an item measures what it is supposed to measure, it has validity. Each test item must also be reliable, that is, give consistent results from one application to another. For a broader discussion of test construction, refer to "Testing for Learning Outcomes" by Deborah Grafinger Hacker, one of the INFO-LINE booklets published by the American Society for Training and Development (revised in 1998). Hacker describes various types of tests, provides directions on writing test items, discusses measuring the validity and reliability of tests, and includes a helpful and extensive resource list.

Make sure the test is meaningful. Instead of asking for simple information or factual recall, ask questions that require the participants to apply or interpret what they learned in the session.

*Question Formats.* All multiple-choice questions consist of a stem and a response. The stem presents a problem, asks a question, or takes the form of an incomplete statement. Responses include possible answers, all of which must be plausible. The

On the WEB

**Table 13.2.  Level 2 Evaluation Methods**

| Method | Advantages | Disadvantages |
|---|---|---|
| **Tests:** | | |
| Objectives tests | Easy to score | Difficult to write |
| Multiple choice | Inexpensive to use | Time-consuming to write |
| Matching | | |
| True-False | | |
| Fill-in | | |
| Subjective tests | Easy to write | Grading is time-consuming |
| Essay | Inexpensive to create | Expensive to grade |
| Short answers | | |
| **Observation:** | | |
| Observe behavior in class | Immediate application | Subjective, open to interpretation |
| Skills demonstrated in skills | Lends itself to on-the-spot | Unable to spend adequate time |
| practices and learning activity | coaching and feedback | observing behavior of all participants |
| **Interviews:** | | |
| Individual interviews conducted | Can gather more detailed | Time-consuming; expensive |
| shortly after the training | information | Must be tightly structured to obtain |
| Random sampling of participants | Instant feedback | quantifiable responses |

*The Trainer's Handbook, Updated Ed.* Copyright © 2009 by Karen Lawson. Reproduced by permission of Pfeiffer, an imprint of John Wiley & Sons, Inc.

greater the number of items, the better the test's reliability. Following are some formats to consider:

- *Correct Answer.* The correct-answer format asks a simple question to which there is only one correct answer. It is used primarily to test the recall of facts. This type of question is appropriate to test product knowledge, for example.

- *Best Answer.* With this type of question, there is more than one correct choice. Some or all of the choices may be correct to some degree. Because the best-answer question requires a higher level of thinking, the respondent must evaluate the choices and draw conclusions. This type of question can create many problems. Because the answer is open to interpretation, the test item can be challenged quite easily, and you might find yourself either arguing with the individual or group and most probably having to give credit for other answers.

- *Combined Response.* This question is the most complicated and time-consuming for both the test writer and the test taker. The choices, one or more that may be correct, are numbered. A second set of choices lists combinations of possible correct responses. This type of question assesses complex cognitive skills and the ability to analyze and evaluate. Exercise a great deal of thought when writing the item. Because of its complexity, the respondent will probably have to spend more time thinking about the item.

*Test-Writing Guidelines.* In most cases, you will probably choose to develop multiple-choice questions. They are easy to grade, but not necessarily easy to write. To help you construct a multiple-choice test that will provide valuable information about the participants' content mastery, consider the following guidelines:

- Avoid "all of the above" and "none of the above" options.

- Make sure the stem (the main part of the question) contains most of the information and defines the problem; place blanks for fill-ins near the end.

- Maintain grammatical consistency or parallel structure for both the stem and the answer choices.

- Try to create choices of equal length.

- Avoid ambiguity and reading difficulty by stating questions in the positive rather than in the negative.

- Keep the sentence stem simple and limit it to one idea.

- Use conversational language when phrasing the item and its choices.

- Arrange the questions in logical order.

- Do not give clues to the correct answer in the question.

To gauge retention of the information learned in the program, administer another test several months following the training.

**Observation.** Trainers can watch participants practicing and applying skills, tools, and techniques during the session. As the trainers observe participant behavior in skill practices, role plays, simulations, case studies, and other activities, they can get a good idea of what the trainees have really learned.

**Interviews.** Shortly after the training, interview the participants and ask them what they learned in the session. Conduct the interviews within the week following the session.

## Level 3: Behavior

The critical question answered by Level 3 is, "How has the training affected the way participants perform on the job?"

Although both managers and training professionals agree that the success of a training program is determined by what the participants do with the information or skills back on the job, these results are often ignored. Level 3 evaluation is both time-consuming and costly. It also requires good organizational and follow-up skills and processes.

**Purpose of Level 3 Evaluation.** Use follow-up evaluation to do the following:

- Measure lasting results of the training

- Identify areas in which trainees show greatest and least improvement

- Compare follow-up and end-of-program responses

**Follow-Up Guidelines.** Use these guidelines for follow-up evaluation:

- Prepare participants. At the end of the training session, tell participants that you will be conducting a follow-up evaluation and what type of evaluation it will be.

- If the training wasn't effective, find out why. Encourage participants to identify reasons why they haven't improved and what factors obstruct their progress. Sometimes there are factors that inhibit or prevent the application of the new knowledge and skills on the job. These barriers might include poor environmental conditions, lack of proper equipment, the supervisor, existing policies and procedures, or even the organizational climate.

- Share follow-up evaluations with participants' managers or supervisors. These individuals should know about program results and follow-up information and should be involved with the participants' practice and application of training.

**Observations.** The trainer or another designated observer can actually observe employees back on the job. Carefully watch employees as they perform their routine job tasks and responsibilities. To facilitate the process and ensure consistency in the data gathering, create a checklist of desired behaviors and then observe whether or not the employee is demonstrating these behaviors.

For example, if you are observing someone who has recently attended a customer service program, your list of customer service behaviors might look like this:

 _____ Smiles.

 _____ Greets customer with "Good morning" or "Good afternoon."

 _____ Uses the customer's name.

 _____ Asks "How may I help you?"

 _____ Offers additional assistance.

 _____ Gives the customer choices.

 _____ States what we can do, rather than what we can't.

**Interviews.** Not only should you interview those who went through the training, but you should interview those who are affected by or closely associated with the program participants. Possible interviewees include the participants' managers, coworkers, customers, or subordinates. The interview questions would have to be carefully constructed and designed to focus on specific applications and behavior changes.

**Surveys.** Surveys are more efficient and less expensive than interviews to find out whether the participants are actually applying what they learned. Once again, do not limit your sources of information. Others who interact with those who participated in the training are often a more reliable source of feedback. You will want to know not only if trainees are using the training on the job but also how they are using it to perform better.

A control group is also helpful for a Level 3 evaluation. To validate your results, choose a control group of employees from the same function as the participants who received the training. Ask the members of the control group to complete the same surveys, questionnaires, and tests as those completed by the participants. Monitor their job performance and compare it with that of employees who received training.

Regardless of which evaluation method(s) you use, make sure you allow enough time for the behavior change to take place. The length of time depends on the program, but three to six months should give the participants ample opportunity to apply what they learned and develop new behaviors.

## Level 4: Results

Level 4 evaluation determines the impact of the training on the organization. Ideally, it shows how the training has contributed to accomplishing organizational goals and objectives—business results. If an organization chooses to conduct a Level 4 evaluation, the area of measurement must be the same as those identified in the needs assessment.

To measure training's impact on the bottom line, return to the data gathered during the needs assessment. Determine your critical success factors up-front. Results measured could include any of the following or any measurable item:

- Production output
- Sales
- Operating costs
- Customer satisfaction
- Quality standards
- Safety record
- Turnover rate
- Absenteeism
- Employee grievances
- Employee satisfaction
- Budget variances
- Promotions

Level 4 evaluation is both difficult and time-consuming. It can also be quite costly. It is difficult to measure because of the many variables that can come into play once the participants leave the session. For these reasons, a Level 4 evaluation is not appropriate for all training. From a practical standpoint, consider Level 4 for those programs that are near and dear to senior management and have been identified as a top priority.

Because of the complexity of Level 4 evaluation and its infrequency of use, it is addressed here only in very basic terms—just enough to give you an idea of what it involves and the purpose it serves. To explore Level 4 in more detail, refer to the listings in Appendix B, including Jack Phillips, Jane Holcomb, Donald Kirkpatrick, and Dana Gaines Robinson and James Robinson.

As a starting point, test your current knowledge of measurement terms by matching the terms in the left-hand column below with the correct definitions in the right-hand column (see Appendix A for the correct answers):

**Term**

_____ 1. Return on Investment (ROI)

_____ 2. Direct Costs

_____ 3. Indirect Costs

_____ 4. Overhead

_____ 5. Development Costs

_____ 6. Hard Data

_____ 7. Soft Data

_____ 8. Compensation for Participants

**Definition**

a. Survey data of employee attitudes

b. Salaries and benefits paid to participants for the time they are attending the program

c. Expenses for creating the training program

d. Involves quantity, quality, cost, time; easily converted to monetary value

e. Costs of shared resources such as heating and building maintenance

f. Expenses of operating the training department that are not directly related to any training program

g. Mathematical formula for calculating the difference between cost and value

h. Costs related to the delivery of the for training program, such as materials and trainer's salary

# Participant Evaluation and Accountability for e-Learning

Unlike traditional evaluations, e-learning evaluations are somewhat difficult because of delivery options and individual learning solutions that often prevent consistency and uniformity in the evaluation process. For example, not all learners will complete self-study courses from start to finish. Some will choose only the modules they think they need. Others may have to go back and repeat a module to gain a greater understanding of its content.

For the most part, however, you can apply the same principles and strategies of traditional evaluation methods and levels discussed earlier in this chapter to the e-learning process. The basic difference, of course, is that the various evaluation methods will be done electronically. The following are types of evaluations that can be adapted to an e-learning environment.

Level 1 evaluation measures participants' reactions. Methods that can be used include questionnaires completed on-screen within the course or as e-mail feedback. Participant reactions can also be captured via online focus groups or in chat rooms.

Level 2, which measures what participants actually learned, uses various tests. Almost all types of tests can be adapted to an electronic format: true-false, multiple-choice, essay, fill-in-blanks, matching. Visit William Horton's website (www.horton.com) for great examples of various testing formats. In addition to testing, you can monitor learners by observing their behavior in learning activities such as simulations and learning games as well as role plays conducted in chat rooms.

To evaluate how well participants apply what they learned (Level 3), you would turn to traditional methods such as observations of the employee's on-the-job performance, surveys completed by the participant and others who interact with him or her, and job performance records. It might also be appropriate to set up control groups: some employees would experience traditional classroom-based training while others would engage in e-learning activities. Employees' individual action plans could also be monitored.

Level 4 evaluation for distance learning is much the same as it is for traditional learning and would involve determining return on investment (ROI) as well as determining benefits such as a decrease in the number of accidents, safety violations, tardiness, absenteeism, turnover, customer complaints, or grievances. Business metrics such as profitability (sales, revenues, profit) and financial health (stock price, market share) might also be targeted for Level 4 evaluation.

As with any evaluation process, it is important to collaborate with the organization's leaders to determine the success criteria. What specifically do the key people want to measure and how will they use the information? In addition to the basic questions addressed in the section on the four levels of evaluation, you may also be interested in evaluating the e-learning process by establishing ways to measure the following:

- How often users log in
- How long they stay
- How long before they receive a response to a question
- How efficient the online system is

# Accountability for Training

Throughout the business world, accountability for all functions is increasing. Staff functions such as training are expected to prove their contribution and value to the organization. Top executives are demanding that training departments offer proof of their worth or take budget cuts. Two approaches to measuring the value of training are covered below: (1) cost/benefit analysis and (2) return on investment.

## Cost/Benefit Analysis

The cost/benefit analysis looks at the total cost to produce a training program and attempts to quantify the benefits. Cost includes everything from the needs assessment, through design, development, delivery, and finally to follow-up. Both direct and indirect costs are used to determine the total cost of the program. As Table 13.3 shows, determining training costs is complex.

Total benefits of the program may be reduced costs or increased revenues directly attributable to the training. In many cases, however, benefits can only be estimated.

Subtract the total costs from the total benefits to find the net benefit of the training program. The program is considered a financial success if the costs are lower than the benefits.

## Return on Investment

The return on investment simply shows what the payback is for the training program. To determine return on investment, you must wait three to six months and even longer for operational results. The formula for determining return on

**Table 13.3. Determining Training Costs**

| | **Direct Costs** | | |
| | **People** | **Facilities** | **Materials** |
|---|---|---|---|
| Design and Development | Salaries, benefits, travel for: course development, clerical support or consultant fee and expense or costs of certifying in-house trainer for purchased programs | | Marketing brochures<br>Participant materials<br>Instructor manual<br>Purchased resource materials<br>Purchased program |
| Delivery | Salaries, benefits, travel for: trainer(s), participants (average salary), clerical support, consultant fees and expenses | Room rental<br>Equipment rental<br>Refreshments | Notebooks<br>Folders<br>Tent cards<br>Paper<br>Pencils/pens<br>Flip charts<br>Handouts<br>Film rental/purchase<br>Transparencies/slides<br>Stationery items<br>Certificates<br>Books<br>Articles reprints |

**Table 13.3. Determining Training Costs, Cont'd.**

### Direct Costs

| People | Facilities | Materials |
|---|---|---|
| Salaries, benefits, travel for: training personnel, participants, clerical support, bosses, subordinates, peers | | Surveys<br>Questionnaires |

*(Evaluation)*

### Indirect Costs

| | | |
|---|---|---|
| Training space<br>Custodial services<br>Utilities<br>Postage<br>Telephone | | Computer time<br>Equipment depreciation<br>Equipment<br>Maintenance/repair<br>Support services |

*The Trainer's Handbook, Updated Ed.* Copyright © 2009 by Karen Lawson. Reproduced by permission of Pfeiffer, an imprint of John Wiley & Sons, Inc.

investment: ROI = (net program benefits/program costs) × 100. Stated simply, if training programs fail to show a reasonable return on the company's investment, future (or even current) training initiatives are at risk. For more information on determining ROI, refer to Jack Phillips's books listed in Appendix B.

## Significance of the Evaluation Process

Evaluation is a complex issue. For one reason, many variables enter into the equation. No matter how hard you try to fine-tune the evaluation process, the reality is that effects can only be estimated, and economic benefits cannot be calculated precisely. As the role of training continues to change and trainers reposition themselves as performance consultants, there will be more pressure to measure the effectiveness of training. The good news, however, is that the field of training and development continues to grow at a rapid pace. This trend will continue to provide many opportunities for training professionals, both internal and external, to make an impact on the growth and development of individuals and organizations throughout the world.

## KEY POINTS

- Evaluation must be tied to the needs assessment process.

- Evaluation should reflect specific business-related or performance-related outcomes.

- Evaluation is an ongoing process.

- Level 1 evaluation measures participant reaction.

- Level 2 evaluation uses tests, observations, and interviews to measure participant learning.

- Level 3 evaluation measures behavior, that is, how the participants apply what they learned back on the job.

- Level 4 evaluation measures results and training's impact on the bottom line.

- A cost/benefit analysis looks at the benefits of a training program compared to the cost to produce a training program.

- Return on investment addresses the degree to which the cost of a program yields a reasonable return on investment.

The training process is a never-ending cycle: analysis, design, development, implementation, and evaluation. As mentioned several times throughout this book, the role of the training professional continues to evolve. Often the trainer fills many roles, including that of a consultant. Whether internal or external, the training consultant must always be mindful of the process and the business of consulting. Chapter 14 addresses the role of the consultant and the key elements of a successful client-consultant relationship.

# Chapter 14

## The Business of Consulting
*Internal and External*

---

**LEARNING OUTCOMES**

In this chapter, you will learn

- To define the role of the training consultant

- To identify the key elements of a successful client-consultant relationship

- To adapt consulting behaviors and strategies to your own client-consultant relationships

---

## The Changing Role of the Trainer

Today's training professionals are expected to do much more than provide good training programs. They are moving from trainer to consultant, from product-centered to client-centered. Their roles are much more focused on meeting business needs and solving business problems. They are seen as change agents and learning leaders.

The growing number of client-consultant relationships means that we need to place a greater emphasis on developing these relationships through various skills and strategies.

Although there are many types and aspects of consulting within the field of human resource development, this chapter will focus on the role and function of the training consultant, both internal and external, as well as the client-consultant relationship.

# Understanding the Client-Consultant Relationship

The key word here is *relationship.* Today's client-consultant relationship, whether internal or external, tends to be one of partnering.

## Defining Terms

Whether internal or external, the definitions are the same, as are the functions. A *consultant* is the person who uses his or her professional expertise to influence, advise, and assist others in solving business-related problems. The *client* is the person who "owns" the business-related problem and who has the authority to implement the solution. While it is true that the participants in your session are also your clients, they are not the decision makers. Their reaction to you and your training, however, can have a profound influence and impact on the success or failure of the project and on the decision maker's reaction to your work.

## Establishing the Relationship

The first step is to identify your client as defined above. Then determine what the client wants/expects from you. This is where your questioning skills come into play.

It is important that you tell your clients what you can do and what you cannot do, based on the desired performance outcomes they have clearly articulated. For example, if a client tells you his or her desired outcome is to provide customer service training to front-line employees and the client wants you to do this in two hours, you need to explain what you can and cannot do given those time constraints.

### EXAMPLE

When I was an internal training consultant for a bank, we had developed a three-week teller training program. Our competency-based program was heavily focused on skill development. As a result, at the end of the three weeks, we could guarantee that each graduate of the program could begin immediately working on a teller window with little or no need for the supervisor to provide additional training. The supervisor, of course, would be expected to conduct ongoing coaching and feedback sessions. One day, a branch manager called me to request that the new teller she hired be sent to her branch after only one week of training. The manager said she was short-staffed and needed someone immediately. I tried to explain to her that it would be better to wait until the new teller had gone through the entire program, but the manager insisted. I then explained (and put in a memo to the manager) what we could do with the teller in only one week of training. I further explained what they could expect of the teller's performance after one week of training and what someone at the branch would need to do to complete the new employee's training. The manager agreed. As it turned out, two weeks after the new teller started at the branch, the manager called, admitted she was wrong not to allow the teller to complete the teller-training course, and requested that the teller return to the program to complete her formal training.

## Use a Collaborative Approach

The most successful client-consultant relationships are collaborative and interdependent. The client and consultant need to view each other as partners, working together for the main purpose of improving performance and meeting a business need. What is the reason for a collaborative approach? This approach establishes mutual responsibility and joint accountability that increases the probability of a more accurate diagnosis of the problem, an assurance that training will be linked to a business need, and a greater likelihood that management will reinforce the training.

As the owner of the problem, the client drives the project; the consultant assumes several roles, including a coach, a change agent, and a learning leader.

At the outset, both parties must participate in establishing the goals for the training project. These goals, however, cannot be established until a needs assessment has been conducted at various levels. In addition to business needs, the consultant should address performance needs, training needs, and environment needs. Performance needs are on-the-job behaviors performed at defined levels of excellence. Training needs focus on what people must know and be able to do in order to succeed at business and performance goals. Environment needs deal with systems and processes within the environment that must be modified for the performance to be achieved. Although the training consultant cannot deal directly with these issues, he or she can make recommendations.

The needs assessment is critical to the success of the project. In some cases, training is not the answer. There may be processes, policies, systems, or even the organization's culture that need to be "fixed," not the people identified for training.

When designing a program, be sure the learning objectives are stated in terms of skills that ultimately will link to the organization's bottom line. Training needs to be positioned not as an activity or an event but rather as a vehicle for accomplishing business results. Successful training consultants will expand their thinking from traditional classroom to "any time, any place, and any way" learning. As discussed in Chapter 10, the consultant may need to embrace other ways of delivering training.

Once the needs assessment has been completed and agreed-on goals have been established, both the client and consultant need to be clear about their level of commitment in allocating the necessary time, money, and people to the project. In today's environment, collaboration may also involve others beyond the actual client such as outside contractors, internal subject-matter experts, and line managers.

## Helping Others Understand What You Can and Cannot Do

Sometimes the greatest challenge in establishing a client-consultant relationship is the way in which the training function is viewed by the decision makers in the organization. Sometimes key people see training as only a support and, therefore, a reactive function. If that is the case, then it is the consultant's job to "enlighten" them. This is particularly true for those who are internal consultants. One way to begin to change the way in which internal consultants function and to help others see the value that an internal consultant brings to the organization is to write a position paper that puts forth the role of training and how training can play a critical role in meeting business needs. Below is a sample outline for a position paper on the role of training and development. All you need to do is to fill in the details.

## Sample Outline for Position Paper

**The Role of Training and Development in XYZ Company**

I. Background

    A. Traditional role of training

    B. Changing role of training

    C. Factors/trends influencing changing role

        1. Competition

        2. Customer sophistication and expectations

        3. Downsizing

        4. Diversity and globalization

     5. Employee skill level and competence

     6. Increased use of technology

   D. Definitions

     1. Training—specific usable skills; current application

     2. Staff development—acquiring of knowledge, skills, attitudes; future oriented

II. Training

   A. Function

     1. Internal consultants

     2. Help solve business problems

   B. Objectives

     1. Advise line managers

     2. Develop programs based on needs assessments

     3. Provide effective and cost-effective training

     4. Meet business needs

   C. Process

     1. Assess needs

     2. Determine appropriate programs

     3. Design, develop, implement programs

     4. Monitor and evaluate selected approach

     5. Reinforce training

III. Staff Development

   A. Administer Career Development Program

   B. Serve as resource center

   C. Help managers provide career counseling

IV. Conclusion

## Communication

Ongoing and open communication is essential to a successful client-consultant relationship. Both parties need to be proficient in several communication skills such as questioning, listening, giving and receiving feedback, and negotiating. To ensure that communication is on target with both the client's and the consultant's expectations, be sure to clearly address the following questions:

- What do we communicate?
- How do we communicate?
- How much do we communicate?
- How often do we communicate?

To avoid any misunderstanding, put communication in writing. This includes schedules, meeting agendas, meeting summaries, and feedback reports or summaries.

## Responsiveness

In a client-consultant relationship, responsiveness relates to the degree and willingness to react to change, answer questions, and provide information. Flexibility is a key characteristic or behavior for both the client and the consultant in responding to each other's needs and building a successful relationship.

Indicators of poor responsiveness include the following:

### On the Part of the Consultant

- Not returning phone calls or responding to e-mail or faxes
- Not understanding the client's needs, goals, and objectives
- Not providing information as requested
- Not being accessible or available for meetings

### On the Part of the Client

- Changing dates or requirements at the last minute
- Canceling meetings
- Not providing requested information
- Delaying payment (in the case of external consultants)

The proposal phase is the first major opportunity for both to demonstrate their responsiveness. Does the consultant respond to the client's request for a proposal within the requested timeframe? Does the client respond to the consultant's proposal in a timely manner, letting the consultant know the status of the proposal submission?

A good proposal should include the following elements:

**Background/Purpose.** This section reflects the consultant's understanding of the client's reason for requesting a proposal and may include references to organizational issues, trends in the industry, and specifically stated development needs.

**Organizational Benefits.** Stated somewhat broadly, this section addresses the benefits to the organization. In other words, what improvements will the organization experience as a result of the consultant's proposed intervention, training, and so on? Examples of benefits include improvements in communication, internal cooperation, employee performance; increased sales; decreased turnover, errors, accidents; and so forth.

**Approach/Design.** In this section, the consultant outlines how he or she will approach the project. A more detailed and involved training or consulting project might present project phases such as needs assessment, program design and development, delivery, evaluation, and follow-up. A fairly simple and straightforward training program might only require the consultant to present a program description that would include an outline of the training session, learning objectives, length of session, number of participants, format, and materials.

**Deliverables.** The client needs to know what he or she will be getting for the money invested. These deliverables could include materials, reports, training delivery, and so on. Often the client will want the consultant to offer several options. For example, the consultant might propose that a training program to be delivered multiple times could be delivered by the consultant (or consultant's associates), or the consultant could conduct a train-the-trainer licensing session to enable the client's internal staff to deliver the training. These various options, of course, need to be clearly reflected in the fee structure.

**Client Investment.** A section should be devoted to consultant fees and other costs, including meetings, development or preparation, delivery, materials, travel expenses, and so forth. The consultant should also address his or her policy regarding payment. Does the consultant expect a portion of the fee at the beginning of the project or will the client be billed for everything at the end? Are participant materials included in the fee or is there a per participant fee?

Although the proposal outline above applies to external consulting, it can be adapted for use by an internal consultant.

## Expectations

Both the client and the consultant should be clear about the expectations each has of the other. Both parties should participate in the contracting stage to set the stage for how they are going to work together. Once they have come to an agreement as to what each party will and will not do, then this understanding should be put in writing in the form of a contract or a letter of agreement. In most cases, the information included in the contract is taken from the proposal.

The following elements should be included in the contract or letter of agreement:

- Description of services
- Deliverables
- Nature and scope of project
- Timetable
- Methods
- What each party will provide
- How client and consultant will work together
- Reporting procedures
- Fees
- Payment terms
- Confidentiality agreement

# Selecting an External Consultant

As more organizations downsize their human resources and/or training departments, they look to outside service providers. This "belt tightening" also results in more service providers competing for business in the marketplace. With so many resources available, how does the client choose the right consultant for the right project? The following section offers some guidelines for selecting an external consultant.

## Trust

Trust is a nebulous term and difficult to define. It is, however, the core of a successful and effective client-consultant relationship. It is actually the result of the other elements already mentioned and is more closely related to professional ethics.

Trust doesn't happen overnight. It takes time to build a relationship that relies on the honesty, integrity, and ability of another person. Think about your client-consultant relationships. How strong is the trust factor? Use the following checklist to evaluate the level of trust that exists in your own client-consultant relationship, with 1 being low and 4 being high.

**What's Your Trust Quotient?**

To what degree do you trust the other person to. . .

| | | | | |
|---|---|---|---|---|
| Maintain confidentiality | 1 | 2 | 3 | 4 |
| Respect your opinions | 1 | 2 | 3 | 4 |
| Give open and honest feedback | 1 | 2 | 3 | 4 |
| Receive feedback without becoming defensive | 1 | 2 | 3 | 4 |
| Deliver what he/she promises | 1 | 2 | 3 | 4 |
| Meet deadlines | 1 | 2 | 3 | 4 |
| Communicate expectations | 1 | 2 | 3 | 4 |
| View/treat you as a partner in the process | 1 | 2 | 3 | 4 |
| Share credit for success | 1 | 2 | 3 | 4 |

An interdependent partnership approach to the client-consultant relationship will produce better results and will often yield benefits that far exceed expectations.

## Sources

In many cases, the person assigned to select an external consultant may not know where to begin the search. The following sources can help save time and money in identifying potential outside resources:

- Internal sources (managers, other human resources professionals)
- Colleagues in other organizations
- Professional organizations
- Consultants organization has used before
- Industry publications

## Selection Criteria

Once you have identified and narrowed the list of potential training consultants, the next challenge is to choose the one with the best "fit" for your particular organization and project. Use the following checklist to help make the right choice:

- Experience in your industry
- Knowledge and experience with the topic
- Length of time in business
- Knowledge of your industry
- Knowledge of your organization
- Knowledge and experience in the field of HRD
- Track record of results
- Quality of materials
- Image/professionalism
- Involvement in professional organizations
- Representative clients
- Publications
- Geographic locations
- Available resources
- Approach/philosophy
- Fees
- Ability to identify need
- Degree of flexibility
- Level of commitment

Begin to evaluate consultant candidates by carefully reviewing each consultant's written material, keeping in mind, however, that these materials have been designed and written as selling tools.

When you interview potential service providers, use behavioral interviewing skills and open-ended questions to identify whether or not the consultant meets a particular criterion. For example, if you want to know about the consultant's track record, you might ask: "Tell me about your most successful client experience." Other probing questions might include:

- "What do you think is the most important aspect of a client-consultant relationship?"
- "What do you know about our organization?"
- "What sets you apart from other consultants?"

- "How long have you been in business?"
- "What has been the most challenging consulting project you have ever had?"
- "How large is your organization?"

# Follow-Up Reports

At the end of a project, the consultant should prepare and submit a follow-up report to the client. Although the content of the report will vary depending on the type and scope of the project, every report should have certain common elements.

### Executive Summary

- An abbreviated, concise, accurate representation of a report, document, or publication
- Spells out the purpose of the report and the approach it will take
- Also called an abstract, overview, or a précis

### Purpose

- Brief explanation of why the project or program was implemented in the first place
- Statement of the problem

### Process

- Methods or approach used to solve problem
- Scope, including length of time, and number of people involved

### Measurable Results/Outcomes

- Present specific outcomes tied directly to the business need
- Reflect any or all of the four levels of evaluation: reaction, learning, behavior, results

### Conclusions and Recommendations

- Outlines next steps
- Suggests further training, interventions, methods or measurement, organizational changes, modifications to existing systems, new policies and procedures

## KEY POINTS

- The consultant is the person (internal or external) who uses his or her professional expertise to help solve business-related problems.

- The client is the person who "owns" the business-related problem and who has the authority to implement the solution.

- Partnership and collaboration are the keys to a successful client-consultant relationship.

- Both the client and the consultant should establish clear expectations for each other.

- Trust is a critical component of the client-consultant relationship.

As you have learned (or perhaps already knew), there is more to training than standing in front of a group and spewing forth information accompanied by a glitzy slide presentation. Training is not an event—it is a process, one that involves thoughtful preparation and purposeful delivery.

Training that makes a difference reflects the following principles and approaches:

- Session content provides participants with what they "need to know" to do their jobs and to succeed.

- There is a balance among affective, behavioral, and cognitive learning.

- The program incorporates a variety of active learning techniques.

- Participants have many opportunities to practice skills and behaviors.

- The program focuses on real-life problem solving and back-on-the-job application.

When training is active, participants do most of the work. They use their brains—studying ideas, solving problems, and applying what they learn. Participants learn to think, not merely absorb. Active training is not only fun, fast-paced, and personally engaging, but it really works!

# Chapter 15

## Training During Tough Times

---

**LEARNING OUTCOMES**

In this chapter, you will learn

- To identify ways to maximize your training dollars

- To use internal resources to reduce training costs

- To leverage technology and nonconventional training to maintain the integrity of the training function

---

When times get tough, training is among the first things to go (or it is considerably scaled back). As workplace learning professionals know, the opposite should happen, but that's not reality. Training dollars as well as training resources are spread thin during economic downturns. So what does that mean for those of us who are committed to keeping the training function "alive" during tough economic times? It means that we have to be even more creative, more resourceful, and most important, more business focused.

We must become not only more agile in adapting to change but more business savvy and further develop our business acumen.

The purpose of this chapter is to give you some techniques and strategies for belt tightening without sacrificing the integrity of your training programs.

## Prove the Value of Training

By far the most important strategy is proving the value of training. As competitive pressures increase and profit margins shrink, training expenses will be more closely scrutinized. As a result, quantifying the impact of training and development programs will be a major priority. Make sure you are practicing the evaluation methods, including ROI, discussed in Chapter 13. It is extremely important to link evaluation to the needs analysis and to make sure that training focuses on performance-based outcomes that can be measured. Arm yourself with figures. You want to be able to show how you can save money by comparing your training plan with past figures. If you have not tracked results, now is the time to start.

Another important consideration in proving the value of training is to tie it to the strategic plan. You need to make a connection between training initiatives and business objectives. As you go forward, document everything you do and quantify whenever possible.

Doing more training with less money requires you to leverage technology and nontraditional methods to stretch training dollars. The following are specific measures you can take to deliver quality training on a shoestring or "no-string" budget.

## Peer Teaching

Peer teaching can be delivered one-on-one or in group settings. Internal experts meet with their colleagues who need to learn about specific skills and acquire an understanding of a particular area or discipline. These sessions can take place within individual departments or across business units. The benefits in both situations are improved communication throughout the organization, a growing sense of teamwork, and an expansion of knowledge about all aspects of the organization.

As mentioned in Chapter 3, technical proficiency alone does not make a trainer. For that reason, you need to be careful in selecting people to train others. Use the checklist in Exhibit 15.1 to select potential trainers.

Once selected, the designated trainers will need some guidance in structuring their approach to training. To help peer trainers teach a task or a procedure, introduce them to the following Model for Teaching a Task or Procedure (Exhibit 15.2) and guide them through the process by using the Worksheet for Teaching a Task (Exhibit 15.3).

**EXHIBIT 15.1.    Checklist for Selecting Peer Trainers**

When selecting potential peer trainers, ask yourself the following questions:
Does this employee . . .

☐  1. Have the appropriate level of technical knowledge and experience?

☐  2. Perform well above average and meet or exceed job standards and
expectations?

☐  3. Communicate well by organizing thoughts, choosing appropriate words,
and speaking clearly and distinctly?

☐  4. Practice good time management by completing assignments on time,
organizing duties logically, and breaking down projects into tasks and
subtasks?

☐  5. Get along well with people at all levels of the organization?

☐  6. Exemplify in both manner and appearance those qualities you want
others to emulate?

☐  7. View training assignments as opportunities for professional development
rather than as intrusions on daily routines?

☐  8. Exercise patience and self-control even when things are not going well?

☐  9. Look for ways to improve the job, welcome new ideas, and regard change
positively?

☐ 10. Display non-arrogant confidence in his or her ability to do the job?

☐ 11. Support the philosophy and goals of the organization?

☐ 12. Practice as well as believe in teamwork?

## EXHIBIT 15.2.   Model for Teaching a Task or Procedure

### Step One: Speculation

- Assemble appropriate materials and equipment.

- Ask the learner to guess how to do the task or procedure or what particular things he or she would think about or consider when completing the task.

- The purpose of this step is to arouse curiosity and help the learner establish a frame of reference for the actual training that will follow.

### Step Two: Observation

- Have the learner watch as you perform the entire task.

- Give no explanation or answer any questions during this step.

- This step is designed to help the learner concentrate all his or her attention visually on the task at hand.

### Step Three: Explanation

- Explain the task or procedure, giving an overview of the entire job.

- Explain the reason(s) for doing the task and how it fits into the "big picture," including other people or departments that will be impacted.

- This step provides a framework by addressing the *what* and the *why*.

### Step Four: Demonstration

- Show step-by-step *how* the task is done, stressing key points along the way.

- Check for understanding by asking open-ended questions as you demonstrate. Don't simply say, "Do you understand?"

### Step Five: Role Reversal

- Ask the learner to assume the role of the trainer for this step.

- The learner tells you what to do and you do it.

- This step will help identify how well the learner understands what he or she is to do.

**EXHIBIT 15.2. Model for Teaching a Task or Procedure, Cont'd.**

- If the learner says something that is incorrect, it is a judgment call whether to do it as instructed and use the negative consequence as a learning tool or to stop and explain why it is incorrect and what could result.

**Step Six: Performance**

- Ask the learner to perform the operation as you observe.
- Correct mistakes as necessary to prevent reinforcement of bad habits.
- Be sure to give feedback and positive reinforcement.

**Step Seven: Practice**

- Put the learner on his or her own to practice.
- Encourage the learner to ask questions and seek help as necessary.
- This step helps the learner become comfortable with the task.

**Step Eight: Monitor and Evaluate**

- Schedule progress checks and gradually taper off.
- Monitor the learner's progress by observing performance and asking questions.
- Measure results against performance standards and objectives.
- Ensure two-way evaluation by giving and soliciting feedback.

## EXHIBIT 15.3.   Worksheet for Teaching a Task

The following is a worksheet to help you prepare to teach someone a task or procedure:

**Preparation**

Name of task/procedure:

Standard of performance (speed, quantity, quality, accuracy, etc.):

Name of learner:

What you know about the learner's experience/skill level relative to this task:

Questions you might ask to find out more about the learner's knowledge, experience, skills level:

Materials/equipment needed for this training:

**Delivery**

Step One: Speculation

   Questions to arouse the learner's curiosity about the task or procedure:

Step Two: Observation

   How you are going to demonstrate the task:

Step Three: Explanation

   What you are going to explain (include key terms, the big picture, and so forth):

Step Four: Demonstration

   Outline the step-by-step procedure:

   Open-ended questions to check for understanding:

| **EXHIBIT 15.3.   Worksheet for Teaching a Task, Cont'd.** |
| --- |

Step Five: Role Reversal

> How you are going to present the role reversal and what you are going to look for from the learner:

Step Six: Performance

> What you expect the learner to demonstrate to you:

Step Seven: Practice

> What you are going to have the learner practice and how much time you are going to allot:

Step Eight: Monitor and Evaluate

> When you will check in with the learner:

> Open-ended questions to ask during follow-up:

---

*The Trainer's Handbook, Updated Ed.* Copyright © 2009 by Karen Lawson. Reproduced by permission of Pfeiffer, an imprint of John Wiley & Sons, Inc.

# Leaders as Teachers

Enlist the services of leaders and other professionals in the organization to serve as guest speakers and trainers. Although for years, training departments have used subject matter experts to deliver very specific content, these folks have been overlooked as valuable resources for so-called soft skills training, notably leadership development. The "leaders as teachers" approach has a two-fold payoff. The most obvious, of course, is that the learners benefit from the leaders sharing their experience, insights, and expertise. The leaders benefit as well by developing their teaching, facilitating, coaching, and mentoring skills far beyond what their normal day-to-day responsibilities require. When they prepare to teach, they gain additional knowledge about various areas of the business, and they come in contact with other leaders in a different context and venue. To ensure the quality of instruction, it is imperative that all internal faculty members participate in a train-the-trainer program. They should also be evaluated on an ongoing basis. Exhibit 15.4 provides a basic outline for a train-the-trainer program.

## EXHIBIT 15.4.    Plan for a Train-the-Trainer Program

**Program Description:**

This program is designed to provide the skills, tools, and techniques necessary to design and deliver a quality training program.

**Time Required:**

Two to three days.

**Learning Outcomes:**

Participants will learn how to . . .

> Assess their learning and training styles.
>
> Write learner-centered, competency-based learning objectives.
>
> Develop a clear and complete plan of instruction.
>
> Develop active learner-centered activities to stimulate learner interaction.
>
> Establish a positive learning climate and increase learner motivation.

**Topical Outline:**

   I.  Introduction and Opening Activities

      A.  Training versus teaching

      B.  Active training principles

      C.  Role of trainer

      D.  Trainer skills, qualities, and characteristics

  II.  Principles of Adult Learning

      A.  How and why adults learn

      B.  Learning styles and teaching styles

 III.  Designing and Developing a Training Program

      A.  Writing instructional objectives

      B.  Writing an instructional plan

      C.  Using active training techniques

| EXHIBIT 15.4. Plan for a Train-the-Trainer Program, Cont'd. |
|---|

IV. Delivering Effective Training

    A. Polishing presentation skills

    B. Using audiovisual aids

    C. Facilitating group discussion

    D. Dealing with difficult participants

V. Closing Activities

    A. Concluding activities

    B. Personal and group action plans

*The Trainer's Handbook, Updated Ed.* Copyright © 2009 by Karen Lawson. Reproduced by permission of Pfeiffer, an imprint of John Wiley & Sons, Inc.

# Negotiate with External Consultants and Service Providers

Most organizations have a relationship with external consultants or service providers. Don't be afraid to contact them and discuss how you can work together to deliver quality training at a reduced cost. Keep in mind that we're all in the same boat. Outside providers, such as independent consultants, consulting firms, and suppliers of packaged training programs, are affected by the same economic conditions that you are. More than likely, they have experienced a decline in their businesses and, therefore, would be more than happy to have some business rather than no business at all. Ask them if they would be willing to take a reduced fee, with the understanding that when the organization's financial situation improves, you can return to normal pricing. You might also suggest that you establish a longer-term payment plan. You could defer payment, spread out payment over a longer period, or transfer part of the cost to the next fiscal budget. Exhibit 15.5 lists areas where you may be able to reduce costs by negotiating with your service providers.

**EXHIBIT 15.5.   Negotiating with Consultants and Service Providers**

The following are some areas where you may be able to cut costs by "cutting deals" with the service provider:

**Fees**

- Reduced fee
- Reduced fee with agreement to "make it up" at a later date
- Reduced fee for delivery by one of the consultant's junior trainers
- Discount for multiple sessions
- Discount for pre-payment

**Payment Schedule**

- Pre-pay in this year's budget for next year's programs
- Defer to next budget year
- Extend payments over longer period

**Cancellation of Postponement Clause**

- "Forgiven" if programs are rescheduled
- Reduced penalty for cancellation or postponement

**Materials**

- Reproduced in-house with no fee
- Licensing fee to reproduce indefinitely or within a certain timeframe

**Expenses**

- Split travel expenses
- Require consultant to use your travel planner
- Establish a standard per diem to cover all expenses

---

**EXHIBIT 15.5.   Negotiating with Consultants and Service Providers, Cont'd.**

---

**Number of People**

- Increase the number of people in a session

- Decrease the number of sessions

- Decrease the length of each session

- Spread out delivery of sessions over a longer period of time

- Deliver shorter sessions "back-to-back"

- Use a variety of delivery methods, such as teleconferencing, to reduce travel expenses and/or participants' time away from work

---

*The Trainer's Handbook, Updated Ed.* Copyright © 2009 by Karen Lawson. Reproduced by permission of Pfeiffer, an imprint of John Wiley & Sons, Inc.

# Supplier/Vendor–Sponsored Training

Many vendors and suppliers offer training as a value-added service. The service may be linked directly or even indirectly to the product or service you are already using. Encourage managers throughout the organization to examine the training options that come with a product and make sure their employees are taking advantage of this service. For example, when I was a training director for a bank, our check supplier offered free mini-training sessions not directly related to the product, such as a two-hour slide presentation on time management.

# Modified Modules

In today's corporate climate, people are under a great deal of pressure to do more with less, and they cannot afford the time away from their job responsibilities to attend an all-day training session. Rather than throwing up your hands in despair at the lack of attendance, adapt to your clients' needs by offering more frequent and shorter sessions. Redesign your programs by chunking them into two-hour modules delivered over a few days or weeks. This approach will also enable you to put more people through the program, although it may be spread out over a longer period of time.

# Lunch and Learn

"Lunch and learn" is a great example of multitasking and is an easy and cost-effective way to deliver training. Very simply, as the name implies, employees bring their lunches and eat them during the training session. Because of their brevity (forty to fifty minutes) and their more informal nature, these sessions should be used for topics such as product training, basic skills training (customer service, for example), personal development, wellness issues, and basic computer skills. These topics could be stand-alone, one-time-only topics, or they could be part of a series. For example, a customer service series might involve the following topics:

- Answering the telephone
- Identifying customer needs
- Dealing with an angry customer
- Solving customer problems

Because of the length and informality, you should not use lunch and learn for heavy or serious topics, such as diversity or sexual harassment, or for training that is mandated, such as compliance. Attendance at a lunch-and-learn session should be voluntary. Exhibit 15.6 is an example of a case study on "Dealing with Interruptions," which can be addressed in a forty-five-minute session. You can use it as a stand-alone piece or as part of a multi-session module on time management.

| EXHIBIT 15.6.    Case Study for "Lunch-and-Learn" Session |

### Dealing with Interruptions

Pat Dawson is a hard-working, dedicated employee, who does whatever she needs to do to meet deadlines. Although she has a lot "on her plate," she readily agreed to work on a special project that her boss asked her to do. This project requires her to devote a significant amount of dedicated, uninterrupted time to think and draft the documents that are needed by her project team. Pat is also the most senior employee in her department and is, therefore, the person others go to for information and help. Pat is a warm, friendly, and helpful person, who graciously drops everything to help someone in need. She believes strongly in internal customer service and responds immediately to people's phone calls and e-mails. In short, Pat is viewed by her boss and colleagues as the ideal employee.

**EXHIBIT 15.6. Case Study for "Lunch-and-Learn" Session, Cont'd.**

On this particular day, Pat is at her desk, frantically working on her portion of the project that is due the next day. Since her boss is on vacation, she has been designated the "go to" person for her department. As she is working on her project, she practices multitasking by responding to her e-mails immediately, answering questions from her co-workers throughout the day, and taking the time to chitchat with several colleagues from other departments who stop by for a brief visit during their breaks.

It is now 6:00 P.M., and Pat has a long way to go to finish her project. She calls home to tell her family she will not be home for hours and that they should have dinner without her. After she hangs up, she sits immobilized, feeling overwhelmed and frustrated.

**Discussion Questions:**

1. What advice do you have for Pat?

2. In what way(s) do you identify with Pat?

3. What should you do or say to those who are interrupting you?

4. What can you do to prevent or minimize your own interruptions in the future?

*Note to Facilitator:* The following are the key learning points you should bring out during the case study discussion:

- Self-management and communication are the most critical skills in dealing with interruptions.

- You cannot completely eliminate interruptions, but you can minimize them.

- You must first exercise self-management by not allowing yourself to be derailed by the interruptions.

- You must tell others what you are doing, explain that you need a certain amount of uninterrupted time in order to work on your task/assignment, and indicate when you will be available.

- If time permits, address other time-management/self-management issues embedded in the case study, such as her inability to say no.

You have a lot of flexibility with delivery. You can deliver the sessions yourself, bring in guest speakers from other areas of the organization, or invite experts from the outside. You will need a room that is private, such as a conference room. Lunchrooms and cafeterias are far too noisy and distracting.

# Podcasting

Podcasting is distributing audio files in a radio-show format over the Internet. It enables you to deliver the right content to the right people—anywhere, anytime. Many people believe that you have to have an iPod to receive and to listen—not so. Many people listen to podcasts on their PCs, portable media players, or smart phones. Podcasting is an economical use of learners' time. They can listen while they are working on something else or during their downtime. Learners can also move at their own pace, choosing to move slower during difficult sections, skimming (or skipping altogether) familiar information. From a dollars-and-cents perspective, podcasting is relatively inexpensive. In fact, you can find low-cost (or even free) software to translate your voice recording into electronic files.

The process is pretty simple:

- Plan what you are going to say and write a script.

- Choose a quiet spot for your recording location.

- Choose a recording device that will enable you to convert your voice into an MP3 format and to upload it to your computer.

- Create electronic files of your voice recording, edit, add music or special effects, and package for distribution.

- Post your podcast and communicate how to access it.

# Teleconferences, Teleseminars, and Web-Casts

Teleconferences and web-casts are efficient and cost-effective ways of delivering training. They are generally delivered in sixty- to ninety-minute segments with very little effort or cost. You can rent bridge lines fairly inexpensively, and some are actually free (with a restriction on number of people). Audioconferencing enables you to deliver training to a large number of people without investing in expensive equipment or paying skyrocketing travel expenses for people to meet at a specific location.

Once again, you might be able to use outside resources, such as your vendors, consultants, or other suppliers. Another source of teleconferences or web-casts might be professional organizations to which people in your organization belong. In most cases, these offerings are no-cost or low-cost to members and their guests. To find out what is available, survey the members of your organization and ask them what professional organizations they belong to. Then research these organizations to find out what educational offerings they have and how your participants can take part.

If you are facilitating teleconferences yourself, use internal experts and just interview them. They will be much more inclined to appear on "your show" if they don't have to prepare much. This is your opportunity to get into the role of a talk-show host. You would, of course, need to think through what information you want the participants to take away, develop your questions, and map out a plan for facilitating the session. You would need to talk briefly with your guest to discuss what you want emphasized and also to go over logistics. You can enhance your teleseminars by expanding to web-conferencing. Web-conferencing allows you to deliver presentations online by providing slides that the participants can download. You also have the capability of making it as interactive as you would like, with activities or question-and-answer segments embedded in the session. For additional ideas on how to make these types of sessions more interactive, refer to Chapter 10.

Also, most companies that offer teleconferencing services have recording capabilities so that the sessions are archived and people can access them at a later time.

The following job aid (Exhibit 15.7) presents guidelines for conducting a teleseminar.

### EXHIBIT 15.7. Guidelines for Conducting a Teleseminar

**Planning**

- Research and select the delivery venue, such as a bridge line or in-house conference capability.

- Determine service features, such as capacity (number of people line can accommodate) and cost, and capabilities, such as recording, muting, access, entry and exit signals.

- Determine topic, length of program, and audience.

- Select presenter(s) and communicate requirements, such as format, timeframe, and materials (handout, slide presentation, etc.).

**EXHIBIT 15.7.  Guidelines for Conducting a Teleseminar, Cont'd.**

- Send announcement and instructions to presenters and participants three to four weeks in advance. Include the following information:

  Date

  Time/length

  Phone number

  Access code

  Links to handouts and/or slides

  Process for connecting to the teleseminar

  Other instructions, such as muting, disabling call waiting, etc.

  Tips on participating

- Prepare presentation. Determine format (lecture, participant interaction, interview, panel, etc.), as well as how you will handle questions.

**Opening**

- Arrive five to ten minutes early so that you are the first to dial in. Test the features (muting, recording, enabling/disabling entry chime).

- Start the call within three minutes of the stated time.

- Greet the participants, introduce yourself, and if appropriate ask the participants to introduce themselves. Set the tone for the session by being upbeat and friendly.

**Facilitating**

- Announce the title of the seminar and explain the format, timeframe, and ground rules, such as muting and how you will handle questions. Questioning options include waiting until the end of the session, asking questions throughout the session, or submitting questions via e-mail or instant messenger.

- Tell the participants that when asking a question or making a comment, the person should state his or her name and then make remarks succinctly.

**EXHIBIT 15.7. Guidelines for Conducting a Teleseminar, Cont'd.**

- Review the agenda and objectives.

- Inform participants that the seminar is being recorded (if it is).

- If applicable, remind them how they can access handouts or slides.

- Introduce the presenter(s). If you are the one presenting the session, tell the audience about yourself as it relates to the topic.

- Throughout the session, generate discussion and engage people by asking questions or asking them to write something down.

- Use your active listening skills to clarify and confirm what the participants are saying.

- Make sure that you do not let one or two people dominate the discussion.

- Maintain your enthusiasm and high energy throughout the session.

- Watch the clock closely and make sure you are staying on schedule.

**Concluding**

- Remind the participants when there are five or ten minutes remaining in the session.

- Summarize the key points of the program.

- Ask participants to share the most important thing they are taking away from the seminar and/or an action item they have identified.

- End the session by thanking the participants and telling them if, when, and how they can access a recording and/or materials.

If you are fairly new to using technology-based delivery methods or are just unsure as to what method to use, refer to Table 15.1 for guidance in making your decision.

**Table 15.1.   Technology-Based Delivery Methods**

|  | **Teleseminar/ Teleconferences**[a] | **Web-Cast/ Web Seminar/ Web Conferences** | **Podcast** |
|---|---|---|---|
| Definition | Using the telephone to deliver seminar—in real time—usually over a bridge line | Sharing what is on your computer desktop with people in other locations—in real time or delayed—over the web; can use telephone and/or Internet for audio | Digital-media files, usually downloaded over the Internet for playback on portable media players and computers |
| Complexity (Developer/Participant) | Low/Low | High/Mid-high | Low/Mid |
| Cost (Developer/Participant[b]) | Low/Low | Mid-high/Free | Low/Free |
| Accessibility: Can "attend"— Anytime Anywhere | No Yes | No/Yes if delayed Yes | Yes Yes |
| Visual presentation | No[c] | Yes | No[c] |
| Level of interaction | Low to Medium | Low to Medium (None if delayed) | None |

[a] Teleseminars can/should be recorded and converted into Podcast.

[b] Presenter can charge for service.

[c] Can be combined with handouts, web downloads, etc.

## Just-in-Time Materials

Training materials such as manuals and assessment tools can be quite costly. Find ways to produce them economically in-house or at your favorite copy center. In both cases, the key to getting a discount is to submit the order weeks or months in advance so there is plenty of time to reproduce them. Keep in mind that the cost is driven by salaries and overhead, not by the actual cost of paper and ink. So the more lead time you can give, the lower the cost to you.

You can also reduce the time and effort on your part, or on members of your staff (particularly if you are short-staffed), by sending materials to participants electronically and asking them to print the materials themselves and bring them to the session. This enables you to eliminate the cost of binders and other hard-copy training aids and materials. Remember that the most important thing is the content, not the packaging.

---

**KEY POINTS**

- Training professionals must be able to prove the value of training.
- Using nonconventional methods is the key to stretching training dollars.

---

According to a song recorded by Billy Ocean in 1985, "When times get tough, the tough get going," meaning that strong people will rise to the occasion. This should be the mantra of all workplace learning professionals who face the daunting task of doing more training with less money. Use the following job aid (Exhibit 15.8) to help you meet this challenge.

**EXHIBIT 15.8.    Tips to Maximize Your Training Dollars**

1.  Quantify the impact of training and development.

2.  Develop a pool of internal peer trainers to be used as needed.

3.  Recruit leaders in your organization to serve as guest speakers and trainers.

4.  Work with external service providers to find ways to reduce costs.

5.  Use free training offered by your vendors and suppliers.

6.  Offer shorter training sessions.

7.  Develop a lunch-and-learn program.

8.  Deliver training in non-classroom formats using technology.

9.  Partner with non-competing organizations to sponsor training programs.

10. Contact your trade associations for free or low-cost education and training offerings.

11. Decrease materials cost by sending the content electronically to participants.

*The Trainer's Handbook, Updated Ed.* Copyright © 2009 by Karen Lawson. Reproduced by permission of Pfeiffer, an imprint of John Wiley & Sons, Inc.

By implementing some of the tips and strategies discussed in this chapter, you will be well positioned to meet the challenge of investing in the training function during a down economy so that the organization is well prepared and well positioned for the next upswing.

# Appendix A

## Answers to Exercises

### Chapter 3: Exhibit 3.3

1. IC
2. IC
3. LC
4. IC
5. IC
6. IC
7. IC
8. LC
9. IC
10. IC
11. IC
12. LC
13. LC
14. IC
15. LC
16. LC
17. LC
18. IC

### Chapter 5: Exhibit 5.1

**Suggested Wording for Each Objective**

1. Explain the leader's role in today's business environment.
2. Distinguish between authority of rank and authority of respect.
3. Explain the three primary theories of motivation.
4. Identify the characteristics of an effective leader.

5. Explain the role of the manager in a team environment.

6. List the advantages and disadvantages involved in group decision making.

7. Identify ten ways to motivate employees.

## Chapter 8: Seating Arrangements

1. Classroom

2. Cluster

3. Horseshoe

4. Single Square or Round

5. Semi-Circle or Full Circle

6. Conference

7. Chevron

## Chapter 8: Active Knowledge Sharing

1. 125–150 words per minute

2. 400–500 words per minute

3. 80 percent; 45 percent

4. 83 percent sight

5. 11 percent sound

6. 6 percent all other sense combined

## Chapter 8: Pre Test

| | |
|---|---|
| 1. F | 4. F |
| 2. F | 5. T |
| 3. T | |

## Chapter 12: Measurement Terms

| | |
|---|---|
| 1. g | 5. c |
| 2. h | 6. d |
| 3. f | 7. a |
| 4. e | 8. b |

# Appendix B

# Recommended Resources

## Books

Allen, M. (2003). *Michael Allen's guide to e-learning*. Hoboken, NJ: John Wiley & Sons.

Aldrich, C. (2003). *Simulations and the future of learning*. San Francisco: Pfeiffer.

Bersin, J. (2004). *The blended learning book*. San Francisco: Pfeiffer.

Carliner, S. (1999). *An overview of on-line learning*. Amherst, MA: HRD Press.

Conrad, K., & Training Links. (2000). *Instructional design for web-based training*. Amherst, MA: HRD Press.

Cohen, G., Eysenck, M.W., & Le Voi, M.E. (Eds.) (1986). *Memory: A cognitive approach*. Philadelphia, PA: Open University Press.

Driscoll, M., & Carliner, S. (2002). *Advanced web-based training strategies*. San Francisco: Pfeiffer.

Gupta, K. (1998). *A practical guide to needs assessment*. San Francisco: Pfeiffer.

Hale, J. (2002). *Performance-based evaluation*. San Francisco: Pfeiffer.

Horton, W. (2000). *Designing web-based training: How to teach anyone anything anywhere any time*. Hoboken, NJ: John Wiley & Sons.

Horton, W., & Horton, K. (2003). *e-Learning tools and technologies: A consumer's guide for trainers, teachers, educators, and instructional designers*. Hoboken, NJ: John Wiley & Sons.

Ingham, J., & Dunn, R. (1993). The Dunn and Dunn model of learning styles: Addressing learner diversity. In J.W. Pfeiffer (Ed.), *The 1993 annual: Developing human resources.* San Francisco: Pfeiffer.

Jacobs, R.T., & Fuhrman, B.S. (1984). Learning-style inventory. In J.W. Pfeiffer & L.D. Goodstein (Eds.), *The 1984 annual for group facilitators.* San Francisco: Pfeiffer.

Kruse, K., & Keil, J. (2000). *Technology-based training.* San Francisco: Pfeiffer.

Lee, W.W., & Owens, D.L. (2004). *Multimedia-based instructional design* (2nd ed.). San Francisco: Pfeiffer.

Mantyla, K. (1999). *Interactive distance learning exercises that really work!* Alexandria, VA: American Society for Training & Development.

Murrell, K.L. (1987). The learning-model instrument. In J.W. Pfeiffer (Ed.), *The 1987 annual: Developing human resources.* San Francisco: Pfeiffer.

Newstrom, J.W., & Scannell, E.E. (1980). *Games trainers play.* New York: McGraw-Hill.

Pfeiffer, J.W. (Ed.). (1972–1996). *Annuals: Developing human resources.* San Francisco, CA: Pfeiffer.

Phillips, J.J. (2002). *How to measure training results: A practical guide to tracking the six key indicators.* New York: McGraw-Hill.

Phillips, J.J., Phillips, P.P., & Hodges, T.K. (2004). *Make training evaluation work.* Alexandria, VA: American Society for Training & Development.

Phillips, P.P. (2002). *The bottom line on ROI.* Atlanta, GA: CEP Press.

Scannell, E.E., & Newstrom, J.W. (1991). *Still more games trainers play.* New York: McGraw-Hill.

Shank, P. (2004). *Making sense of online learning.* San Francisco: Pfeiffer.

Shank, R. (2005). *Lessons in learning, e-learning, and training.* San Francisco: Pfeiffer.

Scott, B. (2000). *Consulting on the inside.* Alexandria, VA: American Society for Training & Development.

Sugar, S. (1998). *Games that teach: Experiential activities for reinforcing training.* San Francisco: Pfeiffer.

Sugar, S., & Willett, C. (2004). *Games that boost performance.* San Francisco: Pfeiffer.

Wacker, M.B., & Silverman, L. (2003). *Stories trainers tell*. San Francisco: Pfeiffer.

Watkins, R. (2005). *75 e-learning activities*. San Francisco: Pfeiffer.

Zahn, D. (2004). *The quintessential guide to using consultants*. Amherst, MA: HRD Press.

Zemke, R., Raines, C., & Filipczak, B. (1999). *Generations at work: Managing the clash of veterans, boomers, xers, and nexters in your workplace*. New York: AMACOM.

## Sources for Assessment Instruments and Simulations

HRDQ
2002 Renaissance Boulevard #100
King of Prussia, PA 19406–2756
(800) 633–4533
www.HRDQ.com

Human Synergistics
39819 Plymouth Road
Plymouth, MI 48170
(313) 459–1030
www.humansyn.com

Pfeiffer
(800) 274–4434
www.pfeiffer.com

TACT^ools
(800) 845–2126
www.tactoolsonline.com

Talico
P.O. Box 3658
Ponte Vedra, FL 32004–3658
(904) 285–7757
www.talico.com

## Props, Toys, and Training Tools

Creative Learning Tools
P.O. Box 37
Wausau, WI 54402
(715) 842–2467
www.creativelearningtools.com

The Trainer's Warehouse
89–I Washington Avenue
Natick, MA 01760
(800) 299–3770
www.trainerswarehouse.com

## Video Distributor

Trainer's Aide, Inc.
163–60 22nd Avenue
Whitestone, NY 11357
(800) 344–6088
www.MonadTrainersAide.com

## Video Producers

American Management Association
1601 Broadway
New York, NY 10019
(800) 262–9699
www.amanet.org

American Media Incorporated
4621 121st Street
Urbandale, PA 50323
(888) 776–8268
www.ammedia.com

CRM Learning
2215 Faraday Avenue
Carlsbad, CA 92008
(800) 421–0833
www.crmlearning.com

The Ken Blanchard Companies
125 State Place
Escondido, CA 92029
(800) 728–6000
www.blanchardtraining.com

Mentor Media
115 West California Boulevard, PMB102
Pasadena, CA 91105
(800) 359–1935
www.mentormediaonline.com

VisionPoint Productions, Inc.
1985 NW 94th Street
Des Moines, IA 50325–6919
(800) 300–8880
www.vppi.com

# Appendix C

## Criteria for Selecting Packaged Programs

Use the following checklist to evaluate packaged programs you are considering. Choose those criteria that are important to you and your organization. Then apply each criterion to the program you are evaluating in order to make the best decision for your particular situation. This is also a valuable tool to use in justifying the cost of purchasing the program.

- Program is based on solid research.
- Absolute, bottom-line price is reasonably low.
- Cost/value ratio is low.
- Payment flexibility, discounts, etc., are available.
- Vendor company has good reputation in the field.
- You *own* course materials, versus renting/leasing them.
- Vendor has client referrals available to be contacted.
- You have good relationship with vendor's rep.

- Vendor's representative is knowledgeable.
- Program can be customized.
- Industry-specific version is available.
- Program is time-tested, has been around a while.
- Program is new or updated.
- You previously worked with vendor.
- Quality of the vendor's formal proposal is high.
- Convenient access to vendor is possible.
- Quality of course materials is high.
- Leader's guide is easy to follow.
- Course materials are immediately available.
- Specific participant is targeted, that is, new or experienced.
- Program has unique concept—"it's different."
- Materials are easy to use—few problems starting up.
- Program's objectives match yours.
- Vendor provides start-up support.
- There is flexibility with participant group size.
- Line manager could present program.
- Program is entertaining/engaging.
- Program is content-rich.
- Overall quality of program is high.
- Vendor offers other programs/services.
- Vendor offers technical support.
- You can contract access to copyright—you could reprint.
- Program is likely to receive high critiques.
- Variety of media are used.
- Reinforcement modules are available.

# References

Allen, M. (2003). *Guide to e-learning: Building interactive, fun, and effective learning programs for any company.* Hoboken, NJ: John Wiley & Sons.

American Council on Education. (1996). *Guiding principles for distance education in a learning society.* Washington, DC: American Council on Education.

Cripple, G. (1996). Instructional styles diagnosis inventory. *The 1996 annual: Volume 2, consulting* (pp. 147–160). San Francisco: Pfeiffer.

El-Shamy, S. (2004). *How to design and deliver training for the new and emerging generations.* San Francisco: Pfeiffer.

Holcomb, J. (1994). *Make training worth every penny: On-target evaluation.* San Francisco: Pfeiffer.

Horton, W. (2000). *Designing web-based training.* Hoboken, NJ: John Wiley & Sons.

James, W.B., & Galbraith, M.W. (1985, January). Perceptual learning styles: Implications and techniques for the practitioner. *Lifelong Learning,* pp. 20–23.

Johnson, D.W., Johnson, R.T., & Smith, K.A. (1991). *Cooperative learning: Increasing college faculty instructional productivity.* ASHE-ERIC Higher Education Report No. 4. Washington, DC: The George Washington University, School of Education and Human Development.

Keller, J.M. (1983). Motivational design of instruction. In C.M. Reigeluth (Ed.), *Instructional-design theories and models: An overview of their current status.* Hillsdale, NJ: Erlbaum.

Kirk, J. (1995). *Trainers' use of games: Some preliminary explorations* (Unpublished manuscript). Cullobee, NC: Author.

Kirkpatrick, D. (1994). *Evaluating training programs: The four levels.* San Francisco: Berrett-Koehler.

Knowles, M. (1990). *The adult learner: A neglected species* (4th ed.). Houston, TX: Gulf.

Kolb, D. (1991). *Learning style inventory.* Boston: Mcber & Company.

Mayer, R.E. (2001). *Multimedia learning.* Cambridge, UK: Cambridge University Press.

Meyers, C., & Jones, T.B. (1993). *Promoting active learning: Strategies for the college classroom.* San Francisco: Jossey-Bass.

Miller, G.A. (1956). The magical number seven, plus or minus two: Some limits on our capacity for processing information. *Psychological Review, 83,* 81–97.

Oppenheim, L. (1981). *Studies of the effects of the use of overhead transparencies on business meetings.* Philadelphia, PA: Wharton Applied Research Center, Wharton School, University of Pennsylvania.

Parkin, M. (1998). *Tales for trainers: Using stories and metaphors to facilitate learning.* London, UK: Kogan-Page.

Peoples. D.A. (1992). *Presentations plus: David Peoples' proven techniques*(rev. ed.). Hoboken, NJ: John Wiley & Sons.

Pescuric, A., & Byham, W.C. (1996, July). The new look of behavior modeling. *Training & Development,* pp. 24–30.

Phillips, K.R. (2004). *Coaching skills inventory* (3rd ed.). King of Prussia, PA: HRDQ.

Piskurich, G. (2000). *Rapid instructional design: Learning instructional design fast and right.* San Francisco: Pfeiffer.

Scannell, E.E., & Newstrom, J.W. (1983). *More games trainers play.* New York: McGraw-Hill.

Silberman, M. (2005). *101 ways to make training active* (2nd ed.). San Francisco: Pfeiffer.

Silberman, M. (2006). *Active training* (3rd ed.). San Francisco: Pfeiffer.

Silberman, M., & Lawson, K. (1995). *101 ways to make training active.* San Francisco: Pfeiffer.

Sterns, H., & Doverspike, D. (1988). Training and developing the older worker: Implications for human resource management. In H. Dennis (Ed.), *Fourteen steps in managing an aging work force.* Lexington, MA: Lexington Books.

Sugar, S. (1998). *Games that teach.* San Francisco: Pfeiffer.

Thomas, K., & Kilman, R. (1974). *The Thomas-Kilman conflict mode instrument.* Sterling Forest, NY: Xicom.

Vogel, D.R., Dickson, G.W., & Lehman, J.A. (1986). *Persuasion and the role of visual presentation support: The UM/3M study.* Minneapolis, MN: Management Information Systems Research Center, School of Management, University of Minnesota.

Walters, L. (1993). *Secrets of successful speakers.* New York: McGraw-Hill.

White, K. (1996, September). Ten most frequently asked questions and their answers. *Training & Development,* pp. *26–30.*

Zemke, R., & Armstrong, J. (1997, May). How long does it take? *Training,* pp. *69–79.*

Zemke, R., Raines, C., & Filipczak, B. (1999, November). Generation gaps in the classroom. *Training,* pp. 48–54.

# Index

# About the Author

**Dr. Karen Lawson** is an international consultant, speaker, executive coach, and author. As founder and president of Lawson Consulting Group, Inc., she has built a successful consulting firm, specializing in organization and management development. She has extensive consulting and seminar experience in the areas of team development, communication, leadership, and quality service, across a wide range of industries. Clients include a variety of prominent organizations from financial services, pharmaceuticals, telecommunications, manufacturing, health care, government, and education. In her consulting work with Fortune 500 companies, as well as with small businesses, she uses her experience and knowledge of human interaction to help leaders at all levels make a difference in their organizations.

Karen is the author of *The Art of Influencing; Improving On-the-Job Training and Coaching; Improving Performance Through Coaching; Involving Your Audience—Make It Active; Skill Builders: 50 Communication Activities; New Employee Orientation Training; Real-World Career Tactics for Women; Leadership Development Basics*; and *101 Ways to Make Training Active* (coauthor). She has also written chapters for many professional edited collections, in addition to numerous articles in professional journals.

She holds a doctor of philosophy degree in adult and organization development from Temple University; a master of arts in English from the University of Akron; and a bachelor of arts from Mount Union College. She is also a graduate of the National School of Banking in Fairfield, Connecticut. She is one of only four hundred people worldwide to have earned the Certified Speaking Professional designation from the four-thousand-member National Speakers Association. She has received numerous awards for her outstanding contribution to the training and speaking professions and was also named one of Pennsylvania's Best 50 Women in Business, as well as one of the Philadelphia region's Women of Distinction.

She has been actively involved in professional organizations such as the National Speakers Association and the American Society for Training and Development, holding leadership positions at both the local and national levels. She is also an active volunteer with the Arts and Business Council of the Philadelphia Chamber of Commerce.

Karen is currently an adjunct professor at Arcadia University in its International MBA program and has taught at several colleges and universities at both the graduate and undergraduate levels. She also teaches at The School of Management Development for the American Bankers Association and has presented at several professional conferences in the United States and Europe.

# Pfeiffer Publications Guide

This guide is designed to familiarize you with the various types of Pfeiffer publications. The formats section describes the various types of products that we publish; the methodologies section describes the many different ways that content might be provided within a product. We also provide a list of the topic areas in which we publish.

## FORMATS

In addition to its extensive book-publishing program, Pfeiffer offers content in an array of formats, from fieldbooks for the practitioner to complete, ready-to-use training packages that support group learning.

**FIELDBOOK** Designed to provide information and guidance to practitioners in the midst of action. Most fieldbooks are companions to another, sometimes earlier, work, from which its ideas are derived; the fieldbook makes practical what was theoretical in the original text. Fieldbooks can certainly be read from cover to cover. More likely, though, you'll find yourself bouncing around following a particular theme, or dipping in as the mood, and the situation, dictate.

**HANDBOOK** A contributed volume of work on a single topic, comprising an eclectic mix of ideas, case studies, and best practices sourced by practitioners and experts in the field.

An editor or team of editors usually is appointed to seek out contributors and to evaluate content for relevance to the topic. Think of a handbook not as a ready-to-eat meal, but as a cookbook of ingredients that enables you to create the most fitting experience for the occasion.

**RESOURCE** Materials designed to support group learning. They come in many forms: a complete, ready-to-use exercise (such as a game); a comprehensive resource on one topic (such as conflict management) containing a variety of methods and approaches; or a collection of like-minded activities (such as icebreakers) on multiple subjects and situations.

**TRAINING PACKAGE** An entire, ready-to-use learning program that focuses on a particular topic or skill. All packages comprise a guide for the facilitator/trainer and a workbook for the participants. Some packages are supported with additional media—such as video—or learning aids, instruments, or other devices to help participants understand concepts or practice and develop skills.

- *Facilitator/trainer's guide* Contains an introduction to the program, advice on how to organize and facilitate the learning event, and step-by-step instructor notes. The guide also contains copies of presentation materials—handouts, presentations, and overhead designs, for example—used in the program.

- *Participant's workbook* Contains exercises and reading materials that support the learning goal and serves as a valuable reference and support guide for participants in the weeks and months that follow the learning event. Typically, each participant will require his or her own workbook.

ELECTRONIC  CD-ROMs and web-based products transform static Pfeiffer content into dynamic, interactive experiences. Designed to take advantage of the searchability, automation, and ease-of-use that technology provides, our e-products bring convenience and immediate accessibility to your workspace.

## METHODOLOGIES

CASE STUDY  A presentation, in narrative form, of an actual event that has occurred inside an organization. Case studies are not prescriptive, nor are they used to prove a point; they are designed to develop critical analysis and decision-making skills. A case study has a specific time frame, specifies a sequence of events, is narrative in structure, and contains a plot structure—an issue (what should be/have been done?). Use case studies when the goal is to enable participants to apply previously learned theories to the circumstances in the case, decide what is pertinent, identify the real issues, decide what should have been done, and develop a plan of action.

ENERGIZER  A short activity that develops readiness for the next session or learning event. Energizers are most commonly used after a break or lunch to stimulate or refocus the group. Many involve some form of physical activity, so they are a useful way to counter post-lunch lethargy. Other uses include transitioning from one topic to another, where "mental" distancing is important.

EXPERIENTIAL LEARNING ACTIVITY (ELA)  A facilitator-led intervention that moves participants through the learning cycle from experience to application (also known as a Structured Experience). ELAs are carefully thought-out designs in which there is a definite learning purpose and intended outcome. Each step—everything that participants do during the activity—facilitates the accomplishment of the stated goal. Each ELA includes complete instructions for facilitating the intervention and a clear statement of goals, suggested group size and timing, materials required, an explanation of the process, and, where appropriate, possible variations to the activity. (For more detail on Experiential Learning Activities, see the Introduction to the *Reference Guide to Handbooks and Annuals*, 1999 edition, Pfeiffer, San Francisco.)

**GAME**  A group activity that has the purpose of fostering team spirit and togetherness in addition to the achievement of a pre-stated goal. Usually contrived—undertaking a desert expedition, for example—this type of learning method offers an engaging means for participants to demonstrate and practice business and interpersonal skills. Games are effective for team building and personal development mainly because the goal is subordinate to the process—the means through which participants reach decisions, collaborate, communicate, and generate trust and understanding. Games often engage teams in "friendly" competition.

**ICEBREAKER**  A (usually) short activity designed to help participants overcome initial anxiety in a training session and/or to acquaint the participants with one another. An icebreaker can be a fun activity or can be tied to specific topics or training goals. While a useful tool in itself, the icebreaker comes into its own in situations where tension or resistance exists within a group.

**INSTRUMENT**  A device used to assess, appraise, evaluate, describe, classify, and summarize various aspects of human behavior. The term used to describe an instrument depends primarily on its format and purpose. These terms include survey, questionnaire, inventory, diagnostic, survey, and poll. Some uses of instruments include providing instrumental feedback to group members, studying here-and-now processes or functioning within a group, manipulating group composition, and evaluating outcomes of training and other interventions.

Instruments are popular in the training and HR field because, in general, more growth can occur if an individual is provided with a method for focusing specifically on his or her own behavior. Instruments also are used to obtain information that will serve as a basis for change and to assist in workforce planning efforts.

Paper-and-pencil tests still dominate the instrument landscape with a typical package comprising a facilitator's guide, which offers advice on administering the instrument and interpreting the collected data, and an initial set of instruments. Additional instruments are available separately. Pfeiffer, though, is investing heavily in e-instruments. Electronic instrumentation provides effortless distribution and, for larger groups particularly, offers advantages over paper-and-pencil tests in the time it takes to analyze data and provide feedback.

**LECTURETTE**  A short talk that provides an explanation of a principle, model, or process that is pertinent to the participants' current learning needs. A lecturette is intended to establish a common language bond between the trainer and the participants by providing a mutual frame of reference. Use a lecturette as an introduction to a group activity or event, as an interjection during an event, or as a handout.

**MODEL**  A graphic depiction of a system or process and the relationship among its elements. Models provide a frame of reference and something more tangible, and more easily remembered, than a verbal explanation. They also give participants something to "go on," enabling them to track their own progress as they experience the dynamics, processes, and relationships being depicted in the model.

**ROLE PLAY**  A technique in which people assume a role in a situation/scenario: a customer service rep in an angry-customer exchange, for example. The way in which the role is approached is then discussed and feedback is offered. The role play is often repeated using a different approach and/or incorporating changes made based on feedback received. In other words, role playing is a spontaneous interaction involving realistic behavior under artificial (and safe) conditions.

**SIMULATION**  A methodology for understanding the interrelationships among components of a system or process. Simulations differ from games in that they test or use a model that depicts or mirrors some aspect of reality in form, if not necessarily in content. Learning occurs by studying the effects of change on one or more factors of the model. Simulations are commonly used to test hypotheses about what happens in a system—often referred to as "what if?" analysis—or to examine best-case/worst-case scenarios.

**THEORY**  A presentation of an idea from a conjectural perspective. Theories are useful because they encourage us to examine behavior and phenomena through a different lens.

## TOPICS

The twin goals of providing effective and practical solutions for workforce training and organization development and meeting the educational needs of training and human resource professionals shape Pfeiffer's publishing program. Core topics include the following:

Leadership & Management

Communication & Presentation

Coaching & Mentoring

Training & Development

e-Learning

Teams & Collaboration

OD & Strategic Planning

Human Resources

Consulting

# What will you find on pfeiffer.com?

- The best in workplace performance solutions for training and HR professionals

- Downloadable training tools, exercises, and content

- Web-exclusive offers

- Training tips, articles, and news

- Seamless on-line ordering

- Author guidelines, information on becoming a Pfeiffer Affiliate, and much more

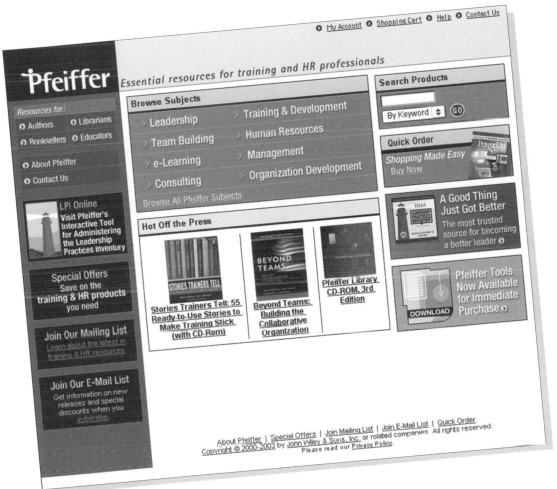

# Discover more at www.pfeiffer.com